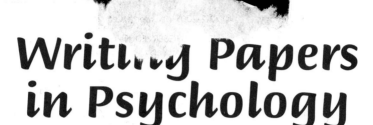

Writing Papers
in Psychology

PROPOSALS, RESEARCH PAPERS, LITERATURE REVIEWS,
POSTER PRESENTATIONS AND CONCISE REPORTS

Ninth Edition

P9-CAR-004

RALPH L. ROSNOW
and
MIMI ROSNOW

WADSWORTH
CENGAGE Learning

Australia • Brazil • Japan • Korea • Mexico • Singapore • Spain • United Kingdom • United States

WADSWORTH
CENGAGE Learning

Writing Papers in Psychology, Ninth Edition

Ralph L. Rosnow and Mimi Rosnow

Senior Publisher: Linda Schreiber-Ganster

Acquisition Editor: Timothy Matray

Editorial Assistant: Lauren K. Moody

Marketing Manager: Marcia Locke

Marketing Communications Manager: Laura Localio

Content Project Management: PreMediaGlobal

Senior Art Director: Pamela Galbreath

Print Buyer: Lind Hsu

Rights Acquisitions Specialist (Image): Thomas McDonough

Rights Acquisitions Specialist (Text): Thomas McDonough

Production Service: PreMediaGlobal

Copy Editor: Margaret Ritchie

Cover Designer: Leonard Bertin

Cover Image: © iStockphoto.com/ Chris Pecoraro

Compositor: PreMediaGlobal

For product information and technology assistance, contact us at **Cengage Learning Customer & Sales Support, 1-800-354-9706.**

For permission to use material from this text or product, submit all requests online at **www.cengage.com/permissions.** Further permissions questions can be e-mailed to **permissionrequest@cengage.com.**

Library of Congress Control Number: 2010943127

ISBN-13: 978-1-111-72613-3

ISBN-10: 1-111-72613-2

Wadsworth
20 Davis Drive
Belmont, CA 94002-3098
USA

Cengage Learning is a leading provider of customized learning solutions with office locations around the globe, including Singapore, the United Kingdom, Australia, Mexico, Brazil, and Japan. Locate your local office at **www.cengage.com/global.**

Cengage Learning products are represented in Canada by Nelson Education, Ltd.

To learn more about Wadsworth, visit **www.cengage.com/ Wadsworth**

Purchase any of our products at your local college store or at our preferred online store **www.cengagebrain.com.**

Instructors: Please visit **login.cengage.com** and log in to access instructor-specific resources.

Printed in the United States of America
1 2 3 4 5 6 7 15 14 13 12 11

To the partnership
that brought this book about

and

to Miles, R.J., Sasha, Matthew, Brendan, Olivia,
and Chloe, whose promise shines

Brief Contents

Contents

CHAPTER SIX Communicating Statistical Information   95

CHAPTER SEVEN Writing the First Draft   111

CHAPTER EIGHT **Producing the Final Manuscript** 133

CHAPTER NINE **Preparing Posters and Concise Reports** 143

APPENDIX A **Jane Doe's Research Report** 155

APPENDIX B **John Smith's Review Paper** 171

Exhibits

Preface for Instructors

This ninth edition of *Writing Papers in Psychology* provides frameworks, citation and referencing examples, tips, guidelines, and sample illustrations for students who are enrolled in psychology courses with writing requirements. The students might be at four-year colleges or community colleges. What all these students have in common is that what they are writing, whether it is a report of empirical research or a detailed literature review, is expected to be in the style recommended in the sixth edition of the *Publication Manual of the American Psychological Association* (hereafter called the APA Manual). This style is customarily referred to as the *APA style*, but the term has come to mean different things. If you know the difference between strictly kosher and kosher-style, you will understand what we mean. In the APA Manual, the term *APA style* is used as a synonym for the formatting guidelines and stylistic rules required of writers, editors, graduate students, and educators who, by necessity, must adhere to the APA strict style when working on manuscripts for APA journals. However, there are prestigious psychology journals outside APA (e.g., the journals of the Association for Psychological Science, or APS) that do not use the "strictly kosher" APA style, although they do adhere to most APA style guidelines for references. That said, what we mean here by *APA style* is that *Writing Papers* applies *most* (not all) of the APA Manual's rules where they seem relevant to papers written by students to fulfill course requirements, that is, papers that will be submitted to the instructor rather to an APA journal editor.

Judging from the feedback that we have received, as well as the experience that one of us has had in teaching research methods and other courses in psychology, the standards that are recommended in *Writing Papers* are not difficult, nor are they a distraction for multitasking students writing papers for course assignments under deadlines. The uniform standards recommended in *Writing Papers* should make it easier for instructors to read and evaluate their students' work. Where we propose departures from the APA's strict style, the standards are intended to streamline the writing process so students are not bogged down by rules that might seem baroque or irrelevant to them. For example, one exception to the strict APA style is the title page of student papers, which can be seen in the sample manuscripts in appendices A and B (at the back of this book). The format of the title pages of the students' manuscripts resembles the format that is recommended in the APA Manual, but the content is different. Title pages of *copy manuscripts* submitted to a journal for publication are expected to provide information that is important to editors, but student papers are *final manuscripts* submitted to instructors who need somewhat different information. For example, the Author Note in the sample papers gives students an opportunity to indicate their responsibility for the originality of the work.

Manuscripts submitted for publication in APA journals are also designed to be compatible with electronic publishing and, in order to be useful to the copy editor and the printer of the hard copy of the journal, to conform strictly to the APA Manual. However, research reports and literature reviews submitted by students reach the instructors exactly as they have been written by the students. For instance, the sample copy manuscript in the APA Manual labels the "running head" as such on the title page. This may be a useful exercise in some unknown way, though it hardly makes sense to tell an instructor that the running head in a student's final paper is the running head.

Another difference is that instructors of research methods courses often prefer that their students' research reports include an appendix with the individual raw scores and, possibly, a more detailed description of the data analysis than the description in the results section of the report. Not every instructor requires this type of appendix, and some may prefer that this information be conveyed in an electronic file or in a supplementary printed copy. The purpose of having students provide this information is that it gives an instructor the option of checking the accuracy of the student's reported results. The procedure in *Writing Papers* is consistent with the spirit of the APA Manual, which stipulates that "researchers must make their data available to the editor at any time during the review and publication process if questions arise with respect to the accuracy of the report." The procedure in *Writing Papers* is also another way of familiarizing students with ethical responsibilities and accountability in science in general.

Later in this book, we have a list of recommended readings in the chapter on communicating statistical information. One of the readings, which may of particular interest to students who plan to continue in psychology or in another area of science, is the recent edition of *On Being a Scientist: A Guide to Responsible Conduct in Research*, published by the National Academy of Science (NAS) and available on the NAS Web site as a free download. Instructors who are teaching research methods or statistics will also find useful links to instructional resources at http://www.teachpsychscience.org, a new Web site edited by Monmouth University professors Gary Lewandowski, Natalie Ciarocco, and David Strohmetz.

Instructors familiar with the previous edition of *Writing Papers* will recognize a number of changes in this ninth edition. For example, as the APA Manual has nothing to say about proposals, we have again streamlined the sample proposals (see Exhibits 11 and 12 in chapter 3). In the previous edition we used the example of looking over the shoulder of a student named Maya as she began the search and retrieval process. We extended this example through several chapters, and we suggest in chapter 2 that students retrace some of Maya's steps on the computer as a guided exercise in finding and retrieving materials. We also moved the discussion of the APA style of citing and referencing source materials to an earlier chapter (chapter 3) in order to familiarize students with this format as they develop their proposals. Chapter 6, on communicating statistical information, has been revised to emphasize not only "how" and "what" to report but also ethical implications.

Within each chapter, we have now numbered the sections to make reference to them easier.

Some exhibits in the previous edition have been dropped and new ones added. For example, in the discussion of poster presentations (in chapter 9), we have added templates for different arrangements (Exhibits 20 and 21), a revised exhibit showing the APA, APS, and AAAS poster design standards (Exhibit 19), and additional sample content in Exhibit 22 for the modified poster arrangement in Exhibit 21.

These are some of the changes in this edition of *Writing Papers*. All of the chapters have been revised and tightened to improve the flow of the narrative, make the focus tighter, and make the book more user friendly.

Acknowledgments

The sample papers in appendices A and B are based on earlier manuscripts that were drafted by two very talented psychology teachers, Anne A. Skleder (who is now the Provost at Cabrini College in Radnor, Pennsylvania) and Bruce Rind (who taught statistics and other courses at Temple University for many years). We thank them both for allowing us to edit those manuscripts in different editions of this book. We especially thank Bruce for the empirical data in the research report (appendix A), which he generously shared with us and permitted us to analyze further. Maya's literature retrieval experience (in chapter 2) began a couple of editions ago when Eric K. Foster, Maya's father, drafted an overview and used Maya's name. With the permission of Maya and her parents, Shobhi and Eric, we have continued the tradition of describing it as "looking over Maya's shoulder." We thank our Wadsworth/Cengage editor, Tim Matray, for his enthusiasm and administrative support, and we thank Tim's editorial assistant, Lauren Moody, for making our task so much easier. Once again, we thank Margaret Ritchie for her skillful and practiced editing of *Writing Papers*, which began years ago with the third edition.

We want to express our gratitude to the following people, whose comments and suggestions improved one or more editions of *Writing Papers:* John B. Best (Eastern Illinois University); Thomas Brown (Utica College of Syracuse University); David E. Campbell (Humboldt State University); Scott D. Churchill (University of Dallas); Stanley Cohen (West Virginia University); Peter B. Crabb (Pennsylvania State University–Abington); Nicholas DiFonzo (Rochester Institute of Technology); Nancy Eldred (San Jose State University); Kenneth Elliott (University of Maine at Augusta); Robert Gallen (Georgetown College); David Goldstein (Duke University); John Hall (Texas Wesleyan University); Donald Hantula (Temple University); James W. Kalat (North Carolina State University); Allan J. Kimmel (Groupe École Supérieure de Commerce de Paris, France); Laura Levine (Central Connecticut State University); Arlene Lundquist (Mount Union College); Joann Montepare (Tufts University); Quentin Newhouse, Jr. (Bowie State University); Ben Newkirk (Grossmont College); Arthur Nonneman (Asbury College); Edgar O'Neal (Tulane University); Rick Pollack (Merrimack College); Maureen Powers (Vanderbilt University); Robert Rosenthal (University of California at Riverside); Gordon W. Russell (University of Lethbridge, Canada); Holly M. Schiffrin (University of Mary Washington); Helen Shoemaker (California State University at Hayward); John Sparrow (State University of New York at Geneseo); Claudia Stanny (University of West Florida); David B. Strohmetz (Monmouth University); Linda M. Subich (University of Akron); Stephen A. Truhon (Winston-Salem State University); Lori Van Wallendael (University of North Carolina).

Finally, we thank the many users of this book for suggestions that have helped us to improve each new edition of *Writing Papers in Psychology*. We very much appreciate your support, and again invite you to send us any comments and suggestions for further improvements (http://rosnow.socialpsychology.org).

Ralph and Mimi Rosnow

1

Getting Started

Writing papers to fulfill course requirements means knowing what the instructor expects and then formulating a plan to accomplish your goal on schedule. Whether you are writing a research report or a literature review, this chapter will help you get started. The chapter also includes some simple dos and don'ts to help you avoid pitfalls and to ensure that the assignment will be completed on time and that it will represent your best work.

1.1   Where to Begin

There was once an intriguing character named Joe Gould, who, after graduating from Harvard in 1911 and trying his hand at a number of futile endeavors, moved to New York City and began to hang around Greenwich Village coffee shops. He told people that he had mastered the language of seagulls—and, in fact, did an uncanny imitation of one—and was translating literature into "seagull." He was best known, however, for an ambitious project he claimed to be compiling, called the "Oral History of Our Times." He boasted of having accumulated a stack of notebooks that stood 7 feet tall, and he carried brown paper bags with him that, he said, contained research notes. Joe Gould died in a psychiatric hospital while doing his seagull imitation. Some years later, in a profile article written by Joseph Mitchell for the *New Yorker* magazine, it was revealed that Joe Gould never started his "Oral History." His notebooks were a myth, and his brown bags contained merely other bags and yellowed newspaper clippings.

For students with required writing assignments, Joe Gould could be a metaphor for the most challenging aspect of any project: how to get started. First of all, familiarize yourself with what is in this book. Exhibit 1 shows a flowchart referring to specific chapters and selections that you

EXHIBIT 1 **Flowchart to walk you through Writing Papers**

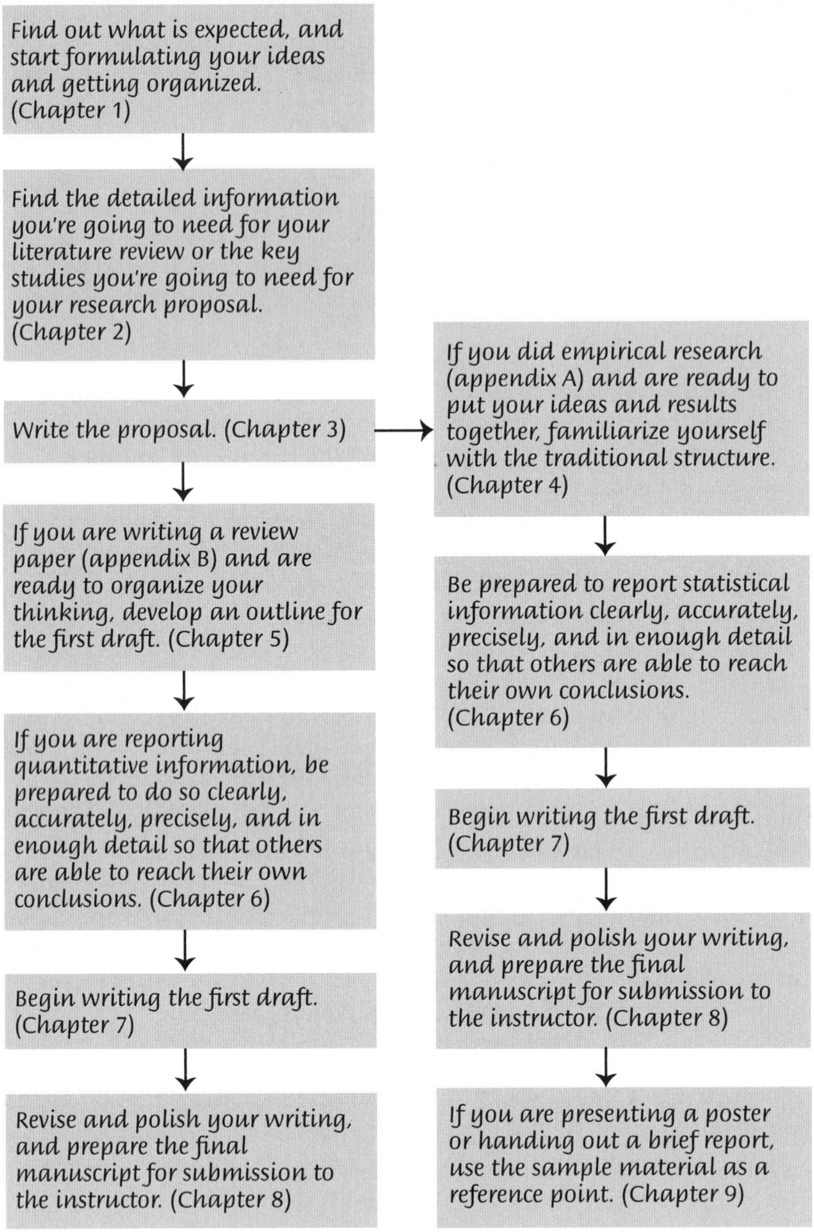

Find out what is expected, and start formulating your ideas and getting organized. (Chapter 1)

↓

Find the detailed information you're going to need for your literature review or the key studies you're going to need for your research proposal. (Chapter 2)

↓

Write the proposal. (Chapter 3) ⟶ If you did empirical research (appendix A) and are ready to put your ideas and results together, familiarize yourself with the traditional structure. (Chapter 4)

↓

If you are writing a review paper (appendix B) and are ready to organize your thinking, develop an outline for the first draft. (Chapter 5)

Be prepared to report statistical information clearly, accurately, precisely, and in enough detail so that others are able to reach their own conclusions. (Chapter 6)

↓

If you are reporting quantitative information, be prepared to do so clearly, accurately, precisely, and in enough detail so that others are able to reach their own conclusions. (Chapter 6)

Begin writing the first draft. (Chapter 7)

↓

Begin writing the first draft. (Chapter 7)

Revise and polish your writing, and prepare the final manuscript for submission to the instructor. (Chapter 8)

↓

Revise and polish your writing, and prepare the final manuscript for submission to the instructor. (Chapter 8)

If you are presenting a poster or handing out a brief report, use the sample material as a reference point. (Chapter 9) can turn to as needed. The table of contents (at the beginning of this book) shows the specialized sections and exhibits and their location in each chapter, and immediately following the table of contents is another separate list of the exhibits. The index (at the back of the book) lists specific terms, should you need to find a particular topic. There are also sample materials throughout. Chapter 3 contains two sample proposals, one for a literature review (Exhibit 11) and the other for a research project (Exhibit 12). Near the end of the book are two appendices (tabbed, so that they're easier to find). Appendix A shows a final research report (Jane Doe's), and appendix B, a final review paper (John Smith's). In chapter 9, you will find templates for poster arrangements (Exhibits 20 and 21), a sample poster presentation (Exhibit 22), and a sample one-page, two-sided handout (Exhibit 23).

Not everything that appears in the sample papers in appendices A and B will be needed in every student paper, but anything you might need is illustrated there or elsewhere in this book. If your assignment is to write a review of a single empirical study, your paper will not be nearly as long or as detailed as John Smith's literature review in appendix B. Your final review of a single empirical study might be only three to five pages long. If your assignment is to write a lab report in an experimental psychology class, your report will not be as long or detailed as Jane Doe's report of original research in appendix A. Even if your required writing assignment is different from John's or Jane's, read both papers anyway because we refer to them throughout this book, and you may get some ideas for your own writing assignment. Both papers are annotated to direct you to the specific section or subsection in this book that discusses the material so noted in more detail. For example, 3.4.21 refers to chapter 3, section 3.4 with the side heading in boldface "**How to Reference Source Materials**," and example 3.4.21 with the italicized side heading "*Entry in Encyclopedia Paginated by Volume*." The manuscripts in appendix A and appendix B also show what a student paper written in the "APA style" looks like.

1.2 Writing in APA Style

The term *APA style* means that the uniform structure and format of a manuscript are consistent with the guidelines in the sixth edition of the *Publication Manual of the American Psychological Association* (called the APA Manual in this book). College instructors in psychology typically require their students to write in APA style, though it is not the only writing style you may encounter in college. In English, language, and literature classes, instructors often require their students to write research papers in a style recommended by the Modern Language Association (called *MLA style*). In that context, the term *research paper* also means something quite different from Jane Doe's research paper in appendix A.

In an English class, you will be "researching the literature" for your paper, whereas in psychology, a *research paper* means you will be writing up the results of an empirical study. You will also be doing some "researching" of the literature for your proposal, but this process is called *searching and retrieving* in this book. Incidentally, the APA style and the MLA style are not the only two styles for the structure and format of manuscripts; there are also the University of Chicago style, the Turabian style, *The New York Times* style, *The Wall Street Journal* style, and so on.

Although we said that both Jane Doe's and John Smith's final papers are in APA style, there are actually some departures from the APA Manual. We will have more to say about these departures, but the difference has to do with the student papers' being thought of as *final manuscripts* rather than *copy manuscripts*. As described in the APA Manual, copy manuscripts are specifically written for editors, reviewers, and typesetters. Once a copy manuscript has been accepted for publication and has gone through the production process, it is discarded. Papers written by students for class assignments are in a final form for the instructor to read. The same is true of theses and dissertations, which are also considered final manuscripts even when the audience goes beyond the student's adviser or mentor. Another important point is that, as the APA Manual cautions, style preferences for some student manuscripts may be diverse and specific to a particular institution. If you are writing a thesis or a dissertation, check with your department for any special style requirements, and ask your adviser to recommend a couple of examples that will give you a sense of what is considered quality work.

Referencing source materials in the APA style is sometimes confusing, but we have tried to simplify the process by referring you to Exhibit 10 in section 3.4. However, if you run into a problem that is not easy to figure out, there are free Web sites that have tried to untangle some of the confusion. There is a blog at APA Style Help to assist those who have encountered difficulties when using the APA Manual: http://blog.apa.style.org and also at http://twitter.com/APA_Style. The blog is also a tacit reminder that you are not alone if you run into problems that the APA Manual does not resolve unambiguously. You will also find useful templates that you can fill in with the citation information to see how to reference it in APA style at Dr. Abel Scribe's Web site at http://www.docstyles.com. You click the style guide you need (APA Psychology, ASA Sociology, Chicago Style, MLA Style) and then just follow the simple directions. Several colleges and universities have Web sites on APA style, which you can access for free. The Owl at Purdue University's Writing Lab is accessed at http://owl.english.purdue.edu/owl/resource/560/01. Similar useful information is available from the Writer's Workshop at the University of Illinois at Urbana-Champaign: http://www.cws.illinois.edu/workshop/writers/citation/apa.

1.3 *Your Instructor's Expectations*

To plan your project, you need some clear objectives and a precise idea of what your instructor expects, which can help you avoid getting bogged down. What is the purpose of your writing assignment, and how long does the instructor expect the final manuscript to be? Do you choose the theme or topic, or will the instructor assign it? Will interim papers (for example, a proposal and progress reports) be required? If so, how long should they be, and when are they due? When is the final paper due? How does this date mesh with your other assignments (e.g., exams and papers in other courses)? You can speak with other students about their impressions, but the person who knows *exactly* what is expected of you is the instructor. Before you boot up your computer, arrange to meet with the instructor, tell the instructor what you understand the assignment to be, talk about your ideas for a topic, and ask if you are on the right path.

One instructor wrote to us that many of his students were reluctant to take this initial step, even though they hadn't a clue about a topic for a required research project. But those who did come in, even without an initial idea, benefited from the meeting and, in most cases, went away with the beginning of a direction for their work. Meeting with the instructor will also give you an opportunity to avoid the anonymity of being another face in the classroom. The instructor will know who you are, and that you are a motivated student. If you later decide to go on to graduate school or law school or medical school, you have introduced yourself to someone you may wish to approach later on to ask for a letter of recommendation.

1.4 *Focusing on Your Objective*

Once you have a topic, it is important to think through the assignment to sharpen your intellectual process. Understanding the differences between the research report and the review paper in psychology classes will help you focus on your particular objective. There are, as we said, variations on these two types, such as reports of lab exercises and reviews of single studies. The APA Manual also notes other types of writing projects in which the goal of the writer (i.e., what the writer wants to achieve) is somewhat different. For example, some review articles are similar to literature reviews but are efforts to advance theoretical thinking rather than to sum up a body of literature. They are called *theoretical articles* in the APA Manual. John Smith's review paper in appendix B is not a theoretical article, but he does propose a term ("multiplex") to theoretically pull together several points of view concerning the "new direction" of thinking about multiple types of intelligence. The APA Manual also talks about *case studies,* such as the in-depth analyses of individuals in clinical case studies and analyses of groups of people with certain shared characteristics in ethnographic research. For this discussion, however, we concentrate on the two types that are exemplified by Jane Doe's research report in appendix A and John Smith's literature review paper in appendix B. Exhibit 2 highlights the typical differences between the two types of writing assignments, so you can begin to focus your efforts on whichever project you have been assigned.

One obvious distinction highlighted in Exhibit 2 is that a literature search forms the core of the review paper and that empirical data form the core of the research report. As noted in the exhibit, empirical research generally requires a preliminary literature review, but it typically involves retrieving only a few key studies that will serve as theoretical starting points. If you are writing a review paper, you can expect to spend more time retrieving abstracts and articles online, and probably more time reading and taking notes. On the other hand, if you are writing a review of a single empirical study, you may not need to do much of a literature search for just a 3- to 5-page paper. However, in some upper-level undergraduate classes that are run like graduate courses, the instructor may expect a 25- to 30-page paper (including the list of references) with a literature review that is as detailed and cohesive as John Smith's paper in appendix B.

The focus and coverage of John Smith's review paper are typical of term papers that are described as *qualitative reviews*. Another kind of literature review, which has become increasingly popular in honors programs and some advanced courses, is the *meta-analytic review*. For such a review, the student uses statistical and graphic methods to sum up quantitatively the results of a group of similar empirical studies. The focus of the review is on the magnitude of the observed effects (called the *effect sizes*) and the variability of the effect sizes. These reviews typically have an exploratory orientation, in which the reviewer looks for conditions (known

---

EXHIBIT 2   *Differences between research reports and review papers*

Research Report	*Review Paper*
1. Is based on data that you have collected; literature search involving only a few key studies.	1. Is based exclusively on literature search; no hard data of your own to interpret, unless you are counting and summarizing the information.
2. Is structured to follow the traditional form described in chapter 4.	2. Is structured by you to fit your particular topic, based on an outline you have prepared (described in chapter 5).
3. Reports your own research findings and conclusions to others in enough detail so they can draw their own conclusions.	3. Puts the literature you review into the context of your own insights to bring coherence to the material.

as *moderator variables*) that alter the magnitude of the effects. A highly cited example of a meta-analytic review in psychology was done by Alice H. Eagly in 1978. Textbooks had long asserted that women were more conforming and more easily influenced than men. Eagly, a specialist in the psychology of gender and the psychology of attitudes, wondered whether the historical period in which the findings were collected might have been a moderator variable. Her meta-analysis revealed that the research done before the era of the women's movement did, in fact, show women as more influenceable than men, but the research that was conducted later uncovered few gender differences in influenceability. You can learn more about Professor Eagly's work in the field of social psychology by visiting her Profile page on the Social Psychology Network at http://socialpsychology.org.

A second distinction in Exhibit 2 is that the typical structure of the research report is expected to conform to a general tradition that has evolved over many years. Usually it includes (a) an abstract (or summary of the research report), (b) an introduction (stating the purpose of the research and the basis of any hypotheses and predictions), (c) a method section (how the research was done), (d) a results section, (e) a discussion of the results, and (f) a list of the references (journal articles, books, etc.) cited in the report. Jane Doe's research report in appendix A contains some additional material, but you will be expected to include at least the six parts listed above. Review papers tend to be much more flexible, depending on the objective of the review, the coverage, and the writer's perspective. You can observe this flexibility in John Smith's review paper in appendix B, where the section headings reflect the organization John developed after he had an opportunity to think carefully about his topic more than just piecemeal.

The final distinction noted in Exhibit 2 is that the review paper puts issues and ideas into the context of a particular theme or thesis, whereas the main objective of the research report is to describe your empirical investigation to others. The principal theme in a research report often involves testable hypotheses with explicit predictions, but the report could be an exploratory study or a purely descriptive investigation (there is more on these distinctions later in this book). If there are hypotheses, then what you found in your empirical research should be put in the context of the predictions, as illustrated in the results and discussion sections of Jane Doe's research report in appendix A.

1.5 Scheduling Time

Once you have a clear sense of your objective, the next step is to set deadlines for yourself so you don't end up like Joe Gould, who was so paralyzed by inertia that he accomplished nothing. You know your own energy level and thought patterns, so play to your strengths. Are you a morning person? If so, block out some time to work on your writing early in the day. Do you function better at night? Then use the late hours of quiet to your advantage. Allow extra time for other pursuits by setting up realistic deadlines for the completion of each major part of your assignment. Write the dates on your calendar. Some students prefer to post the dates over their desks as daily reminders. Others post the due dates of assignments over their bathroom mirror, a place they are sure to look more than once a day.

In planning your schedule, give yourself ample time to do a good job. Patience will pay off by making you feel more confident as you complete each task and move on to the next one. How do you know what tasks to schedule? Because writing a thorough literature review requires spending time online (and also probably in the library) finding sources, reading them, and accumulating your notes, you will need to leave ample time for these tasks. Here are some ideas about what to schedule on your calendar if you are writing a review paper and are first required to submit a proposal:

- ◆ Completion of preliminary literature search for proposal
- ◆ Completion of proposal
- ◆ Completion of literature search
- ◆ Completion of library work
- ◆ Completion of an outline and first draft
- ◆ Completion of final draft and proofing

If you are writing a research report based on an empirical investigation, you need to set aside time for the ethics review, the implementation of the research, and the data analysis. Here are some scheduling suggestions for these and other tasks if you will be doing empirical research and are first required to submit a proposal:

- ◆ Completion of preliminary literature search for proposal
- ◆ Completion of proposal for research
- ◆ Completion of ethics review
- ◆ Implementation of the study
- ◆ Completion of data analysis
- ◆ Completion of a first draft
- ◆ Completion of final draft and proofing

Researching, organizing, writing, and revising will take time. A book or journal article that you need might be unavailable, and not all articles are available online. The data collection and analysis can also run into snags. Other problems might be that the ethics review takes a lot longer than you expected, or you may be asked to resubmit your proposal, or not all your research subjects show up, or the hard drive on a computer suddenly gives up the ghost, or research material you need is hard to find. In your schedule, allow yourself time to cope with unforeseen problems.

Also allow enough time between the first and final drafts so that you can distance yourself from your writing and return to your assignment with a fresh perspective, as you polish the first draft and check for errors in logic, flow, spelling, punctuation, and grammar. If you schedule your time in this way, you should not feel pressured by an imaginary deadline—or surprised as the real deadline approaches.

If you get started early, you will have time to track down hard-to-find material or to locate a test you need. In the reference section of the research report in appendix A, it is evident that Jane Doe had to find some older source materials, many that were unavailable to her in an electronic form but that she found using the resources in her college library. It is also evident in John Smith's review paper in appendix B that he needed access to a lot of books and had to spend time in the library.

You may want to use a test or instrument that is protected by copyright, and getting permission will take time. Though tests that require advanced training to administer or interpret are usually unavailable to college students, many others are available to students. For example, there are books with sample measures and literature reviews, such as *The Science of Self-Report*, edited by a team led by Arthur A. Stone (published by Erlbaum in 2000), and another titled *Measures of Political Attitudes*, edited by John P. Robinson, Phillip R. Shaver, and Lawrence S. Wrightsman (published by the Academic Press in 1993). In chapter 2, we discuss ways of tracking down books like these, which, if they are not available in your library, can frequently be obtained through an interlibrary loan. For a comprehensive catalog of available tests and measures that you can look up in journal articles and other reports, there is the *Directory of Unpublished Experimental Mental Measures* (published by the American Psychological Association). The word *unpublished* in the title of this series (which was edited by Bert A. Goldman, David F. Mitchell, and their colleagues) simply means that the instruments are usually available without a fee or special credentials. A huge database of information on questionnaires, interview schedules, checklists, coding schemes, rating scales, and so on in the fields of health and psychosocial science was created by Evelyn Perloff. Called *Health and Psychosocial Instruments* (HaPI), it is available on the EBSCO and Ovid databases (host systems that also offer PsycINFO, discussed in the next chapter in section 2.4).

Should you encounter a problem, discuss it early with the instructor to ensure that you can finish on schedule. Starting early may also give you time to tackle data analysis procedures that are not in the course textbook. If you feel the need, you might also want to e-mail a researcher and request any still-unpublished articles that follow up previous research you've been reading, or to request permission to reprint or reproduce something. In John Smith's paper in appendix B (see the Author Note on his title page), he acknowledges that he received permission to reproduce a graphic. Jane Doe had to get permission from the restaurant owner and the server to conduct her experiment (see her title page in appendix A). Another word of advice: Instructors have heard all the possible excuses for a late or badly done final manuscript, so don't expect much sympathy if you miss the deadline. If you need to ask the instructor for a letter of recommendation later on, you don't want to create the impression that you are unreliable.

1.6 Choosing a Topic

The next step is to come up with a research idea or choose a suitable topic for a literature review. The selection of a research idea or review topic is an integral part of learning, because usually you are free to explore experiences, observations, and ideas for questions or issues that will sustain your curiosity and interest as you work on your project. There are lots of ways of getting ideas. For example, John notes in his proposal for a literature review (Exhibit 11) that he first became interested in the idea of multiple intelligences when the instructor in his psychological testing course mentioned her own research on a facet of that work. Jane Doe, in her proposal for a research study (Exhibit 12), describes a similar situation involving her instructor's research on tipping behavior. Jane also mentions her intrinsic interest in the topic (because she has a summer job as a waitress).

If you are a psychology major or minor, you probably have lots of questions and ideas regarding why people behave, perceive, or think as they do. But if you are looking around for an idea, and the psychology department invites guest lecturers to present their research in colloquia that are open to undergraduate students (most usually are), you may get some research ideas of your own while listening to the speaker (so take a pencil and paper to jot down your ideas). Students also frequently have an opportunity to chat informally with the speaker after the colloquium presentation. Another way to stimulate your creative mind is to approach your everyday experiences with an open, inquisitive mind. One of us (Ralph) got interested in the psychology of rumor years ago when there was a rumor circulating about Paul McCartney of the Beatles. This particular rumor was not behaving at all in the way that some classic textbooks insisted that rumors behaved. The discrepancy between the classic account of rumor and what was visible to the naked eye became the launching point for a renewed program of research on the psychology of rumor.

In considering a suitable topic, beware of a few pitfalls. The following dos and don'ts may make your life easier as you start choosing a topic:

- Choose a topic that piques your curiosity and will sustain your interest over the long haul.
- Make sure your topic can be covered in the available time and in the assigned number of pages.

◆ Assuming you are expected to work independently, don't choose a topic that you know other students have chosen, or you will be competing with them for access to the library's source material.
◆ If you are not already knowledgeable on a topic, read about it before you begin to narrow your objective.

1.7   Narrowing the Topic

For students who must write papers with quickly approaching deadlines, choosing too broad a topic or question for either a literature review or a research project will add difficulties and anxiety and will mean an unsatisfactory result. A proposed review that is too broad—for example, "Sigmund Freud's Life and Times" or "B. F. Skinner's Life and Times"—would involve trying to cover too much material within the limited framework of the assignment and the time available to complete it. A specific aspect of Freud's theoretical work (assuming you are interested in psychoanalytic writings and the instructor approves your choice of a topic) will prove a more appropriately narrowed focus for a review paper in a course on personality theories, abnormal behavior, or psychopathology. Writing a paper about how the experimental psychologist B. F. Skinner's pioneering ideas became the basis of his novel, *Walden II* (which describes a whole society organized according to known principles of psychological conditioning), will prove a more narrowed focus for a course on the history and systems of psychology.

In narrowing the literature review topic, do not limit your discussion just to facts that are already well known. Ask yourself what is special about how you plan to approach the assignment. For example, John Smith's review paper is not just a listing of other people's conclusions, but an effort to incorporate his own perspective. This approach not only will give the project a specific focus but will also make the paper stand out when the instructor grades it. Here are two further guidelines for narrowing your topic:

◆ Be sure that your topic is not so narrow that reference materials will be hard to find.
◆ Be guided by your instructor's advice, because the instructor can help you avoid taking on an unwieldy topic.

If you approach instructors with several concrete ideas, you will usually find them glad to help you tailor your ideas so that you, the topic, and the project assignment are all compatible. Here are examples of how a student who was assigned to develop an idea for a literature review sharpened the focus of a paper on Sigmund Freud:

Unlimited Topic (Much Too Broad)
"An examination of Freud's theories of personality and abnormal behavior."

Limited to 20-Page Paper
"An examination of Freud's theory of oedipal conflict applied to mental health."

Limited to 10-Page Paper
"An examination of Freud's theory of infantile sexuality."

Here is the concentration of another student's focus on a different topic, in this case for a one- or two-semester research project:

Unlimited Topic (Too Broad for a Term Project)
"An empirical investigation of how nonverbal stimuli are deciphered."

Slightly Limited Topic
"An empirical investigation of how certain kinds of nonverbal stimuli are deciphered differently by women and men."

Adequately Limited Topic
"An empirical investigation of whether female and male volunteer subjects at Podunk U. differ in their ability to identify photographed facial expressions of joy, disappointment, anger, and fear in a sample of female and male actors."

If you are currently enrolled in a research methods course, the assigned textbook probably discusses criteria for assessing the scientific merits of hypotheses. A detailed discussion is beyond the scope of this book, but we can mention three criteria:

1. *Good hypotheses are plausible, or credible.* That is, they are grounded in credible ideas and facts, the assumption being that well-grounded hypotheses will have a higher payoff potential when tested. Thus, you must do a preliminary literature search to find out whether your ideas are consistent with accepted findings in the scientific literature. If they are not consistent, you will need to think about these inconsistencies and decide (with the help of the instructor) whether you really do have a fresh insight or will need to develop some other hypothesis.
2. *Good hypotheses are succinct, logically coherent, and consistent with the facts, and the technical terms are used correctly and precisely.* To see whether you are using a technical term correctly, consult the APA *Dictionary of Psychology* or an encyclopedia of psychology (or whatever area you are interested in), but don't just rely on a lazy online search. To ensure that your hypothesis is succinct and coherent, consult your instructor, who will show you how to cut away unwieldy words. This word-trimming and

focusing process is known as using Occam's razor—named after a 14th-century Franciscan philosopher, William of Ockham, who cautioned against wordy explanations. It is sometimes said that using Occam's razor should be like trimming a beard, not like cutting off a piece of chin.

3. *Good hypotheses are testable, and they are empirically falsifiable if incorrect.* It is possible for anyone with a fertile imagination to concoct "support" for even the most preposterous belief. The assumption of most scientists is that hypotheses that cannot be refuted by *any* means are not within the realm of science. For example, the statement "All behavior is a product of the good and evil lying within us" does not qualify as a valid scientific hypothesis, because it is so vague and amorphous that it cannot be subjected to empirical refutation.

1.8 Knowing Your Audience and Topic

All professional writers know that they are writing for a particular audience. This knowledge helps them determine the tone and style of their work. If you were a major in journalism, you would be taught about how to write a news story, maybe a story about a local house fire. If you were an English major, you might write a short story on a similar theme, but the expectation is that the facts will be couched in telling literary details that will draw your audience into the narrative. Knowing your audience is no less important when you are writing a literature review or a research report in psychology. The audience is the instructor, who is not just any reader, but someone who is quite knowledgeable in the area. You are writing to demonstrate your own acquired knowledge and also to give evidence of your insights as well as your ability to express your ideas coherently in an appropriate framework.

If you have questions about the instructor's grading criteria, find out what they are before you start to work. For example, in a course on research methods, one instructor's syllabus listed the following grading criteria for different parts of the finished report (the numbers in parentheses are percentages):

Abstract
   Informativeness (5)
Introduction
   Clarity of purpose (10)
   Literature review (10)
Method
   Adequacy of design (10)
   Quality and completeness of description (10)
Results
   Appropriateness and correctness of analysis (10)
   Use of tables or figures (5)
   Clarity of presentation (10)

Discussion
    Interpretation of results (10)
    Critique/future directions (10)
Miscellaneous
    Organization, style, references, etc. (5)
    Appendix for raw data and calculations (5)

This information enabled the students to develop checklists to make sure that they concentrated on important parts of the assignment, just as the instructor would concentrate on them when evaluating the reports. As you get deeper into this book, you will find lists that you can use as reminders to attend to different parts of your writing assignment.

1.9 Cultivating an Understanding

Let us assume that you know what your main audience—your instructor—expects of you. Now you must try to develop more than a superficial understanding of your topic. The more you read about it and discuss your ideas with friends, the more you will begin to cultivate an intuitive understanding of the topic. In the next chapter, we describe how to use computerized and library resources to nurture this understanding. Here are two tips to get you started:

- Some writers find it helpful to keep several 3 × 5-inch cards handy, or to use sticky notes, for jotting down relevant ideas that suddenly occur to them. This is a good way to keep your topic squarely in your mind.
- You need to understand your source material, so equip yourself with a good desk dictionary, and turn to it routinely whenever you come across an unfamiliar word. This habit will serve you well.

The most comprehensive dictionaries are described as *unabridged,* which means they have not been shortened by the omission of terms or definitions. They can be expensive but are readily available in college and local libraries, and some are available online through your library's Web site. The most comprehensive of all dictionaries in the English language is the multivolume *Oxford English Dictionary* (the OED, for short). It gives the origin and history of words in the English language from the year 1150 to the publication of the OED. Suppose you were interested in writing a paper about the psychology of gossip and began by looking the term up in the OED. You would find that the word *gossip* began quite innocently as *god-sibbs,* for "godparents," meaning those with spiritual affinity to the child being baptized. Christenings were occasions for distant relatives to be present and an opportunity to share news. In the same way that the *d* in *God's spell* was dropped to form *gospel, god-sibbs* led to *gossip.* Incidentally, a book that might whet your interest in the OED is Simon Winchester's *The Professor and the Madman: A Tale of Murder, Insanity, and the Making of the Oxford University Dictionary.*

2

Finding and Retrieving Reference Materials

The literature search is an indispensable step in preparing a review paper; it is also an essential aspect of a research proposal as it puts your own ideas into a context, building on the existing work of others. Knowing about the many online and print resources that are available will allow you to gauge the effort it will take to find credible information. This chapter also provides advice on taking notes and tips on observing conventions of etiquette as you search for and retrieve materials.

2.1   Looking Over Maya's Shoulder

We begin by looking over the shoulder of a student, named Maya, who needs to choose a topic for a literature review and gather key studies for the proposal. First, we describe how Maya gets an idea for her review paper and has a preliminary talk about it with her instructor. She knows that she must produce a written proposal, and in the next chapter we illustrate the process of developing and writing a proposal. Before she can begin to draft it, however, she will need to identify and retrieve the relevant work on the topic. We will describe, step by step, how Maya goes through the process of doing a literature search. Afterward, we will examine in more detail the resources she used and others that may be available in your college library, or electronically through the library's Web site, or by means of a search engine that takes key words or questions and returns a list of Web sites. Not all reference materials are available in all libraries, but the sources that Maya uses are those that are generally available. Later, we provide an exhibit with a more detailed list of selected reference databases for psychology students, although not all will be available in all libraries. (For definitions of common technical terms and jargon used on the Web, see Exhibit 3.)

EXHIBIT 3 *Common terms and jargon on the Web*

---

attachment: a digitally coded file that is downloaded when you open an add-on to an e-mail message; the attachment might contain words, images, or, in a worst case scenario, a hidden virus.

browser: a program that is used to display Web pages.

cache: a place on the computer's hard drive where images and text from visited Web pages are stored to speed up the process of downloading the next time they are visited. Caches can, however, clutter the hard drive, particularly when information on the Web pages is constantly updated, so it is a good idea to clean the cache occasionally.

cookies: bits of personalized information left on the hard drive by some Web sites so they can track visitors online (some Web sites will not admit visitors who do not agree to accept a cookie). There are cookie cleanup programs to send this clutter into oblivion.

database: a collection of data, such as the reference databases shown in Exhibit 7.

firewall: a system that protects online computers from outside hackers who want to steal information or create a launching pad for destructive signals to Web sites.

full-text database: a collection of textual material that can be electronically perused in its entirety, such as the complete content of the journals in the database.

html: the coded language (hypertext markup language) used to create Web pages.

http: acronym for hypertext transfer protocol, the prefix (http://) of many URLs; it signifies how computers communicate with one another on the Internet.

hyperlink: a coded image (an icon or a button) or a coded word or phrase (usually in blue and underlined) that changes to a hand when you move your mouse pointer over it; clicking the hyperlink transports you to another place.

Internet service provider: the company or organization providing access to the Internet.

JPEG: acronym for Joint Photographic Experts Group, which is the most popular format on the Internet for photos because it supports 24-bit color and subtle variations in brightness and hue.

online search: the use of a computer and a search engine to retrieve information.

PDF: acronym for portable document format, which retains the look of the original document and is viewed by means of the Acrobat Reader installed on your computer (or available free from http://www.adobe.com).

search engine: a program (such as Google.com) that takes key words, queries an internal index, and returns a set of Web documents. Usually, if you click on "Help," you will find search help instructions, terminology, and advanced search tips.

spam: unsolicited e-mail that is automatically sent to all those on an address list.

URL: acronym for uniform resource locator, or another name for the Web address. For example, the URL of a helpful Web site that is sponsored by the Library of the University of Waterloo is http://www.lib.uwaterloo.ca/society/psychol_soc.html. There are links on this Web site to a great many national and international psychological societies, some of which provide information of interest to students who plan to go to graduate school (such as information about funding and career planning).

viruses: damaging codes that invade a computer's hard drive when an infected attachment or a contaminated file is opened. Some viruses, called *worms*, copy themselves and spread rapidly in the hard drive; others, called *Trojan horses*, assume the appearance of normal files but secretly wipe the hard drive clean. As a safeguard against viruses, be cautious about what you download or open. Install (and routinely update) antivirus software to automatically check attachments before you open them and, in a worst case scenario, to find and try to repair damage to your hard drive.

In one of the instructor's lectures, he explained what he called the "Pygmalion experiment," a classic research study by Robert Rosenthal and Lenore Jacobson. In a book the instructor mentioned, *Pygmalion in the Classroom,* Rosenthal and Jacobson described how, in the 1960s, they had given a standard nonverbal intelligence test to the children in a public elementary school in South San Francisco. The teachers were told only that the test was one of "intellectual blooming." Approximately 20% of the children, whose names the investigators had picked at random, were represented to the teachers as capable of marked intellectual growth based on their performance on this test. In other words, the difference between the supposed potential "bloomers" and the other students existed solely in the minds of their teachers. The children's performance on the intelligence test was measured after one semester, again after a full academic year, and again after two academic years. The results revealed that although the greatest differential gain in total intelligence appeared after one school year, the "bloomers" held an advantage over the other children even after two years. Maya's instructor described these results as an example of what are frequently referred to in psychology as *expectancy effects* and *the Rosenthal effect* (because Robert Rosenthal conducted extensive experimental investigations of how people's expectations sometimes become *self-fulfilling prophecies,* a term that was coined earlier by Robert Merton, a noted sociologist).

Maya is interested in going into teaching and thinks that a literature review paper on expectancy effects might be a good topic. She knows that it may be too broad a topic and that she needs to narrow it, but the Pygmalion experiment could be a launching point for a more focused review. She begins by making an appointment with the instructor in order to discuss her idea. She brings a pad of paper to the meeting to make notes, so she won't have to rely on her memory alone. At the meeting, the instructor encourages her to pursue her idea, and he recommends that she start by reading the Rosenthal and Jacobson book and, afterward, a journal article by Stephen Raudenbush. Raudenbush performed an early meta-analysis of the research on teacher expectancy effects, and he was successful in identifying a plausible moderator variable, the instructor tells Maya. The instructor does not recall the journal or the year of the Raudenbush article, but he believes that it was published in an APA journal, probably in the 1980s as there were several follow-up studies by then that could be meta-analyzed. He recommends that Maya use PsycINFO to search for the article, and he tells her that she will be able to get an abstract of the work on PsycINFO and possibly the full-text article as well. He also mentions a book edited by Peter Blanck, with "interpersonal expectations" in the title. The instructor tells Maya that she can readily track down detailed information about this book, as well as more detailed information about *Pygmalion in the Classroom,* using the online catalog at the Library of Congress. She can also look in any encyclopedias of psychology in the library to see what they have to say about expectancy effects, or teacher expectancy effects, or interpersonal expectations, or the Rosenthal effect. "Good luck, and keep taking careful notes," he tells her. "And stay focused; it is easy to get distracted by the mountain of literature on expectancy effects."

The instructor gave Maya good advice when he said "stay focused," because there really is a mountain of literature not only on expectancy effects, but in the field of psychology in general, and it continues to proliferate by leaps and bounds. Without a clear objective for her literature review, as well as the will to stay focused on that objective, Maya could be overwhelmed by the assignment she faces. This is the reason it is so important to narrow the focus of your literature review or empirical research, and to manage your time efficiently.

2.2   Using the Online Catalog

When Maya returns to her room that afternoon, she uses her computer to begin the search and retrieval process. By using your own computer to retrace her steps in this and section 2.4, you can easily teach yourself how to access the electronic resources described here. You will also have an opportunity to learn about the resources that are available to you at your college. If some full-text databases are unavailable, you can ask a librarian about the availability of printed copies of material you need. The library may have access to other resources, or the librarian may have some suggestions. As you find particular databases, such as those mentioned in sections 2.4–2.6, you can put a checkmark next to each of the names in this chapter. If you don't have your own computer, you need to find the location of areas in your college where computers are available for students' use. Let's now see how Maya progresses in her search and retrieval process.

Going online and using a search engine (such as www.google.com), Maya begins typing "Library of Congress online catalog" (no quotation marks). Before she can finish, she sees a list of suggestions, one of which is *Library of Congress Catalog*. Clicking it reveals thousands of Web sites; the first one is exactly what she was looking for, and clicking it immediately takes Maya to http://catalog.loc.gov. She is presented with two options: a Basic Search (using a fill-in box where she can search by title, author, subject, keywords, etc.) and a Guided Search (where she can use a series of form menus). There is also a space labeled "Quick Search." Maya types in "Pygmalion in the classroom" (without the quotes), chooses the "Keyword (All)" option, and clicks "Search." The next screen gives her information about several books, and the top two are both titled *Pygmalion in the Classroom*. One has a 1968 publication date (it's the original edition of Rosenthal and Jacobson's book) and the other, a 1992 date (a later, updated edition). Clicking on each of them in turn gives her a "brief record" for each book, which she prints out for later use.

Maya clicks the tab labeled "New Search" and starts over again, this time searching for information about the other book her instructor mentioned. Had she put off this search for another day, she could return by going online and typing in the Library of Congress's URL: http://catalog. loc.gov. She decides to do a Basic Search by using the keywords that the instructor mentioned ("interpersonal expectations"). She clicks on the Basic Search option and sees a space called "Search Text." She types *interpersonal expectations*. There is a space below it that lists further options, and Maya chooses "Title Keyword" and clicks on "Search." She is given a list of books, one of which is exactly the book she was looking for, and clicking on it gives her the brief record that is shown in Exhibit 4. She notices there are links on the page for "Sample text," "Publisher description," and "Table of contents." She clicks on "Table of contents," peruses

EXHIBIT 4   Brief record from Library of Congress online catalog

the various chapter titles in the book, and concludes that it will be a useful resource in her literature review.

Maya notices that the call number of the book is also indicated. She decides to be prudent and print the brief record, in case there is information she needs in the future. The ISBN number noted in the exhibit refers to the International Standard Book Number; you will usually see these numbers printed on the back covers of books or in the front matter on the same page as the publication information. The rest of the information is either self-explanatory or specialized for librarians, such as the description indicating that this book has 18 (xviii) prefatory pages, is 500 pages (p.) long, contains illustrations (ill.), and stands 24 cm high on the shelf.

2.3   Print Resources in the Library

The next day, Maya goes to her college library to find out whether the books that she needs are in the library's stacks (the shelves throughout the library). While there, she also asks about the location of encyclopedias of psychology. (She learns this information is available on the library's online catalog, which in the future she can access back in her room). The 1968 edition of the Rosenthal and Jacobson book was borrowed by someone and not returned. If it is overdue, she can request that the library contact the borrower to ask that the overdue book be returned for another patron. Neither the 1992 edition of the Rosenthal and Jacobson book nor the book titled *Interpersonal Expectations* was ever in the library's collection, but Maya can order them through *interlibrary loan,* a system in which groups of libraries share services and materials with one another. (Many libraries have interlibrary loan forms on their Web sites; these forms can be filled out and submitted online.) Maya is aware that it will take time for the library to receive material she orders through interlibrary loan, and she is on a tight schedule to submit a proposal. However, she decides to order *Interpersonal Expectations* through interlibrary loan and, while she is waiting for it, see if she can find a paperback copy of the 1992 edition of *Pygmalion in the Classroom* that she can purchase online and begin reading.

While she is in the library, Maya checks out the encyclopedias of psychology and browses the stacks for anything valuable but unexpected. Not all libraries allow students to browse the stacks. Instead some request that you submit a form listing the material that you want to use; a staff member will then retrieve it for you. If your library permits you to browse the stacks, see the information in Exhibit 5. It shows the two systems used in the United States to catalog psychological materials in libraries. Though most now use the Library of Congress system, there may be some old-timers that still use the Dewey Decimal System. The Library of Congress *call number* in Exhibit 4 is BF323.E8. It means that this book is shelved in the BF section of the stacks and, next, in numeric (323) and, then, in alphanumeric

EXHIBIT 5 *Cataloging of psychological materials*

Library of Congress System		*Dewey Decimal System*	
BF	Abnormal psychology	00-	Artificial intelligence
	Child psychology	13-	Parapsychology
	Cognition	15-	Abnormal psychology
	Comparative psychology		Child psychology
	Environmental psychology		Cognitive psychology
	Motivation		Comparative psychology
	Parapsychology		Environmental psychology
	Perception		Industrial psychology
	Personality		Motivation
	Physiological psychology		Perception
	Psycholinguistics		Personality
	Psychological statistics		Physiological psychology
HF	Industrial psychology	30-	Family
	Personnel management		Psychology of women
HM	Social psychology		Social psychology
HQ	Family	37-	Educational psychology
	Psychology of women		Special education
LB	Educational psychology	40-	Psycholinguistics
LC	Special education	51-	Statistics
Q	Artificial intelligence	61-	Psychiatry
	Physiological psychology		Psychotherapy
QA	Mathematical statistics	65-	Personnel management
RC	Abnormal psychology		
	Psychiatry		
	Psychotherapy		
T	Personnel management		

order (E8). The call number is written on the bottom of the spines of books in the stacks. Exhibit 5 shows various areas where psychology-related books are shelved.

Maya's instructor cautioned her that there was a mountain of literature and not to lose sight of her objective. At this point, however, she has only a very general idea, which she will need to narrow and then sharpen. Knowing about the many print resources in the library, including dictionaries and reference sources, can be useful when she gets deeper into her project. For example, the *Annual Review of Psychology* is another potentially useful reference source, and it is available online as well as in print in many libraries. It is part of the *Annual Review* series, which is a *serial publication* (i.e., one published at regular intervals) that provides authoritative reviews on just about every subject in science. Other useful reference books in libraries are called *handbooks;* if you search on this term in the library's online catalog, you are likely to find specialized handbooks. These books have detailed reviews by experts in the field. A handbook chapter tends to be more idiosyncratic than the subject reviews in the *Annual Review of Psychology* or the brief articles in encyclopedias.

Some journals also specialize in integrative reviews. For example, the Association for Psychological Science (APS) publishes two such journals: *Perspectives on Psychological Science* (described by the APS as "an eclectic mix of reports and articles," which include integrative reviews, meta-analyses, theoretical statements, and other sorts of articles) and *Psychological Science in the Public Interest* (a monograph series that has reviews of issues of public interest). The APS also publishes a journal of research articles called *Psychological Science* and a journal of brief reviews of research and content areas, *Current Directions in Psychological Science.* The American Psychological Association sponsors a large number of journals, including two highly respected ones that publish literature reviews (*Psychological Bulletin*) and theoretical papers (*Psychological Review*). Another important journal that contains integrative reviews is *Behavioral and Brain Sciences* (published by Cambridge University Press). A special feature of this journal is a section after each article called "Open Peer Commentary," which has lively commentary on the article by other authors. There are specialty journals in virtually any general area you can think of, and librarians can point you to these and other works that you may find useful. Professional librarians are highly skilled in helping people find the material they need, so don't be shy about approaching a librarian for help in finding resource material.

2.4   Using PsycINFO

Maya's instructor had also suggested that she look up a meta-analysis by Stephen Raudenbush, but all he could remember was that it was about "teacher expectancy effects" and thought it was published back in the 1980s in an APA journal. He recommended that Maya use an electronic database called PsycINFO. This APA database has bibliographic records from the 1800s to the present. Maya finds that she can access this database in the library and in several other areas of the college where there are computers and printers for student use, and she can also use her own computer and save what she needs in a file. Libraries purchase site licenses from vendors, who then provide PsycINFO and, possibly, other APA databases. These vendors (or hosts) include companies called EBSCO, OVID Technologies, DIALOG, DIMDI (Germany), Hogrefe (Switzerland), and ProQuest. Maya's library uses the EBSCO host system for PsycINFO, which she finds listed in her library's record of databases available to students.

When she chooses this database, the screen has a field of information, including a blank space and the option to "Select a Field" (author, title, journal title, series title, keywords, year of publication, ISBN, and so on). Other options that she can check (or ignore) allow Maya to limit the results by publication date (month, year), publication type (all journals, peer-reviewed journals, etc.), age groups, language, and so on. Maya is interested in the path of least resistance, and so she types "Raudenbush" (no quotes) and chooses "Author," and below it, in another space, she types "teacher expectancy" (again no quotes) and chooses "Title." Clicking "Search" gives her the bibliographic reference, and she has the option of requesting the abstract or the full-text article, which she can then save or print. Had Maya typed "Raudenbush" and clicked "Author," she would have been provided a long list of publications by Raudenbush, including many that were not available in full text on PsycINFO. There would be additional information for all the publications, so that she could retrieve them by using other electronic databases, or by going to the printed journals in her college library, or for older ones that may not be available in these two formats, by using microfilm archives that she can read in the library and print.

Exhibit 6 shows the entire PsycINFO record for the particular Raudenbush article that Maya retrieved. Although the term *moderator variable* does not appear anywhere in the record, reading the abstract confirms that Raudenbush found a moderator variable, which was that the magnitude of teacher expectancy effects on pupil IQ was moderated by how well the teachers knew their pupils at the time of the expectancy induction. Maya now has an idea about how to narrow the focus of her literature review on *moderators of Pygmalion expectancy effects*. While still using PsycINFO, Maya experiments by typing in "Pygmalion" and choosing "Keywords," and below it typing "moderator" and choosing "Abstract." She is given two relevant bibliographic references: an article in the *Journal of Organizational Psychology* (2000, *21*, 913-928) by Nicole M. Kierien and Michael A. Gold, titled "Pygmalion in Work Organizations: A Meta-Analysis," and an article in the *Journal of Applied Psychology* (1995, *80*, 253-270) by Taly Dvir, Dov Eden, and Michal Lang Banjo, titled "Self-Fulfilling Prophecy and Gender: Can Women Be Pygmalion and Galatea?" The second article was in an APA journal, and she retrieves and saves the PDF full-text article. PsycINFO does not offer a PDF full-text copy of the first article, but it tells her how to "Find Full Text." Maya clicks it and sees that she has other options for finding the full-text version of this article.

Notice in Exhibit 6 that there is an entry called "Digital Object Identifier." It refers to information that Maya will need when she includes the Raudenbush reference in either her proposal or her final paper. Symbolized as *DOI*, or in the references formatted in the APA style as *doi,* it is an identification number used for intellectual property in the digital environment.

EXHIBIT 6 PsycINFO *record of journal article*

Record: 1

Title:	Magnitude of teacher expectancy effects on pupil IQ as a function of the credibility of expectancy induction: A synthesis of findings from 18 experiments.
Authors:	Raudenbush, Stephen W., Harvard U Graduate School of Education
Source:	Journal of Educational Psychology, Vol 76(1), Feb, 1984. pp. 85-97.
Publisher:	US: American Psychological Association.
Other Publishers:	US: Warwick & York
ISSN:	0022-0663 (Print) 1939-2176 (Electronic)
Language:	English
Keywords:	meta analysis of expectancy induction, effect of teacher expectancy on student IQ, 1st–7th graders, implications for theories & future meta-analytic research
Abstract:	Meta-analysis was used to examine the variability in the outcomes of experiments testing the effects of teacher expectancy on pupil IQ. The tenuous process of expectancy induction, wherein researchers supply teachers with information designed to elevate their expectancies for children actually selected at random, is viewed as problematic in "Pygmalion" experiments, as developed by R. Rosenthal and L. Jacobson (1968). It was hypothesized that the better teachers know their pupils at the time of expectancy induction, the smaller the treatment effect would be. Data strongly support this hypothesis. Hypotheses that the type of IQ test (groups vs individual) and type of test administrator (aware vs blind to expectancy-inducing information) influence experimental results were not supported. The hypothesis that expectancy effects are larger for children in Grades 1 and 2 than for children in Grades 3–6 was supported. However, significant effects reappeared at Grade 7. Theoretical implications and questions for future meta-analytic research are discussed. (57 ref) (PsycINFO Database Record © 2009 APA, all rights reserved)
Subjects:	*Elementary School Students; *Experimental Methods; *Intelligence Quotient; *Junior High School Students; *Teacher Expectations; Age Differences; Literature Review; Statistical Analysis; Theories
Classification:	Classroom Dynamics & Student Adjustment & Attitudes (3560)
Population:	Human (10)
Age Group:	Childhood (birth-12 yrs) (100) School Age (6-12 yrs) (180) Adolescence (13-17 yrs) (200)

EXHIBIT 6 *Continued*

Methodology:	Empirical Study; Literature Review
Format Availablability:	Electronic; Print
Format Covered:	Print
Publication Type:	Journal; Peer Reviewed Journal
Document Type:	Journal Article
Release Date:	19840101
Copyright:	American Psychological Association. 1984.
Digital Object Identifier:	10.1037/0022-0663.76.1.85
Accession Number:	1984-16218-001
Number of Citations in Source:	57
Database:	PsyclNFO
Full Text Database:	

The APA style of referencing cited electronic materials is to show these doi numbers for each of the references that you obtained electronically, assuming that there is a doi number for the reference. In chapter 3 we provide examples of how to indicate the doi numbers, but to anticipate a little, see the reference sections of Jane Doe's final report in appendix A and John Smith's review paper in appendix B. Notice that the doi appears at the end of the particular reference and there is no period, the reason being there was no period as part of the doi. In full-text journals, the doi is now usually indicated on the first page of the article. Maya will need to keep a record of the doi numbers for all electronic information she cites and references.

Maya has made impressive progress in a very short time. She has discovered what a time saver the library and electronic resources are. Just the process of using PsycINFO and reading the abstract of the Raudenbush article focused Maya's thoughts and made her writing assignment more manageable.

2.5   PsycARTICLES, PsycBOOKS, PsycEXTRA, and PsycCRITIQUES

Maya used PsycINFO, the American Psychological Association's primary abstract database. The advantage of electronic databases like PsycINFO and the Library of Congress's online catalog, as Maya discovered, is that you can search to your heart's content. Even if you do not have your own computer, libraries have a bank of computers reserved for students. Because you may have to wait your turn to use one, you also need to know whether there are computers in other locations that you can use to communicate with the library's automated system. If you have your own computer, you need to find out how to access these resources from your room. PsycINFO and other electronic databases each have their own limited vocabulary, which is appropriate to the particular database. There is a print version of PsycINFO's limited vocabulary, called *Thesaurus of Psychological Index Terms,* that is typically available in libraries that subscribe to PsycINFO. But it is pretty easy to use PsycINFO, and many journal articles and chapters in handbooks come with keywords that you can use in the online search and retrieval process. When you use a term that is not exactly right, often the search engine will suggest some alternatives for you to consider. Most students find the search and retrieval process easy to use and very intuitive, and before too long they are sufficiently comfortable with the process to assist other students who are new to it.

There are many full-text databases for journal articles and books, but few are free online unless you are a student who can access them through your library's Web site. The best way to proceed is to find out what electronic databases are available to you and how to access them. There may be so many at your college that you need to scroll down pages and pages of names. To make it easier for students, many library Web sites also sort these databases by academic discipline. Textbook publishers often provide links to electronic databases as well, but they may not have the journals or sourcebooks that you are looking for. PsycINFO has extensive records of books and articles published by psychologists, including bibliographic records that give the full citations of work that was not published by APA. PsycINFO typically has a "journal link" that takes you to the journal home page on the publisher's site, where you find out if the full text is free or not. Some publishers (not all) put their journals up for free after an embargo period, and there are electronic databases that provide these materials.

PsycARTICLES is another APA database, which is linked with PsycINFO in the libraries that subscribe to both. PsycARTICLES is a database of full-text articles from the APA journals, journals of the Canadian Psychological Association (CPA), and a group of journals published by Hogrefe. You can find out more about these journals and the years of coverage at www.apa.org/databases. PsycBOOKS, another APA database, provides subscribers with electronic access to the full text of scholarly books from APA and some other publishers, including a number of classic resources in psychology and the electronic version of the APA's *Encyclopedia of Psychology.* PsycEXTRA, another APA database, provides subscribers with records and some full-text access to unpublished and/ or "hard-to-find work" (called the "gray literature") that is not covered in PsycINFO and is outside the peer-review literature (conference papers, newspapers, technical reports, government reports, etc.). The term *peer review* means that the literature passed through a systematic review process in which expert authorities in the field assessed the originality, validity, and significance of the work and recommended it be accepted or rejected for publication. PsycCRITIQUES, also an APA database, provides reviews of psychology books, videos, films, and software, including the historical file of an APA journal of book reviews called *Contemporary Psychology* (which existed from 1956 to 2004).

2.6 Tips on Using Other Electronic Databases

Once you are familiar with how to use PsycINFO, you should find it easy to use other electronic databases to search for information. Exhibit 7 shows some of the many electronic databases that may be available to students through their library's Web site. Databases exist for just about every discipline and area of interest. If you are confused about which database has the information you are looking for, ask one of the information specialists in your college library. Many college library Web sites have a link that you can click, after which you type the name of the journal and/ or the title of the article, and you are told whether it is in an electronic database subscribed to by your college. Here are some tips for using these databases:

- ◆ Begin by writing down the questions you have, and then make a list of words or phrases you want to try as search terms.
- ◆ Scan the list of the databases that are available to you online; print the list if you can, to avoid having to remember the databases or to endlessly go back and forth.
- ◆ Put a check mark next to any other databases that look relevant—or that might be of interest later on.
- ◆ As you search, keep a record so that you don't backtrack without realizing it; list the abstract or index, the years you searched, and the search terms that you used.
- ◆ If you can, copy what you find into a file that you can open again later. You can use your antivirus program to make sure the file is not infected.
- ◆ Don't just make a citation list of relevant work. Read what you are going to cite, because the instructor will wonder whether you have read it.

Notice at the bottom of Exhibit 7 a database called the Web of Science. If you need to do a more comprehensive search for a meta-analysis or a dissertation, the Web of Science will provide access to relatively recent records in the Social Sciences Citation Index (SSCI), Science Citation Index (SCI), and Arts & Humanities Citation Index (A&HCI). These databases are useful if you want to track down studies that followed up on an older study you've read about in your textbook. Once you are into

EXHIBIT 7 *Reference databases available electronically*

Name	Coverage
Academic Search Premier	Full-text data from many scholarly publications in social science, the humanities, education, computer science, engineering, language and linguistics, arts and literature, medical science, and ethnic studies.
Annual Reviews Online	Full-text literature reviews of the significant research in 32 disciplines.
Britannica.com	Full-text database for *Encyclopedia Britannica* and *Merriam-Webster's Collegiate Dictionary*.
Cambridge Journals Online	Full-text database of Cambridge University Journals.
Census Lookup	Access to data tables for specific types of geographic areas from the most recent Census of Population and Housing; produced by the U.S. Census Bureau.
DSM Library	*Diagnostic and Statistical Manual of Mental Disorders.*
Electronic Human Relations Area Files	Database of a nonprofit institution at Yale University, a consortium of educational, research, cultural, and government agencies in over 30 countries that provides ethnographic and related information by culture and subject; the acronym is eHRAF.
ERIC	Bibliographic records of research reports, conference papers, teaching guides, books, and journal articles in education, from preschool to the doctoral level; ERIC is an acronym for Educational Resources Information Center.
Ingenta Connect	Article summaries from thousands of journals.
JSTOR	Full text of back issues of periodicals across all disciplines.
LEXIS-NEXIS Academic UNIVerse	Full text of news reports, including business, medical, political, financial, and legal; a convenient source of news reports by topic areas.
Mental Measurements Yearbook	Information and evaluations regarding commercially available testing instruments.
NCJRS Database	National Criminal Justice Reference Service database, including summaries of publications on criminal justice.
OED Online	Full text of 20-volume *Oxford English Dictionary* and additions.

EXHIBIT 7 *Continued*

Oxford Scholarship Online	Full text of selected books published by Oxford University Press.
Periodicals Archive Online	Full-text database of back issues of over 500 journals.
Periodicals Index Online	Index to millions of articles published in over 5,000 journals going back over 300 years.
ProQuest Dissertations & Theses	Full-text database of more than two million doctoral dissertations and master's theses.
PsycARTICLES	The American Psychological Association's full-text database of APA journal articles.
PsycBOOKS	The American Psychological Association's full-text database of chapters in books published by the APA, some historic books in the public domain, and the APA's *Encyclopedia of Psychology.*
PsycCRITIQUES	APA database of book and film reviews.
PsycEXTRA	APA database of hard-to-find documents and records, such as conference papers and technical reports that exist outside psychology's traditional peer-reviewed literature.
PsycINFO	The American Psychological Association's abstract database, including every abstract created by the APA from 1887 to the present.
Sage Journals Online	Full-text database of journals from Sage Publications, including those of the Association for Psychological Science (APS): *Psychological Science, Current Directions in Psychological Science, Psychological Science in the Public Interest,* and *Perspectives on Psychological Science.*
Science Online	Full-text access to *Science,* published by the American Association for the Advancement of Science (AAAS).
Social Science Research Network	A worldwide collaborative effort of scholars, which is devoted to the rapid dissemination of social science research.
Web of Science	Access to Social Sciences Citation Index (SSCI), the parent source of titles of works and names of authors in psychology and related fields.

the Web of Science, you can click on the "Tutorial" button for guidance, or you can click on the "Full search" button (for a general search) or the "Easy search" button (which allows a more limited search of articles on a specific topic, person, or address). This kind of search is called an *ancestry search* because you are tracking down "ancestral" citations of an older article or a book.

Here are some more tips:

- Don't start out by using Google or Yahoo or Bing for your search and then only rely on any documents that appear. Search engines like these generally seek what are called *statistic Web pages*, or thin, digitized layers of information that do not have search functions of their own. The electronic databases in Exhibit 7 are part of what is called the *deep Web*, which means they surface only when you make database queries from within the sites.

- However, Google does have a search engine called Scholar, which might provide some sources you won't run across elsewhere. Click on www.googlescholar.com. As is typical of Google searches, you'll get thousands of returns, but chances are good that the first few dozen will suit your purpose. (Maya typed in "classroom environment" and got over 500,000 hits.) The links may take you to other sites and require "Save/E-mail/Print" procedures that are different from (and usually not as convenient as) the procedures on PsycINFO, but they are certainly worth exploring.

- If you go to www.googlescholar.com and enter a scholar's name, you will see the number of citations of each work listed—a measure of how important and useful the work has been to others interested in the topic. You will notice that sometimes there is a PDF link to a full-text copy of the work. Another source of information for the number of citations is www.harzing.com/pop.htm. For some names, you may get different results if you type the person's full name or the first initial and the last name, but you can experiment.

- Finally, if you are in a department that has many active researchers on the faculty, one of them may be working on the very problem that interests you. To find out, ask your instructor, and also ask if it would be OK to approach that person. If the answer is yes, set up an appointment to discuss your interests, but be sure to do your homework on the topic (and on the department's Web page) first. List for yourself the questions you want to ask, and then take notes during the interview.

2.7 Taking Notes in the Library

We have discussed retrieving abstracts and full-text material online and locating original material in the library, but not taking notes. If you have the funds, the best way to make sure that your notes are exact is to photocopy the material you need. But be sure to write down in a conspicuous place on the photocopy the complete citation of everything you copy. You will still need to interpret what you copied, and it is often easier to make notes of your interpretation at the time you first have the material in hand. Having notes like these will enable you to write an accurate paper as well as one that is organized efficiently. You can write your interpretations on the back of your photocopies so that your notes are handy when it is time to organize all your work. Making detailed notes of all the material you use will also help you avoid committing *plagiarism* accidentally.

We will have more to say about plagiarism later in this book, but you plagiarize *intentionally* when you knowingly present someone else's work as your own. *Accidental plagiarism* means that the writer copied someone's work but forgot to credit it or to put it in quotation marks with an accurate citation. Plagiarism is illegal, and you should guard against it by following three simple rules:

1. Keep accurate notes.
2. Give credit to others when it is due.
3. Do not claim someone else's work as your own.

If you are taking extensive notes on a laptop computer, you need some way to distance yourself from pages and pages of notes in order to bring coherence to them. The same is true if you are taking handwritten notes in the library. Some writers like to use a separate index card for each idea that they find as they uncover relevant material. Some prefer making notes on 5 × 8-inch index cards. Many students find that they can usually get all the information they want on the front of a 5 × 8-inch index card, so it is easier to find what they want later. If you are using a computer to take notes, you can print them out and cluster them in logical batches (as you would large index cards). For each note, be sure to include the full reference of the material, including all the information you will need for the reference section of your paper, as well as the page numbers of verbatim quotes (to cite in the narrative of your paper).

If you have made an outline for a literature review (as described in chapter 5), you can code each card or printout with the particular outline section where the material will be used (or you can use color coding). An alternative is to use a folder for each section of your literature review, and then to file the relevant batches of note cards or printouts in the appropriate folder. In this way, you can maintain a general organization of your notes and avoid facing a huge stack of miscellaneous bits and pieces of information that you must sort and integrate into a useful order. If you have devised your own code of reference numbers to sort material, be consistent, because a haphazard arrangement will only slow you down when it is time to write your first draft.

The most fundamental rule of note taking is accuracy, which means that anything you quote must be exactly true to the original, including the spelling and punctuation that were used in the original. We will have more to say about the use of quoted material later in this book, but to anticipate a little, there are procedures for indicating a spelling mistake, or a punctuation error, or a grammatical problem in the original quote (the italicized word *sic,* for "thus," is inserted in brackets) or for indicating that words in the original are omitted in the quote (the use of three spaced dots, called *ellipsis points*). Here are further tips that will serve you well:

- Try to be as thorough and systematic as you can so that you do not waste time and energy having to return to the same book or article.
- It is better to photocopy or record too much than to rely on your memory to fill in the gaps, because human memory can be faulty.
- Be sure your notes will make sense to you when you examine them later.

2.8 Source Credibility

Not all information is reliable, and the question is how to separate the credible from the suspect. This question is not easy to answer: A source of information that one person views as reliable may not be perceived by another the same way. The way this problem is addressed in academia is to subject manuscripts submitted to journals to *peer review* (that is, as already mentioned, the editors send them out to experts in the same field for independent evaluations and recommendations). It is not impossible for a poorly done study to slip by occasionally, but as a general rule, scientists and other scholars give greater weight to peer-reviewed journal articles than to unpublished manuscripts and technical reports. Textbooks are sent out for review, but mostly because the prospective publisher wants to find out whether they will be saleable.

Even within the peer-reviewed literature, there is a pecking order of journals in any field. Manuscripts that are rejected by one journal may be sent to a second or third journal, until they finally find a home. Articles in journals at the top of the pecking order are not automatically more reliable than those in other journals, but a social hierarchy of journals does exist in every field, and the toughest journals in which to publish are those at the top of the social structure. In some cases, 85% or more of manuscripts submitted to the most prestigious journals are rejected by the editors based on peer reviews, but some manuscripts may be returned without review because, in the editor's judgment, they seem to be inappropriate for that particular journal. Journals that are cited a lot are usually also regarded as higher in the pecking order, information that can be found online by going to "Harzing's Publish or Perish" Web site (www.harzing.com/pop.htm).

Some information is especially suspect, however, such as that in chat rooms on the Web. There is, in fact, a growing literature in psychological science on the nature of these chat rooms and the fertile ground they provide for rumors to take root. Because in a given instance it might be hard to decide whether something you read online is a fact or a rumor (that is, an unsupported allegation) or maybe even a boldfaced lie, the saying about "buying a pig in a poke" is applicable to much of this information. A useful Web site that specializes in debunking false rumors is www.snopes.com. However, the best guidance we can give you about assessing the credibility of information that you are thinking about citing in your research report or review paper is this: When in doubt, ask your instructor for guidance.

2.9 Additional Tips for Starting Your Literature Search

As you get started on the literature search, try to be realistic in assessing how much material you will need in your review. Too few journal articles or books may result in a weak foundation for your project, but too much material and intemperate expectations may overwhelm you and your topic. You are writing not a doctoral dissertation or an article for a journal but a required paper that must be completed within a limited amount of time. How can you find out what is a happy medium between too little and too much? Talk with your instructor before you start an intensive literature search. Ask whether your plan seems realistic.

Here are some more tips to get you started on the literature search and retrieval and to do it efficiently:

- Ask the instructor to recommend any key works that you should read or consult. Even if you feel confident about your topic, asking the instructor for specific leads can keep you from going on a wild goose chase.
- Do not expect to finish your literature search and retrieval in one sitting. Students with unrealistic expectations make themselves overly anxious and rush a task that should be done patiently and methodically.
- Suppose you can't locate the original work that you are looking for in the library. Some students return repeatedly, day after day, seeking a book or journal article before discovering that it has been lost or stolen or is being rebound. Ask a librarian to find the elusive material. If the original work you need is unavailable, the librarian may consult another college library. However, the material could take so long to arrive that you might miss the deadline set by your instructor (this kind of delay is not an acceptable excuse).
- If you are looking for a specialized work, you probably will not find it in a small public library, so don't waste your time. When students spend a lot of time off campus in public libraries and bookstores looking for source material, they usually come back with references from general texts or current mass-market books and periodicals, and these rarely constitute acceptable sources.

- Remember to keep a running checklist of the sources you searched and the search terms you used so that you don't accidentally retrace your steps.
- And finally, remember the advice that Maya's instructor gave her: *Stay focused!*

2.10 Library and E-mail Etiquette

Before we turn to the basics of developing your proposal for a review paper or a research project, here is some final advice about using the library. The golden rule of library etiquette is to respect your library and remember that others also have to use it:

- Be quiet.
- Never tear pages out of journals or books.
- Never write in library journals or books.
- Do not monopolize material or machines.
- Return books and periodicals as soon as you finish with them.

Many students are surprised to learn that they can communicate with busy researchers. There is no guarantee that you will get a reply, but if you do make a request by e-mail, here are some dos and don'ts of e-mail etiquette:

- Don't ask for something readily available in most college libraries, because it is going to sound as if you were too lazy to look for it.
- Indicate in the subject space the nature of your e-mail message (for example, "Reprint request"), or else it may be deleted as spam without ever being opened.
- Don't write an overly detailed message; say who you are and what you are "requesting" (the polite way of asking), and thank the person in advance.
- Don't expect a lengthy response.
- If you are requesting a reprint, it is likely to be transmitted as a PDF or Word file, so make sure that your computer can open both of these kinds of files.
- If you receive a response, thank the person.

3

Developing a Proposal

Once you settle on an objective, the next step is to develop a proposal. Some instructors feel that an oral presentation is sufficient, but most require a written proposal as a way of ensuring that they and their students have a common understanding of the direction of the proposed research or literature review, the importance of originality, and a clear sense of all ethical issues involved in the proposed research. As you will be citing source materials, this chapter will familiarize you with the APA style of citing and referencing your sources. The chapter also contains sample proposals for a literature review and an empirical research study.

3.1   Settling on an Objective

In the previous chapter we saw how Maya started the process of finding and then retrieving reference material. Had we continued to look over her shoulder, we would see that she came up with several directions for her literature review. Exhibit 8 shows what is called a *cluster outline* in high school English. In the center of the cluster is the study that inspired Maya. The arrowed lines that emanate from the center represent four options that Maya is considering. One option would be to focus her review on the moderator variables (this term was explained in chapter 1 in section 1.4), starting with the Raudenbush article (Exhibit 6 in chapter 2) and continuing with the other work that she uncovered when she was using PsycINFO (section 2.4). Not all that work was available in full text in the APA full-text database (PsycARTICLES), but it could be retrieved by means of some other electronic databases that might be available through her library, or she could consult a librarian about obtaining print versions of the work (some may already be in her college library's stacks). A second

EXHIBIT 8   *Maya's perceived options for a research proposal*

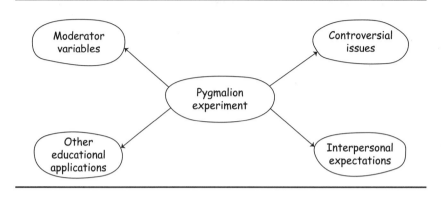

option for Maya's review paper would be to emphasize interpersonal expectations, using some of the work in Peter Blanck's book (Exhibit 4 in chapter 2) as a starting point. Browsing through that book also gave Maya a third option: to focus on educational applications. A fourth option would be a review of controversial issues in the literature on the Pygmalion experiment.

As she ponders the four options in Exhibit 8, Maya is further guided by her need to pull together ideas for a written proposal that is not diffuse or unwieldy. There is more to writing a proposal, however, than telling the instructor what you would like to study. An additional objective is to tell the instructor what you believe to be the significance of the project you are proposing (i.e., why it is of interest) and how you plan to proceed. Maya might justify the significance of a paper on the Pygmalion effect on practical grounds if she concentrates on the educational applications. If she decides to explore controversial issues, she might justify this emphasis on theoretical or methodological grounds. If Maya were writing a research proposal (rather than a literature review paper), she would need only a few key studies to help her formulate one or two hypotheses and then draft a plan for how she proposes to do the research and analyze the data. In the research proposal, she would be expected to anticipate and discuss any ethical issues that the research raises.

3.2   The Accepted Proposal as a "Letter of Agreement"

The term *proposal* means that you are suggesting something for acceptance. Thus, the proposal is not just a one-way communication from you to the instructor. It is also an opportunity for the instructor to provide you with feedback and to raise questions that you may need to address before your proposal is accepted. You might think of the accepted proposal as a sort of letter of agreement between you and the instructor. It is understood that you will consult the instructor if you wish to make any significant changes. However, there is no need to anticipate the conclusions in your final review paper or final research report; they are not carved in stone. It would be unreasonable to expect you to know already what you will conclude. But your instructor will assume that you have given enough thought to your assignment to formulate some preliminary ideas about the direction of the project. It is unacceptable to simply show up on the day the paper is due with a manuscript that is clearly different from what you and the instructor agreed on. If your proposal has outlined an empirical study, you may encounter problems in doing the study that you did not anticipate in the proposal. In such a case, it is essential that you discuss these problems with the instructor and obtain the instructor's approval before making any changes.

As you will see later in this chapter, the proposal for a literature review has more room for flexibility than the proposal for an empirical research study. Therefore, instructors may require submissions in addition to a written proposal if you are planning to conduct empirical research. For example, the instructor might give you a form or a questionnaire dealing with the ethics of the research, as required by the institutional review board (IRB) at your college or university, and you will need to complete the form or questionnaire. Jane Doe (appendix A) was also required to obtain the written permissions of the owner of a restaurant and a waitress in the restaurant who agreed to let Jane do her research there. The instructor's purpose in asking students to discuss not only their general ideas but also how they came up with the ideas and why the topic is worth studying are (a) to stimulate students to formulate and think about their assignments, (b) to encourage students to choose topics that they find intrinsically interesting, and (c) to make sure these are the students' ideas. We will have more to say about the third point later on in this book, but it is absolutely essential that the work be your own even though it builds on the work of others or might be a partial replication of a previous study.

In the case of empirical research, many instructors welcome students' proposals for replications of previous studies. The reason is that replication is an essential criterion of reliable knowledge, as it continues the discovery process by clarifying and expanding both the meaning and the limits of theories, hypotheses, and observations. Replications are described as *successful* when they duplicate an earlier scientific observation or extend the observed relationship. They are described as *unsuccessful* when they fail to duplicate or extend an earlier observation or relationship. Someone once compared the scientist to a person who is looking for the right key to open a door and see what is behind it. In a successful replication, another competent researcher has tried a similar "key" and observed something similar behind the door. When researchers say that a replication "failed," it should not be taken to mean that the follow-up study failed to reproduce the original p value. The p value is sensitive to the number of sampling units (e.g., the total number of people who participated as subjects), the magnitude of the research finding (the *effect size*), the variability of the scores, and so forth. We will have more to say about statistical concepts in a later chapter (chapter 6), but successfully replicating a finding means observing something similar when you use a similar key.

Replications are sometimes the basis of senior theses and course projects. The student is expected to add a creative touch to the design, usually in the form of a new hypothesis or some other innovative aspect. For example, if the research study you are proposing to replicate used two levels of an independent variable, you might propose to experiment with three or four levels in order to explore whether there is a curvilinear relationship between the independent and dependent variables. If you hypothesized a variable that alters the size of the relationship between the independent and dependent variables, you can design a replication around your hypothesis of a moderator variable. Or you might choose a different measure of the dependent variable to explore whether the relationship is generalizable beyond the particular measurement that was used in the original study. You will still need to design your study so that it is similar in important respects to the original study, even though you are exploring your own innovative idea. Otherwise, you will find yourself in a logical bind if you need to explain discrepancies between your results and the earlier study's results. If you are writing a proposal for a replication study, it is a good idea to tell how you plan to compare the results. Do you propose a statistical comparison of the effect sizes, or a qualitative comparison based on theoretically relevant characteristics, or a combination of both?

3.3   How to Cite Source Materials

Later in this chapter, we provide sample proposals to give you a clear idea of one form of a research proposal or a proposal for a literature review. You will see that the two proposals differ in terms of the content emphasized, but one basic they have in common is that they use the APA style for citing source materials. The final research report in appendix A and the final review paper in appendix B also use this same style for citing source materials. The purpose of citations is to make it easy for readers to identify sources and to locate them in the list of references. To familiarize you with this style, which you will be using in your proposal and final paper, we pause here to illustrate how to cite the source materials you use when writing papers in APA style.

The author-date method is the APA's style of citing materials. The surname (last name) of the author (or the name of an institutional author, or a group that authored the work) and the year that the work was

EXHIBIT 9   Types of citations illustrated in section 3.3

One Work by One Author
  3.3.1 *Author's Name as Part of Narrative*
  3.3.2 *Parenthetical Citation*
  3.3.3 *Quoted Author*
  3.3.4 *Authors with Same Surname*
Multiple Coauthors
  3.3.5 *Two Coauthors*
  3.3.6 *Three, Four, or Five Coauthors*
  3.3.7 *Six or More Coauthors*
Secondary Sources
  3.3.8 *Secondary Citation of a Classic Work*
  3.3.9 *Two Secondary Citations in the Same Sentence*

copyrighted or issued are inserted in the text at the appropriate point. One very basic rule is not to list any publication in your reference list that you do not cite. A corollary rule is not to cite anything without placing it in the references. However, there are exceptions. If you were developing an extensive bibliography and wanted to list all relevant articles and books on the subject, then you would list some references that are not actually cited in the manuscript. However, you will not be expected to compile such a bibliography for a review paper or a research report in a college course. Another exception is a *personal communication* that you cite but do not include in the references. You will find an example in the Author Note on the title page (page 1) of John Smith's paper in appendix B. Exhibit 9 lists the various types of citations that are discussed in detail in the remainder of this section.

One Work by One Author

3.3.1 Author's Name as Part of Narrative
When the author's name appears at the beginning of a sentence or as part of the narrative, the surname is followed by the year of publication in parentheses. If the author is a group or an institution, the name of the group or institution is treated in this same way.

  (a) *Beginning of sentence:*
    Piaget (1952) called the developmental period of birth up to 2 years the sensorimotor stage.
  (b) *Possessive case at beginning of sentence:*
    Piaget's (1952) theory of development describes the period of birth up to 2 years as the sensorimotor stage.

(c) Beginning of clause:
In the field of developmental psychology, Piaget's (1952) concept of the sensorimotor stage of development (viz., the period of birth up to 2 years) has been highly cited.

(d) Group as author:
The National Commission for the Protection of Human Subjects of Biomedical and Behavioral Research (1979) recommended that the Belmont Report be adopted in its entirety.

3.3.2 Parenthetical Citation

The author's surname followed by a comma and the year of publication are all in parentheses.

(a) Surname of author:
In the field of developmental psychology, the sensorimotor stage of development refers to the period of birth up to 2 years (Piaget, 1952).

(b) Group as author:
The recommendation was that the Belmont Report be adopted in its entirety (National Commission for the Protection of Human Subjects of Biomedical and Behavioral Research, 1979).

3.3.3 Quoted Author

For quotations that are shorter than 40 words, the format above (3.3.1 and 3.3.2) is used and the page (p.) number of the quoted material is added at the end of the quotation (in parentheses) or, if the full citation appears after the quotation, is inserted after the date of publication.

(a) Author's name not in parentheses:
In *Aggression and Crimes of Violence*, Goldstein (1975) stated, "Perhaps no area of the criminal justice system is in as much need of revision as correctional facilities" (p. 137).

(b) Author-date in parentheses:
In *Aggression and Crimes of Violence*, the author stated, "Perhaps no area of the criminal justice system is in as much need of revision as correctional facilities" (Goldstein, 1975, p. 137).

3.3.4 Authors with Same Surname

If you cite two or more authors with the same surname (e.g., a book by Jeffrey H. Goldstein and a journal article by David Goldstein), each cited author's initials are given.

(a) Author's name not in parentheses:
In *Aggression and Crimes of Violence*, J. H. Goldstein (1975) stated, "Perhaps no area of the criminal justice system is in as much need of revision as correctional facilities" (p. 137).

(b) Author-date in parentheses:
In *Aggression and Crimes of Violence*, the author states, "Perhaps no area of the criminal justice system is in as much need of revision as correctional facilities" (J. H. Goldstein, 1975, p. 137).

Multiple Coauthors

3.3.5 Two Coauthors
Give both names each time the coauthored work is cited. The word and *is spelled out in a narrative citation, and an ampersand (&) is used in a citation in parentheses.*

(a) Authors' names not in parentheses:
In their book, *Wittgenstein's Poker,* Edmonds and Eidinow (2001) described a 10-minute argument between Ludwig Wittgenstein and Karl Popper, which has become legendary in modern philosophy.

(b) Authors-date in parentheses:
Wittgenstein's Poker describes a 10-minute argument between Ludwig Wittgenstein and Karl Popper, which has become legendary in modern philosophy (Edmonds & Eidinow, 2001).

3.3.6 Three, Four, or Five Coauthors
All the names are given in the first citation; all subsequent citations use the first author's name followed by et al.

(a) First citation of Shadish, Cook, and Campbell (2002):
Shadish, Cook, and Campbell's (2002) *Experimental and Quasi-Experimental Designs for Generalized Causal Inference* is a comprehensive overview of recent thinking about threats to causal inference since Campbell and Stanley's classic chapter in Gage's (1963) *Handbook of Research on Teaching.*

(b) Subsequent citation of Shadish, Cook, and Campbell (2002):
Internal validity implies "the validity of inferences about whether observed covariation between A (the presumed treatment) and B (the presumed outcome) reflects a causal relationship from A to B as those variables were manipulated or measured" (Shadish et al., 2002, p. 38).

3.3.7 Six or More Coauthors
Give the surname of the first author followed by et al. *(not italicized) and the date. For example, an article in* Psychological Science *(2010) was coauthored by 10 people (J. C. Ziegler, D. Bertrand, D. Tóth, V. Csépe, A. Reis, L. Faísca, N. Saine, H. Lyytinen, A. Vaessen, and L. Blomert). The article would be cited as Ziegler et al. (2010) or as (Ziegler et al., 2010) in the first citation as well as in subsequent citations.*

Secondary Sources

To cite a source that you did not read in its original form, make it clear that you are using someone else's citation (called a secondary citation). Use a secondary source only if the original source is unavailable to you; otherwise examine and cite the original source yourself, as there is no guarantee that the material you want to cite was described or quoted correctly in the secondary source.

3.3.8 Secondary Citation of a Classic Work

In Virgil's epic poem, *The Aeneid* (as cited in Allport and Postman, 1947), the following characterization of Fama appears: . . .

3.3.9 Two Secondary Citations in the Same Sentence

Hasher, Goldstein, and Toppino's finding (as cited in Kendzierski & Markey, 2002) is also consistent with the traditional idea that merely being exposed over and over to the same message, even if it is blatantly false, is usually enough to instill confidence in its credibility (McCullough, Murphy, & Schwartz, 1911, as cited in Baldwin & Baldwin, 2004).

Here are some additional guidelines that will cover most of the cases that you are likely to encounter:

- If you are citing a series of works, the proper sequence is alphabetical order by the surname of the first author and then by chronological order. If the surnames are the same for two authors, then the citation is alphabetized by the first name: (M. Baenninger, 2007, 2009; R. Baenninger, 2003; Brecher, 2009; DiClemente, 2010; E. K. Foster, 2009; S. Foster, 2009; Frei, 2008; Wells & Lafleur, 2007).
- Two or more works published by the same author in the same year are designated as *a, b, c,* and so on (Hantula, 2002a, 2002b, 2002c). In the references section, the alphabetical order of the works' titles determines the sequence when there is more than one work by an author in the same year.
- Work accepted for publication but not yet printed is designated *in press:* (Stern, in press; Terlecki, in press). In a list of citations of work by the same author, the rule is to place this work last: (Crabb, 2009, 2010, in press). In this case, three works by Crabb are cited, one published in 2009, another published in 2010, and a third work that has been accepted for publication but not yet published.
- If there is more than one cited work in press by the same author(s), the work is indicated by the suffixes *a, b, c,* and so on according to the alphabetized titles. Suppose that DiFonzo and Bordia have three articles accepted for publication but not yet published. The title of one is "Inside rumor," another is titled "Outside rumor," and the third is titled "Gossip and rumor." The alphabetized order is (a) "Gossip

and rumor," (b) "Inside rumor," (c) "Outside rumor." The citation is: (DiFonzo & Bordia, in press a, in press b, in press c).

- To cite a specific document obtained from a Web site, use a format similar to that for printed material (as shown above). If you want to cite a particular Web site but not a specific document from a Web site, give only the address (URL) of the site.

Finally, if you run into a problem that these guidelines do not address, keep one general idea in mind: Ask yourself whether you could identify a reference based on the citation you have provided. In other words, put yourself in your reader's shoes, and try to be consistent.

3.4   *How to Reference Source Materials*

The list of references starts on a new page, with the title "References" (in bold, no quotes, upper and lower case) centered at the top of the page. The list of references is illustrated in the sample papers in appendices A and B (and later on in this chapter, in the proposals that are illustrated). The references are arranged alphabetically by the surname of the first author and then by date of publication. Prefixes (*von, Mc, Mac, de, du*) can give students pause as they try to figure out how to alphabetize them, and the APA Manual has specific rules based on whether or not the prefix is *customarily used* when referring to the person. If you find yourself struggling with this distinction, we suggest you alphabetize by the particle preceding the name and be consistent when you add names to your list of references.

The standard style guidelines in the APA Manual are as follows:

- Invert all authors' names (that is, last name, first initial, middle initial).
- List multiple authors' names in the exact order in which they appear on the title page of the cited work.
- Use commas to separate multiple authors and an ampersand (&) before the last author.
- Give the year the work was copyrighted (the year and month for magazine articles and the year, month, and day for newspaper articles).
- In titles of books, chapters in books, and journal articles, capitalize only the first word of the title and of the subtitle (if any) as well as any proper names.
- Give the issue number of the journal in parentheses if the article cited is paginated by issue.
- Italicize the volume number of a journal article and the title of a book or a journal.
- Give the city and state for a U.S. book's publisher, using the postal abbreviations for the state (Exhibit 18 in chapter 8). For a foreign city, give the country name.

- In chapter 2 (section 2.4), we mentioned the digital object identifier (DOI), the numerals used to identify intellectual content in a digital environment. If what you are referencing has a DOI, list it at the end of the reference as "doi:xxxxxx" without a period.
- If there is no DOI, and you retrieved the information electronically, APA style is to list the home page URL for the journal or other source of the information.

The rule of thumb is to be clear, consistent, and complete in referencing your source materials. Don't reference anything you have not cited in your paper (i.e., unless you are that rare student who is compiling a bibliography). Exhibit 10 is a summary list of the examples in this section.

EXHIBIT 10   Types of references illustrated in section 3.4

Authored Book
  3.4.1   *Single Author, One or More Editions*
  3.4.2   *More Than One Author*
  3.4.3   *Institutional Author and Publisher the Same*
  3.4.4   *Digital Version of Print Book or Electronic-Only Book*

Work in Press
  3.4.5   *Edited Volume in Production but Not Yet Published*
  3.4.6   *Journal Article Accepted for Publication but Not Yet in Print*
  3.4.7   *Article Posted on the Internet in a Preprint Version*
  3.4.8   *Chapter in Edited Book in Production but Not Yet in Print*
  3.4.9   *Authored Book in Production but Not Yet in Print*
  3.4.10 *Monograph in a Journal Issue Not Yet in Print*

Edited Published Work
  3.4.11 *Single Editor of a Book, One or More Editions*
  3.4.12 *More Than One Editor, More Than One Volume, Revised Edition*

Work Republished at a Later Date
  3.4.13 *Book of Collected Work*
  3.4.14 *Single Volume in Multivolume Series of Collected Work*
  3.4.15 *Chapter in an Anthology*

Article or Chapter
  3.4.16 *Article by a Single Author in Journal Paginated by Volume*
  3.4.17 *Article by Up to Six Authors in Journal Paginated by Volume*
  3.4.18 *More Than Six Authors*
  3.4.19 *Chapter in Edited Book*
  3.4.20 *Chapter Author with Hyphenated First and Last Names*
  3.4.21 *Entry in Encyclopedia Paginated by Volume*
  3.4.22 *Article in Newsletter Paginated by Issue*
  3.4.23 *Article in Journal Paginated by Issue*

EXHIBIT 10 Continued

Non-English Publication
  3.4.24 Book
  3.4.25 Journal Article

Chapter in Multivolume Edited Series
  3.4.26 Different Author and Editor
  3.4.27 Same Author and Editor

Mass Media Article
  3.4.28 Magazine Article
  3.4.29 Newspaper Article (Author Listed)
  3.4.30 Newspaper Article (No Author Listed)

Dictionary or Encyclopedia
  3.4.31 Dictionary (No Author Listed)
  3.4.32 Encyclopedia (More Than One Volume, Two Publishers in Two Locations)

Doctoral Dissertation or Master's Thesis
  3.4.33 Doctoral Dissertation, from Commercial Database
  3.4.34 Master's Thesis, from Commercial Database
  3.4.35 Dissertation or Thesis in Print Copy

Other Unpublished Material
  3.4.36 Technical Report, Unpublished
  3.4.37 Unpublished Manuscript on a Personal Website
  3.4.38 Manuscript in Preparation

Meetings and Symposia
  3.4.39 Paper Presented at a Meeting
  3.4.40 Presentation in Chaired Symposium
  3.4.41 Poster Presentation at a Meeting
  3.4.42 Published Proceedings of Meeting

Audiovisual Media
  3.4.43 Motion Picture
  3.4.44 Television Broadcast
  3.4.45 Music Recording

Electronic-Only Source Materials
  3.4.46 Abstract Retrieved from PsycINFO
  3.4.47 Article in Open-Access Electronic Journal
  3.4.48 Article in Limited-Access Electronic Journal
  3.4.49 Information Retrieved from Web Site

Authored Book

3.4.1 Single Author, One or More Editions

Invert the author's name, using initials for the first and middle names, and give the year of publication, the italicized title of the book (capitalizing the first word of the title and subtitle and ending with a period), and then the location (using the United States Postal Service abbreviation for the state) and name of the publisher in its shortened form. If there is more than one edition of the book, the edition number is inserted in parentheses after the title. In the second illustration below, the abbreviation **EKG** *(for* **electro-cardiogram***) is all in caps just as it appeared in the book.*

(a) One edition:
> Strogatz, S. (2009). *The calculus of friendship: What a teacher and a student learned about life while corresponding about math.* Princeton, NJ: Princeton University Press.

(b) Sixth edition:
> Thaler, M. S. (2010). *The only EKG book you'll ever need* (6th ed.). Philadelphia, PA: Lippincott.

3.4.2 More Than One Author

Insert a comma followed by an ampersand (&) before the last author's name. In the first example (two coauthors), notice that the country name is given for a publisher outside the United States.

(a) Two coauthors:
> Stewart, P. J., & Strathern, A. (2004). *Witchcraft, sorcery, rumors, and gossip.* Cambridge, England: Cambridge University Press.

(b) Three coauthors:
> Shadish, W. R., Cook, T. D., & Campbell, D. T. (2001). *Experimental and quasi-experimental designs for generalized causal inference.* Boston, MA: Houghton Mifflin.

3.4.3 Institutional Author and Publisher the Same

Give the full name of the institution, and list the publisher's name as "Author" when it is the same as the institutional author.

> American Psychological Association. (2010). *Publication manual of the American Psychological Association* (6th ed.). Washington, DC: Author.

3.4.4 Digital Version of Print Book or Electronic-Only Book

If you retrieved an electronic version of a book online, add the statement "Retrieved from" and the URL (no period) after the title. If there is a document number (not the case here), include it in parentheses after the title (before the period), but the electronic retrieval statement takes the place of the publisher and location.

National Commission for the Protection of Human Subjects of Biomedical and Behavioral Research. (1979). *The Belmont Report: Ethical principles and guidelines for the protection of human subjects.* Retrieved from http://ohsr.od.nih.gov/guidelines/belmont/html

Work in Press

3.4.5 Edited Volume in Production but Not Yet Published

An edited volume or book that has been accepted by the publisher and is in the process of production is considered "in press." Insert in parentheses the abbreviation "Ed." (if one editor) or "Eds." (if more than one editor), followed by a period, and then "in press" (no quotes) in parentheses, followed by a period. This volume was in press at the time of this writing. Once the book is published, the copyright date (usually found on the reverse side of the title page of the book) replaces "in press."

Panter, A. T., & Sterba, S. K. (Eds.). (in press). *Handbook of ethics in quantitative methodology.* London, England: Taylor & Francis.

3.4.6 Journal Article Accepted for Publication but Not Yet in Print

A manuscript that has been officially accepted for publication by the editor of a journal is considered "in press." (This article has been published, but we use it here as an illustration of the APA style for a journal article that is in press.)

Frei, R. L., Racicot, B., & Travagline, A. (in press). The impact of monochromic and type A behavior patterns on faculty research productivity and job-induced stress. *Journal of Managerial Psychology.*

3.4.7 Article Posted on the Internet in a Preprint Version

The APA Manual recommends showing the exact URL used, the idea being that the article was "informally published" in the preprint version. You may find that articles in a preprint version often list the DOI, a permanent identifier that may be preferable to the URL.

Spielmans, G. I., & Parry, P. I. (2010). From evidence-based medicine to marketing-based medicine: Evidence from internal industry documents. *Journal of Bioethical Inquiry.* doi:10.1007/s11673-010-9208-8

3.4.8 Chapter in Edited Book in Production but Not Yet in Print

A chapter that has been accepted by the editor of a book that, in turn, has been accepted by the publisher is considered "in press." Notice that the

editors' names are not inverted, whereas the chapter authors' names are inverted as usual.

> Myung, J., Cavagnaro, D. R., & Pitt, M. A. (in press). Mathematical modeling. In Social comparison processes in the physical health domain. In A. T. Panter & S. K. Sterba (Eds.). *Handbook of ethics in quantitative methodology.* London, England: Taylor & Francis.

3.4.9 Authored Book in Production but Not Yet in Print
A book manuscript that has been accepted by the publisher and is in the process of being prepared for publication is considered "in press."

> Fine, G. A. (in press). *Mushroom worlds: Naturework and the taming of the wild.* Cambridge, MA: Harvard University Press.

3.4.10 Monograph in a Journal Issue Not Yet in Print
A monograph is a lengthy manuscript that the journal publishes either separately as a supplement or as a whole issue of the journal. Once the monograph is published, the issue number and the supplement or part number (if it is published separately) are indicated in parentheses after the volume number, followed by doi (colon) and no period. (This monograph has been published, but we use it here as an illustration of the APA style.)

> Lana, R. E. (in press). Choice and chance in the formation of society. *Journal of Mind and Behavior.*

Edited Published Work

3.4.11 Single Editor of a Book, One or More Editions
After the editor's name, insert Ed. in parentheses, followed by a period, the italicized title of the book, and so forth.

(a) One edition:
> Morawski, J. G. (Ed.). (1988). *The rise of experimentation in American psychology.* New Haven, CT: Yale University Press.

(b) Third edition:
> Kazdin, A. E. (Ed.). (2003). *Methodological issues and strategies in clinical research* (3rd ed.). Washington, DC: American Psychological Association.

3.4.12 More Than One Editor, More Than One Volume, Revised Edition
To indicate more than one editor, Eds. is inserted in parentheses, followed by a period. Revised edition (Rev. ed.) and the numbers of the volumes cited (after the abbreviation Vols.) are noted in parentheses after the title.

> Gilbert, D. T., Fiske, S. T., & Lindzey, G. (Eds.). (1988). *The handbook of social psychology* (Rev. ed., Vols. 1–2). Boston, MA: McGraw-Hill.

Work Republished at a Later Date

3.4.13 Book of Collected Work
The date that the original work appeared is included in parentheses after the full citation of the current edition.

> *(a) Collection of modern lectures:*
> Feynman, R. P. (1995). *Six easy pieces: Essentials of physics explained by its most brilliant teacher.* Reading, MA: Addison-Wesley. (Original lectures from 1961 to 1963)
> *(b) Collection of classical orations:*
> Demosthenes. (1852). *The Olynthiac and other public orations of Demosthenes.* London, England: Henry G. Bohn. (Original work written 349 B.C.)

3.4.14 Single Volume in Multivolume Series of Collected Work
The number of the particular volume is indicated in parentheses after the title of the series. The original date of publication of a classical work is indicated in parentheses at the end.

> Lessing, G. E. (1971). *Gotthold Ephraim Lessing: Werke* (Vol. 2). München, Germany: Carl Hanser Verlag. (Original work published 1779)

3.4.15 Chapter in an Anthology
The pages on which the classical work appears in the anthology are indicated in parentheses after the title of the anthology, followed by a period. The original date of publication of the classical work is indicated in parentheses at the end.

> Pope, A. (1903). Moral essays: Epistle I. To Sir Richard Temple, Lord Cobham, of the knowledge and character of men. In H. W. Boynton (Ed.), *The complete poetical works of Pope* (pp. 157–160). Boston, MA: Houghton Mifflin. (Original work published 1733)

Article or Chapter

3.4.16 Article by a Single Author in Journal Paginated by Volume
The journal name and volume (42) are written in italics, followed by the page numbers (97–108, not in italics) of the article. The doi (colon) is given without a period.

> Scott-Jones, D. (1994). Ethical issues in reporting and referring in research with low-income minority children. *Ethics and Behavior, 42,* 97–108. doi:10.1207/s15327019b0402-3

3.4.17 *Article by Up to Six Authors in Journal Paginated by Volume*
An ampersand (&) is placed before the last author's name, and only the journal name and volume are italicized. The doi (colon) is given without a period.

> Coppin, G., Delplanque, S., Cayeux, I., Porcherot, C., & Sander, D. (2010). I'm no longer torn after choice: How explicit choices implicitly shape preferences of odors. *Psychological Science, 21,* 489–493. doi:10.1177/09567797610364115

3.4.18 *More Than Six Authors*
In the new APA Manual, if there are seven or more authors, only the first six are listed, followed by a comma and spaced ellipsis points (. . .), and then by the last author. In the case below, the article was coauthored by ten people (J. C. Ziegler, D. Bertrand, D. Tóth, V. Csépe, A. Reis, L. Faísca, N. Saine, H. Lyytinen, A. Vaessen, and L. Blomert). The doi (colon) is given without a period.

> Ziegler, J. C., Bertrand, D., Tóth, D., Csépe, V., Reis, A., Faísca, L., . . . Blomert, L. (2010). Orthographic depth and its impact on universal predictors of reading: A cross-language investigation. *Psychological Science, 21, 551–559.* doi:10.1177/0956797610363406

Some journals continue to use a format described in the previous APA Manual for seven or more authors, where the convention was to list the first six, followed by a comma and et al.

> Ziegler, J. C., Bertrand, D., Tóth, D., Csépe, V., Reis, A., Faísca, L., et al. (2010). Orthographic depth and its impact on universal predictors of reading: A cross-language investigation. *Psychological Science,* 21, 551–559. doi:10.1177/0956797610363406

3.4.19 *Chapter in Edited Book*
The authors' names are inverted, but not the editors' names. The page numbers of the chapter (not italicized) are placed in parentheses immediately after the italicized title of the book, followed by a period.

(a) One editor:
> Zhong, C.-B., Liljenquist, K. A., & Cain, D. M. (2009). Moral self-regulation: Licensing and compensation. In D. De Cremer (Ed.), *Psychological perspectives on ethical behavior and decision making* (pp. 75–89). Charlotte, NC: Information Age.

(b) Two editors:
> Haynes, S. N., Kaholokula, J. K., & Yoshioka, D. T. (2008). Behavioral assessment. In A. M. Nezu & C. M. Nezu (Eds.), *Evidence-based outcome research: A practical guide to conducting randomized controlled trials for psychosocial interventions* (pp. 67–93). New York, NY: Oxford University Press.

3.4.20 Chapter Author with Hyphenated First and Last Names
Hyphens in the first name and last name are retained, with all other information presented as before.

> Perret-Clermont, A.-N., Perret, J.-F., & Bell, N. (1991). The social construction of meaning and cognitive ability in elementary school children. In L. Resnick, J. M. Levine, & S. B. Teasley (Eds.), *Perspectives on socially shared cognition* (pp. 41–62). Washington, DC: American Psychological Association.

3.4.21 Entry in Encyclopedia Paginated by Volume
The volume and page numbers of the article or entry (not italicized) are indicated in parentheses after the italicized title of the encyclopedia.

> Foster, E. K. (2009). Gossip. In H. T. Reis & S. K. Sprecher (Eds.), *Encyclopedia of human relationships* (Vol. 2, pp. 768–770). Thousand Oaks, CA: Sage.

3.4.22 Article in Newsletter Paginated by Issue
Immediately after the italicized volume number (23), the issue number is indicated (4, no italics) in parentheses.

> Camara, W. J. (2001). Do accommodations improve or hinder psychometric qualities of assessment? *The Score Newsletter, 23*(4), 4–6.

3.4.23 Article in Journal Paginated by Issue
The format is the same as the one in 3.4.22.

> Valdiserri, R. O., Tama, G. M., & Ho, M. (1988). The role of community advisory committees in clinical trials of anti-HIV agents. *IRB: A Review of Human Subjects Research, 10*(4), 5–7.

Non-English Publication

3.4.24 Book
Diacritical marks (an umlaut in Störeffekte *in this example) and capital letters are used for non-English words in the same way they were used in the original language. The English translation of the book's title is included in brackets, not italicized, followed by a period.*

> Gniech, G. (1976). *Störeffekte in psychologischen Experimenten* [Artifacts in psychological experiments]. Stuttgart, Germany: Verlag W. Kohlhammer.

3.4.25 Journal Article
The same rule referring to the use of diacritical marks and capital letters applies to the non-English title of the article and the name of the journal (however, the name of the journal is not translated into English). If the

DOI is known, it is given as doi (colon) as illustrated in 3.4.16, 3.4.17, and 3.4.18.

> Foa, U. G. (1966). Le nombre huit dans la socialization de l'enfant [The number eight in the socialization of the infant]. *Bulletin du Centre d'Études et Recherches Psychologiques, 15,* 39–47.

Chapter in Multivolume Edited Series

3.4.26 *Different Author and Editor*
Volume and page numbers of the chapter are indicated in parentheses after the italicized series title.

> Kipnis, D. (1984). The use of power in organizations and interpersonal settings. In S. Oskamp (Ed.), *Applied social psychology* (Vol. 5, pp. 171–210). Newbury Park, CA: Sage.

3.4.27 *Same Author and Editor*
Notice that the chapter author's name is inverted, but the same name is not inverted when the author is also the editor of the series in which the chapter appears.

> Koch, S. (1959). General introduction to the series. In S. Koch (Ed.), *Psychology: A study of a science* (Vol. 1, pp. 1–18). New York, NY: McGraw-Hill.

Mass Media Article

3.4.28 *Magazine Article*
In parentheses followed by a period, the year and month(s) (if published monthly) and the day (if published more frequently than monthly) are indicated. If the volume number is known, then it is indicated as shown here in italics (29), followed by the page numbers.

> Csikszentmihalyi, M. (1996, July/August). The creative personality. *Psychology Today, 29,* 36–40.

3.4.29 *Newspaper Article (Author Listed)*
All the page numbers are indicated for an article that appears on discontinuous pages, and the page numbers are separated by a comma.

> Carey, B. (2010, May 18). Can an enemy be a child's friend? *The New York Times,* pp. D1, D6.

3.4.30 *Newspaper Article (No Author Listed)*
When no author's name is listed in a newspaper article or editorial, the work is referenced by the title of the article and alphabetized in the list of references by the first significant word in the title. In this example, toast *is the first significant word.*

> A toast to Newton and a long-lived "Principia." (1999, October 11). *The New York Times,* p. F4.

Dictionary or Encyclopedia

3.4.31 Dictionary (No Author Listed)

When no author's name is listed on the title page of a dictionary or an encyclopedia, the work is referenced by the title of the work and alphabetized by the first significant word in the title.

> Random House dictionary of the English language. (1966). New York, NY: Random House.

3.4.32 Encyclopedia (More Than One Volume, Two Publishers in Two Locations)

After the name of the general editor of the encyclopedia, Ed. is inserted in parentheses, followed by a period. The number of volumes appears in parentheses following the title and then a period. In this case, the title page of the encyclopedia lists two publishers in two locations.

> Kazdin, A. E. (Ed.). (2000). Encyclopedia of psychology (Vols. 1–8). Washington, DC: American Psychological Association. New York, NY: Oxford University Press.

Doctoral Dissertation or Master's Thesis

ProQuest Dissertations & Theses (see also Exhibit 7 in Chapter 2) was the commercial database used for 3.4.33 and 3.4.34. The title of the work is given in italics, followed by the type of work (in parentheses), the name of the database, and finally (in parentheses) the identifying code used in the database (no period).

3.4.33 Doctoral Dissertation, from Commercial Database

> Foster, E. K. (2003). Researching gossip with social network analysis (Doctoral dissertation). Available from ProQuest Dissertations & Theses. (AAT 3112272)

3.4.34 Master's Thesis, from Commercial Database

> Roeder, M. B. (2009). Emotional influence on cross-modal attentional capture (Master's thesis). Available from ProQuest Dissertations & Theses. (AAT1465792)

3.4.35 Dissertation or Thesis in Print Copy

For referencing the print copy of a doctoral dissertation or a master's thesis, put the title in italics, write "Unpublished doctoral dissertation" or "Unpublished master's thesis," and give the university and location. Notice in the second example that the title contains a British spelling ("organisational"), which a spell check program may try to "correct," but "organisational" is the appropriate spelling here.

(a) University in the United States:
   Mettetal, G. W. (1982). *The conversation of female friends at three ages: The importance of fantasy, gossip, and self-disclosure.* (Unpublished doctoral dissertation). University of Illinois, Urbana, IL.
(b) University outside the United States:
   Hunt, E. (2000). *Correlates of uncertainty during organisational change.* (Unpublished master's thesis). University of Queensland, St. Lucia, Queensland, Australia.

Other Unpublished Material

3.4.36 Technical Report, Unpublished
The title of an unpublished technical report (not retrieved electronically) is italicized and followed (in parentheses) by the number or other identifying information (no italics), and by the location and name of the organization that issued the report.

   LoSciuto, L. A., Aiken, L. S., & Ausetts, M. A. (1979). *Professional and paraprofessional drug abuse counselors: Three reports* (DHEW Publication No. 79-858). Rockville, MD: National Institute on Drug Abuse.

3.4.37 Unpublished Manuscript on a Personal Website
The title of an unpublished manuscript retrieved from a personal Website is indicated in italics, followed by "Unpublished manuscript" and the URL (without a period at the end).

   Strick, M., Dijksterhuis, A., Bos, M. W., Szoerdsma, A., van Baaren, R. B., & Nordgren, L. F. (2009). *A meta-analysis on unconscious thought effects.* Unpublished manuscript retrieved from www.unconsciouslab.com/publications/Paper_Meta.doc

3.4.38 Manuscript in Preparation
Indicate "Manuscript in preparation" and the author's institutional affiliation or location.

   Mithalal, C. (2010). *Protocols of telephone therapy.* Manuscript in preparation, Institute for Telephone Therapy, New Rochelle, NY.

Meetings and Symposia

3.4.39 Paper Presented at a Meeting
The month of the meeting is listed, the title of the paper is italicized, and the name of the sponsoring organization and location of the meeting are indicated.

Hantula, D. A. (2010, May). *A risk too far: Behavioral economics of escalating commitment to a failing course of action.* Paper presented at the meeting of the Association for Psychological Science, Boston, MA.

3.4.40 Presentation in Chaired Symposium
The title of the symposium is italicized, but not the title of the presentation.

Higa-McMillan, C. K., Daleiden, E. L., Pestle, S. L., & Mueller, C. W. (2008, November). Evidence-based practice and practice-based evidence: Using local and national data to encourage youth provider behavior change in a public mental health system. In L. D. Osterberg (Chair), *Implementation of EST's in clinical service settings: What do services look like following dissemination efforts?* Symposium presented at the meeting of the Association of Behavioral and Cognitive Therapies, Orlando, FL.

3.4.41 Poster Presentation at a Meeting
Same format as 3.4.40.

Bess, J. P., & Hantula, D. A. (2010, May). *Going for broke? Staying in the game? Sunk-cost effect depends on measurement.* Poster presented at the meeting of the Association for Psychological Science, Boston, MA.

3.4.42 Published Proceedings of Meeting
In the second example, the paper was retrieved electronically, in which case the retrieval statement takes the place of the publisher's location and name.

(a) Not retrieved electronically:
Esposito, J. L. (2005). "Primum non nocere": An oath for survey practitioners? *Proceedings of the Fifth QUEST Workshop* (pp. 151–165). Heerlen, Netherlands: Statistics Netherlands.

(b) Retrieved electronically:
Esposito, J. L. (2005). "Primum non nocere": An oath for survey practitioners? *Proceedings of the Fifth QUEST Workshop* (pp. 151–165). Retrieved from www.quest.ssb.no/meetings/200504workshops/529286_bookmarks.pdf

Audiovisual Media

3.4.43 Motion Picture
After each primary contributor, the particular contribution is noted in parentheses, and "Motion picture" is inserted in brackets after the italicized title of the film. The country of origin (where the film was primarily made or released) and the motion picture studio are indicated.

Zinneman, F. (Director), & Foreman, C. (Screenwriter). (1952). *High noon* [Motion picture]. United States: Universal Artists.

3.4.44 Television Broadcast

The key here is to provide sufficient information to identify the broadcast as best you can, without omitting any significant identifying detail.

> Doyle, W. (Producer). (2001, November 3). *An American insurrection* [Television broadcast]. New York: C-Span 2.

3.4.45 Music Recording

The information in this example includes the artist's name, the date of copyright, the title of the piece, the recording artist, the title of the album (Mahler–Bernstein), the medium of recording (CD, record, cassette, etc.), and the location.

> Mahler, G. (1991). Symphonie No. 8. [Recorded by L. Bernstein & Wiener Philharmoniker]. On *Mahler–Bernstein* [CD]. Hamburg, Germany: Deutsche Grammophon.

Electronic-Only Source Materials

3.4.46 Abstract Retrieved from PsycINFO

Instructors usually assume that you have read the full-text article that you are citing, but if you are citing only the abstract you retrieved from PsycINFO, the APA style is to give the URL. As the URL can sometimes be incredibly detailed, we suggest you provide the full citation as it appears in PsycINFO and state "Abstract retrieved from PsycINFO."

> Stupak, N., DiFonzo, N., Younge, A. J., & Homan, C. (2010). Social sense: Graphical user interface design considerations for social network experiment software. *Computers in Human Behavior, 26*(3), 365–370. Abstract retrieved from PsycINFO.

3.4.47 Article in Open-Access Electronic Journal

Open access means that the electronic journal is available to anyone on-line. The URL that an interested person would use to retrieve the article is given at the end of the reference (no period). In this example, the article was authored by a group of editors at PLoS Medicine.

> PLoS Medicine Editors. (2009, Sept.). Ghostwriting: The dirty little secret of medical publishing that just got bigger. *PLoS Medicine, 6,* Issue 9, e1000156. Retrieved from http://www.plosmedicine.org. static/ghostwriting.action

3.4.48 Article in Limited-Access Electronic Journal

Limited access means that retrieval of the article is limited to those who subscribe to the database, for example, institutions that subscribe to a host system that provides such access.

Lewandowski, Jr., G., & Strohmetz, D. B. (2009). Actions can speak as loud as words: Measuring behavior in psychological science. *Social and Personality Psychology Compass, 3*(6), 992–1002. doi:10.1111/j.1751-9004.2009.00229.x

3.4.49 Information Retrieved from Web Site
The Web site host or institutional provider of this information is given, followed by the date (in parentheses, followed by a period), and then the title (period), and finally the URL (no period).

Social Psychology Network. (2010, April 28). Free Offerings from SPN sites. Retrieved from www.socialpsychology.org/free.htm

3.5 The Proposal for a Literature Review

Exhibit 11 illustrates one particular format for the proposal for a literature review. The proposal should present an organized argument that leads to a reasoned approach to your topic. In the opening paragraph of John Smith's proposal, he states the objective of the review as he envisions it now, knowing that it may change slightly as he gets deeper into the project. John shows that he has the project neatly organized in his mind from the general ("contrast two theoretical orientations") to the specific ("focus on the theoretical work of Howard Gardner").

In the next section of his proposal, the background section, John tells how he got the idea for his proposal and soon afterward began to consider relevant source materials. He also begins to sketch a picture of what the final paper might look like, though it must be tentative because he cannot anticipate all aspects of the final paper. What is so striking is that John shows that he has ideas of his own, and instructors are attuned to the issue of originality in student writing assignments. John has an impressive selection of citations, which shows that he is not floundering and, instead, has a clear direction for finding and retrieving further information. In the next section, he states that he plans to use PsycINFO and other online databases to continue his search for any relevant materials. However, he wisely qualifies that statement by noting that, because of the constraints of the academic semester and the press of other course requirements, there are limitations to how much he can read for this project.

Notice that John's full name is typed above each page beside the page number. This insertion serves as a safety device if any pages get accidentally detached. John gives his e-mail address or other contact information, so that the instructor can communicate with him efficiently rather than by torturously delayed communications. The proposal ends with a preliminary list of references. We are left with the impression that John has put effort and thought into the assignment and that he manages his own expectations realistically.

EXHIBIT 11 *Sample proposal for a literature review*

Proposal for a Literature Review

John Smith (e-mail address or other contact information)

(Date the proposal is submitted)

Objective of the Proposed Review

I propose to contrast two theoretical orientations regarding the nature of human intelligence. One orientation assumes that a general trait (g) is at the core of every valid measure of intelligence, such as the WAIS. The other orientation is the view that there are types of intelligence that are not measured by these traditional tests. In regard to the latter view, I propose to focus on the theoretical work of Howard Gardner on multiple intelligences.

Background

My interest in this project initially grew out of something that Prof. Skleder discussed when she was lecturing on the concept of intelligence. She described research that she had done on a facet of work by Howard Gardner on what he called *interpersonal intelligence*. Using the Library of Congress online catalog, I found that Gardner had written a number of books on "multiple intelligences" (e.g., Gardner, 1983, 1991, 1993a, 1993b, 1999). From what I have read so far, starting with the textbook that we use in this course (Kaplan & Saccuzzo, 2009) and other reference sources, my understanding is that Gardner's work represents a movement away from the traditional view of IQ that predominated in psychology and education for many years. Other leading psychologists who have argued that IQ tests overlook aspects of intelligence are Robert Sternberg (1985, 1988, 1990) and Stephen J. Ceci (1990, 1996; Ceci & Liker, 1986).

Whereas the traditional view has emphasized a general factor (called the g factor) that is common to all standard measures of intelligence and IQ (Spearman, 1927), the alternative view assumes there are several distinctive types of intelligence. Gardner (1983) differentiated seven types of intelligence: logical-mathematical, linguistic, spatial, bodily-kinesthetic, musical, interpersonal, and intrapersonal intelligence.

EXHIBIT 11   *Continued*

John Smith 2

From my limited reading so far, I have found that there are controversial issues, which I propose to give a sense of in my review paper. Kaplan and Saccuzzo (2009) stated that "of all the major concepts in the field of testing, intelligence is the most elusive" (p. 230), and I think that I will use this idea of the elusiveness of the concept of intelligence as a principal theme.

Literature Search Strategy

The textbook in this course has a long discussion of intelligence (Kaplan & Saccuzzo, 2009), and as noted above, I have begun reading and taking notes from additional resource materials. Browsing in the library, I came across an encyclopedia of education that had an article about intelligence tests (Gilbert, 1971). The article implied that the concept of intelligence has been awash in controversy for many years. I plan to use PsycINFO (and possibly other online databases) to search for additional relevant articles.

Having taken a psychological statistics course, I believe I can understand any basic quantitative information in the material I read. On the following pages are books and articles that I have uncovered so far, but I may not cite all of them. As I get deeper into this project, I expect to add many more references. I am also, of course, open to suggestions for additional leads, but I expect that I will only be able to skim some of the work because of the press of other course requirements.

EXHIBIT 11   Continued

John Smith 3

References

Ceci, S. J. (1990). *On intelligence . . . more or less: A bioecological treatise on intellectual development.* Englewood Cliffs, NJ: Prentice Hall.

Ceci, S. J. (1996). *On intelligence: A bioecological treatise on intellectual development* (Expanded ed.). Cambridge, MA: Harvard University Press.

Ceci, S. J., & Liker, J. (1986). Academic and nonacademic intelligence: An experimental separation. In R. J. Sternberg & R. Wagner (Eds.), *Practical intelligence: Origins of competence in the everyday world* (pp. 119–142). New York: Cambridge University Press.

Gardner, H. (1983). *Frames of mind: The theory of multiple intelligences.* New York: Basic Books.

Gardner, H. (1991). *The unschooled mind: How children think and how schools should teach.* New York: Basic Books.

Gardner, H. (1993a). *Creating minds: An anatomy of creativity seen through the lives of Freud, Einstein, Picasso, Stravinsky, Eliot, Graham, and Ghandi.* New York: Basic Books.

Gardner, H. (1993b). *Multiple intelligences: The theory in practice.* New York: Basic Books.

Gardner, H. (1999). *Intelligence reframed: Multiple intelligences for the 21st century.* New York: Basic Books.

Gilbert, H. B. (1971). Intelligence tests. In L. C. Deighton (Ed.), *The encyclopedia of education* (Vol. 5, pp. 128–135). New York: Macmillan & Free Press.

Kaplan, R. M., & Saccuzzo, D. P. (2009). *Psychological testing: Principles, applications, and issues* (7th ed.). Belmont, CA: Wadsworth/Cengage Learning.

Spearman, C. (1927). *The abilities of man.* New York: Macmillan.

Sternberg, R. J. (1985). *Beyond IQ: A triarchic theory of human intelligence.* New York: Cambridge University Press.

Sternberg, R. J. (1988). *The triarchic mind: A new theory of human intelligence.* New York: Viking.

Sternberg, R. J. (1990). *Metaphors of mind: A new theory of human intelligence.* New York: Cambridge University Press.

3.6 *The Proposal for a Research Project*

Exhibit 12 illustrates one form of a proposal for a course research project. As in the sample proposal in Exhibit 11, Jane Doe begins by concisely stating the objective of the research she proposes. In the next section, she puts the objective into a practical context that communicates the importance of the research. She also describes how the idea for this research came to her and why she is especially interested in it. Her statements again emphasize the issue of originality (just as in John Smith's proposal). She sketches her idea for the hypotheses she will test and then takes us step by step through her thinking. In this way she prepares us for the next section, where she describes the method that she proposes to use.

In the method section, Jane begins by mentioning that, after getting the instructor's approval, she contacted the owner of a local restaurant where she was hoping to conduct the study. She has already informed the restaurant owner and the server about the nature of her proposed research and has got their written approval (which she mentions is attached to the proposal). Jane should be able to get started quickly once her instructor has approved her proposal. Her three experimental hypotheses are well reasoned and precisely stated, another indication of her motivation and diligence. The more thorough Jane is, the more focused the instructor's comments can be as he continues to shepherd Jane toward her goal. If you plan to develop a questionnaire or an interview schedule, put a verbal sketch of it into the proposal so the instructor can give you specific feedback.

In the beginning of the method section, where she describes the participants, Jane tells why she has settled on a total N of 80 dining parties. In discussing the procedure she will use, she tells how the four conditions in her experiment will be randomly chosen by the waitress and what the particular procedure will be in each condition. She then turns to the scoring and analysis, where she begins by telling how the dependent variable will be measured. She mentions advice given to her by the instructor, who suggested how to deal with nonsignificant results due to possibly underpowered tests. In describing her plan for computing a contrast to test the overall prediction, Jane shows her understanding of the data analysis. There is a brief discussion of ethical considerations, but some instructors may require that you complete a standard form or questionnaire that was prepared by an institutional review board (IRB) at your college or university. Jane's proposal concludes with a list of the studies that she has cited.

The level of detail in Jane's proposal reflects the considerable amount of time that she has spent and her consultations with the instructor on more than one occasion. If there is a problem, this student is not someone who will be shy about asking for guidance. She is clearly energetic and goal directed.

EXHIBIT 12   *Sample proposal for a research project*

Jane Doe 1

Proposal for a Research Project

Jane Doe (e-mail address or other contact information)

(Date the proposal is submitted)

Objective of the Research

I propose to conduct a randomized experiment in a naturalistic situation to investigate whether the presentation of after-meal candies to dining parties influences their tipping behavior. There will be several treatment conditions, so that I can investigate whether tipping increases when more candies are presented to dining parties in order to create an impression of the server's friendliness, and when the presentation of candies implies the server's generosity and friendliness.

Background and Hypotheses

According to the Bureau of Labor Statistics (2010–2011), there were 2,381,600 workers who held jobs as waiters and waitresses in 2008. Most of the jobs were part time, "attracting many young people to the occupation." This summer I have a job as a waitress in a restaurant in Ogunquit, Maine. When Prof. Rind told about the experiments he had done on tipping behavior (Rind & Bordia, 1995, 1996), it got me thinking that this topic might be appropriate for my research project. Prof. Rind directed me to an article by Lynn (1996) as well as work on restaurant tipping by Garrity and Degelman (1990), Hornik (1992), Lynn and Mynier (1993), and Tidd and Lockard (1978). In a social psychology course last semester, we learned about reciprocity theory, a formulation that also has implications for the empirical research that I am proposing.

Research findings in the articles cited above are consistent with the idea that servers who are seen as friendly are likely to receive larger tips. For example, techniques such as a friendly touch or a smiling face drawn on the check have been found to increase the resulting tip percentages. My proposed research will use another simple procedure for fostering an impression of server friendliness, which will be to have the server personally offer each diner an after-meal treat of a complimentary chocolate candy. There will

EXHIBIT 12 *Continued*

Jane Doe 2

be a control (no candy) condition and three experimental conditions (as described below) based on the interaction between the server and the diners when the check is presented.

Three experimental hypotheses will be tested. My first hypothesis is that offering each diner one piece of candy (called the *1-piece condition*) will have the effect of increasing tips, compared with the *no-candy control*. Second, assuming that this effect is cumulative, I hypothesize that offering each diner two candies (called the *2-piece condition*) will further increase tipping in comparison with the control. Third, as people often feel obligated to return a favor (Regan, 1971), I hypothesize that creating the impression that offering a second piece of candy reflects a generous impulse on the part of the server will elicit even larger tips (called the *1 + 1 condition*). To sum up, I predict that tips will increase from the control, to the 1-piece, to the 2-piece, to the 1 + 1 condition.

Proposed Method

Research Participants

After discussing the proposed research with Prof. Rind, who gave me approval to proceed to the next stage, I spoke with an acquaintance who owns a restaurant regarding the possibility of conducting my study there. Attached to this proposal are the written permission of the restaurant owner and also the written permission of a female server who has agreed to participate. They have agreed to let me randomly assign 80 dining parties to the four conditions. Based on a power analysis using a table in the course text, the power of three t tests of simple effects will be approximately .80 (which was the recommended level), assuming an effect size of approximately $r = .5$.

Procedure

The conditions (control, 1-piece, 2-piece, 1 + 1) will be written on 80 index cards, so each card describes one of the four conditions. The cards will be shuffled and given to the server, who will select a card blindly from her apron pocket just before presenting the check. The server will also be given a basket containing an assortment of wrapped miniature chocolates. In the *control condition,* the server will hand over the check, thank the dining party, and immediately leave the table in order to avoid any nonessential interaction. In the remaining three conditions, the server will bring the basket of candy when presenting

EXHIBIT 12 *Continued*

Jane Doe 3

the check. In the *1-piece condition*, the server will offer each person in the dining party one candy of his

or her choice, will thank the diners after their selection, and will leave the table. In the *2-piece condition*,

the server will offer each person two candies, thank the diners after their selections, and leave. In the *1 +*

1 condition, the server will offer each person a candy and then say, "Oh, have another piece," in order to

create the impression that the treat was a generous afterthought; the server will then thank the diners and

leave the table. After the party has left the restaurant, the server will record on the same index card that

was used to specify the condition (a) the amount of the tip, (b) the amount of the check before taxes, and

(c) the size of the dining party.

Scoring and Analysis

The dependent measure will be the tip percentage, the amount of the tip divided by the amount of

the bill before taxes, then multiplied by 100. The basic results will be reported in the form of means, 95%

confidence intervals, and standard deviations. Three independent-sample *t* tests will be used to compare

each of the three treatment conditions (1-piece, 2-piece, and 1 + 1) against the control. I will also report

the effect sizes and their 95% confidence intervals.

Prof. Rind raised the possibility that the observed effects may not be as large as $r = .5$, in which

case I will not have the benefit of working with power of .8. Although there is not much I can do about

increasing the total N (because of time constraints and the agreement with the owner of the restaurant and

the server), Prof. Rind suggested I think of the *t* tests as a posteriori tests after an overall ANOVA. This

option would justify using the pooled S^2 and its associated degrees of freedom ($df = N - k = 80 - 4 = 76$)

for each *t* test. For the effect size correlations computed from these *t* tests, the *df* would still be defined by

the groups being compared ($df = n_1 + n_2 - 2 = 20 + 20 - 2 = 38$), as described in the course text.

Prof. Rind also recommended that I compute a 1×4 contrast F (or *t*) to test the prediction that the

tip percentage increased from control to the 1-piece to the 2-piece to the 1 + 1 condition (using lambda

weights of −3, −1, +1, +3, respectively). I realize that also reporting an overall ANOVA will not address

my specific predictions, but the ANOVA summary table would be a way to show how the contrast F can

be carved out of the overall between-groups sum of squares. I can compute the overall ANOVA using the

EXHIBIT 12 *Continued*

statistics program we have been taught, and it would be a convenient way to obtain the pooled S^2 (i.e., the MS_{within}).

Ethical Considerations

The study involves what I would describe as a mild deception, in that the diners will be unaware that they are participating in an experiment. I do not propose to debrief them, because no potential risk is involved. I cannot ask people who are dining whether they will agree to "participate in an experiment," because that would destroy the realism of the treatments and render the results meaningless. I have agreed to give the owner and the server full details of the results when I submit the final research report. I have promised not to mention their names or the name of the restaurant in any research reports. All tips will be the property of the server.

EXHIBIT 12   *Continued*

Jane Doe 5

References

Bureau of Labor Statistics. (2010–2011). *Occupational outlook handbook.* Retrieved from

http://www.bls.gov/oco/ocos162.htm

Garrity, K., & Degelman, D. (1990). Effect of server introduction on restaurant tipping. *Journal of*

Applied Social Psychology, 20, 168–172. doi:10.1111/j.1559-1816.1990.tboo405.x

Hornik, J. (1992). Tactile stimulation and consumer response. *Journal of Consumer Research, 19,* 449–

458. Retrieved from http://www.jstor.org/stable/2489401

Lynn, M. (1996). Seven ways to increase servers' tips. *Cornell Hotel and Restaurant Administration*

Quarterly, 37(3), 24–29. doi:10.1177/001088049603700315

Lynn, M., & Mynier, K. (1993). Effect of server posture on restaurant tipping. *Journal of Applied Social*

Psychology, 23, 678–685. doi:10.111/j.1559-1816.1993.tb01109.x

Regan, D. T. (1971). Effects of a favor and liking on compliance. *Journal of Experimental Social*

Psychology, 7, 627–639. doi:10.1016/0022-1031(71)90025-4

Rind, B., & Bordia, P. (1995). Effect of server's "thank you" and personalization on restaurant tipping.

Journal of Applied Social Psychology, 25, 745–751. doi:10.1111/j.1559-1816.1995.tb01772.x

Rind, B., & Bordia, P. (1996). Effect on restaurant tipping of male and female servers drawing a happy,

smiling face on the backs of customers' checks. *Journal of Applied Social Psychology, 26,* 218–225.

doi:10.1111/j.1559-1816.1916.tb01847.x

Tidd, K., & Lockard, J. (1978). Monetary significance of the affiliative smile: A case for reciprocal

altruism. *Bulletin of the Psychometric Society, 11,* 344–346.

3.7 Ethical Considerations

As noted above, Jane's discussion of ethics is brief, but other proposals may call for a more detailed discussion or a standard form that needs to be filled out, signed, and submitted. The student may be asked to provide a stronger rationale or to provide other relevant information. The reason that instructors require a detailed discussion of ethics is that ethical accountability is an important consideration in every aspect of research. The three absolute requirements of ethical accountability are (a) that you, the researcher, will protect the dignity, privacy, and safety of your research participants; (b) that your study will be technically sound (so as not to waste valuable resources, including the research participants' time and effort); and (c) that the research will not be detrimental in any way to the participants or to society.

Here are some specific questions to get you thinking about the ethics of your proposed study:

- Might there be any psychological or physical risks to the research participants? How do you propose to avoid these risks?
- Will any deception be used, and if so, is it really necessary, or can you think of a way to avoid using deception? If you believe that you *must* use a deception, how do you propose to debrief the participants, and how can you be sure the debriefing procedure has been effective?
- If you are planning to use volunteer subjects, how do you propose to recruit them in a way that is honest, forthcoming, and noncoercive? How do you propose to use informed consent and to ensure that the participants understand they are free to withdraw at any time without penalty?
- What steps will you take to ensure the confidentiality of the data?

3.8 Tempus Fugit!

Because time flies when you are writing an assigned paper, here are two final tips:

1. *Turn in your proposal on time.* Instructors are also very busy people, and they (like you) schedule their work. Turning in a proposal late is like waving a red flag that signals the wrong message to your instructor. Instead of communicating that you are someone responsible and reliable, who thinks clearly, this red flag signals that you may be none of the above.
2. *Be precise.* In Lewis Carroll's *Through the Looking Glass*, Alice (of *Alice in Wonderland*) comes upon Humpty Dumpty, who uses a word in a way that Alice says she doesn't understand. He smiles

contemptuously and says, "Of course you don't—till I tell you. . . . When *I* use a word, it means just what I choose it to mean—neither more nor less." Unlike Humpty Dumpty, you do not have the luxury of telling your instructor to "take it or leave it." Nor do you have the extra time to keep resubmitting the proposal if your initial description was not precise enough.

4

Planning the
Research Report

The structure and form of research reports in psychology
have evolved over many years. In this chapter we describe this
structure in the context of the sample report in appendix A.
Although the arrangement is similar in most reports of
individual studies, the way that you choose to explain
your study will partly reflect the descriptive, relational, or
experimental orientation of the research. Familiarity with these
matters will enable you to organize your thoughts and prepare
the first draft (discussed in chapter 7).

4.1 Three Types of Research Orientations

Once you have conducted your research and are working on the data
analysis, it is time to think some more about the final research report.
Research methods texts routinely cover data collection and data analysis,
and we will assume that you are mastering these techniques (though we
have more to say about reporting statistical information in chapter 6).
What primarily remains in planning the research report is to think about
how you can explain in clear language (a) what you did, (b) why you did
it, (c) what you found out, (d) what your results mean, and (e) what you
have concluded. Research methods texts make fine distinctions among the
various kinds of research strategies, such as the laboratory or field experiment, the sample survey, the case study, and the archival approach.
Over and above these differences is another distinction regarding three
broad types of research, or what you might think of as the "big picture"
orientations. Termed *descriptive, relational* (also called *correlational*), and
experimental, each has its own objective and limitations. Understanding
these parameters is important when you discuss what the results mean
and what conclusions can be drawn, because it is important not to stretch

your interpretations and conclusions beyond the objectives and inherent limits of your research.

The purpose of research that has a *descriptive orientation* in human psychology is to map out an aspect of how people feel, think, or behave. In other words, the primary objective of this type of research is the description of "how things are." This description might be in the form of a narrative portrayal in what is often called *qualitative research*, or it might instead be in the form of numbers and statistics in what is called *quantitative research*. In both cases, the interpretation of the results is strictly limited by the fact that the orientation is descriptive. Of course, it is quite possible for research that is primarily relational or experimental to contain descriptive information as well. For example, in the opening paragraph of Jane Doe's experimental research report (appendix A), she presents descriptive information when, citing government labor statistics, she mentions that over two million people in the United States work as waiters and waitresses in restaurants.

The purpose of research that has a primarily *relational orientation* is to identify relationships among variables. For example, Jane could also have explored the incomes of servers in restaurants by gender, region, age, and so on. Usually in relational research, we are interested not only in the magnitudes of relationships (indicated, for example, by the correlations between variables), but also in patterns of relationships. We want to know, for example, whether the relationship resembles a straight line (a linear relationship), or whether it is not linear but instead a curvilinear relationship (for example, resembling a U or an upside-down-U, or resembling another pattern). In other words, the objective of this type of research orientation is the quantitative description of "how things are in relation to other things." It is important when writing about relational research findings not to fall into the trap of implying causality when all that can be reasonably claimed is the form of the relationship. This is usually expressed by correlations and confidence intervals, but it is always important to plot the data in order to inspect the form of the relationship.

The purpose of research that has an *experimental orientation* is to learn whether changes in one variable (X) are *responsible* for changes in another variable (Y). In other words, the objective in this case is to learn not only "how things are in relation to other things," but to learn "what leads to what." A problem with trying to tease out the answer to the "What leads to what?" question in relational research is that an unknown variable (Z) might be the reason why X and Y were statistically related. An example of this *third-variable problem* mentioned by the mathematician John Paulos, in his popular book *Innumeracy*, is that children's spelling ability is correlated with the size of their feet; that is, the bigger their feet (X), the more proficient is their spelling ability (Y). It would, of course, be absurd to infer that using foot stretchers will improve a child's spelling ability. There was a third (composite) variable that was responsible for the statistical relationship between X and Y, namely, the children's age and educational experience. Older children have bigger feet and can generally spell better than younger children.

Going back to Maya's assignment in chapter 2, we can further flesh out the three broad research orientations by imagining that she is developing descriptive, relational, and experimental research ideas. You may recall that Maya is thinking about becoming a teacher. Let us suppose that she is especially interested in the study of children's failure in school. An example of descriptive research would be to observe the classroom behavior of children who are doing poorly and then to describe that behavior as carefully as possible. The careful description of behavior is usually a first step in the development of a program of research, but it is rarely seen as sufficient. Sooner or later, someone will want to know *why* something happens or *how* what happens is related to other events or circumstances.

Here is an example of relational research: Trained observers make coordinated observations on a sample of students. These students are in classrooms that adequately represent a population of students about whom some correlational conclusions are to be drawn. For example, those observers could note for each student whether the student appears to be learning anything and the degree to which the teacher appears to be exposing the student to new material to be learned. From the coordinated observations, we could quantify the probable relationship between the amount of students' exposure to material to be learned and the amount of the material they did in fact learn.

Suppose that the students exposed to less information were also those who tended to learn less. Upon discovering this relationship, we might be tempted to conclude that children learn less because they are taught less. It is a plausible hypothesis but is not warranted by the statistical relationship reported. For example, it might be that teachers teach less to those they know to be less able to learn. In other words, the differences in teaching behavior may be as much a *result* of students' learning as a *causal agent* of that learning. Dilemmas like these are traditionally addressed by experimentally manipulating the variables that are suspected to be responsible for the effect.

For example, Maya might select a sample of students and then, using a randomizing method, divide them into two presumably similar groups. One of the groups would have more information given them by their teachers, while the other group would be given less information. She could then assess which group learned more. If the two groups differed, she would be in a better position to attribute the difference to the different treatments—more, compared to less, information. There would still be a question of what it was about the better treatment that led to the improvement in learning. Was the improvement due to the extra material; to the increased attention from the teacher while presenting the material; to the increases in eye contact, smiles, and warmth; or perhaps to still other correlates of the teachers' behavior? Each of these possibilities could be investigated in additional studies involving relational and experimental observations.

4.2   The Basic Structure

So far, we have seen that the answers to questions about what the results mean and the conclusions that can be reasonably drawn will partly reflect the orientation of the research. We leave the fine details of the design, implementation, and analysis of specific research strategies to your research methods textbook. Whatever are the "big picture" orientations and the specific strategies, well-written reports of research reflect a logical progression in thought as they address the kinds of questions mentioned at the beginning of the previous section. To encourage this logical order, and to make it easier to read individual studies and generalize across different fields, the uniform style that is used generally adheres to the following basic structure (where the appendix, footnotes, tables, and figures are collectively described as the *end material*):

Title page
Abstract
Introduction
Method
Results
Discussion
References
Footnotes
Tables
Figures
Appendix

Not all reports of individual studies require all those parts. For example, not all reports use footnotes, or an appendix, or both tables and figures. Instructors generally expect reports of individual studies to include (a) an abstract, (b) an introduction, (c) a method section, (d) a results section, (e) a discussion of the results, and (f) a list of references. In Jane Doe's report in appendix A, there are more parts in her manuscript than these six, and your instructor might require still another variation, or you may want to report some results in a figure rather than (or in addition to) a table. In chapter 8, in which we focus on the production of the final manuscript, we will have more to say about the title page. You can also anticipate that discussion by glancing at the title page of Jane Doe's report. In the remainder of this chapter we concentrate on the other parts of the research report that we have listed. Like Jane, you will be writing a final manuscript to submit to your instructor. Therefore, there are some departures from the strict APA style that we describe in this chapter and again later on, and that are illustrated in Jane's research report.

4.3   The Abstract

The purpose of the abstract is to provide the instructor with a summary of your final manuscript. The abstract appears at the beginning of the final report (immediately after the title page), but it should be written after you have completed the other sections. Think of the abstract as a distillation into one paragraph of the important points covered in the body of the research report. In chapter 2, for example, the summary of the Stephen Raudenbush article (Exhibit 6 in section 2.4) illustrates the APA form of an abstract. It is, as the APA Manual would describe it, "dense with information." That is, the Raudenbush abstract is packed with details and emphasizes keywords (such as *teacher expectancy, Pygmalion experiment,* and *pupil IQ*), which would make the article easier to find if you were searching on these keywords.

The APA Manual lists four essentials of good abstracts. First, they are accurate in the way they report the purpose and content of the paper. Second, all they do is to report this information; they do not evaluate it. The evaluation is saved for discussion of the results in the body of the manuscript. Third, they contain no jargon. Fourth, they are not long-winded, but concise and to the point. Ideally, the abstract for a research report will describe the purpose or goal of the research in a single sentence. Word limits for published abstracts vary, but they range from 150 to 250 words. The author is expected to describe the participants, the method used, the basic findings, and the conclusions. In the abstract of Jane's research report (appendix A), she relates the basis of her research, what she did, what she found, and the relationship of what she found to what she predicted, and she ends by stating that "limitations to the study and suggestions for further research" are also discussed.

In planning your abstract after you have written your report, answer the following questions as accurately, coherently, clearly, and concisely as possible:

- What was the objective or purpose of my research study?
- What principal method did I use?
- Who were the research participants?
- What were my major findings?
- What did I conclude from these findings?
- Without going into details that are included in the discussion section, can I report in one sentence that there will be limitations discussed later on?

More detailed and specific statements about methods, results, and conclusions are given in the body of your report. Just remember that the purpose of the abstract is to give the reader an idea of what your report is about. This is why the abstract is presented first.

4.4 The Introduction

The introduction is the foundation for the research. It describes the problem that you investigated and thus prepares the reader for the methods you chose. In planning your introduction, think about the history or the background of your topic and how you might go from that kind of opening into your hypotheses or questions. You will be making an *evidence-based argument,* a line of reasoning in which you build an empirical case for your hypotheses or questions. In this way, you establish the underpinning for the objective of your study and what you predicted. Suppose you planned your research as an improvement on a previous study, and let us assume that the previous study by researcher X had been criticized by researcher Y, who claimed there was a serious methodological flaw in X's research. It would not be good evidence-based writing to state something like "X (2006) reported an effect of interpersonal expectations on companion choice, but this experiment of X's was criticized by Y (2009) because of a methodological flaw." This statement fails to adequately describe the effect reported by X and does not identify the methodological flaw that Y criticized. The statement is concise, but it is imprecise and uninformative. Simply presenting a string of loosely related summary statements like these, without showing that you understand what you are citing and how it supports a particular view or position, would be a weak evidence-based argument.

In her opening paragraph, Jane starts out with a descriptive finding that becomes an underpinning that she uses to establish the importance of studying tipping behavior. The following paragraphs pick up the thread from her first paragraph. Jane summarizes the results of a series of studies precisely (she gives the percentages) and succinctly. It is easy for us to follow the flow of her argument. Some students simply assert conclusions advocated by authors of cited studies and fail to describe the evidence that the researchers used to support those assertions. Jane, however, deftly leads us into her three hypotheses. She takes nothing for granted and, instead, walks the reader (the instructor) step by step through the reasoning behind each of her hypotheses. It is a strong introduction, because it states not only the problem but also the hypotheses in such a way as to make the method section seem a natural consequence of the introduction. That is, it is the kind of introduction that is bound to get the reader to think when she or he reads the method section, "Yes, of course, that's what this researcher had to do to answer this question."

Here are some questions to ask yourself as you plan the introduction:

◆ What was the purpose of my study, and why did it seem important to choose this particular problem?

◆ How did my study derive from other studies, and also how does it build on those studies?

◆ What were my hypotheses, predictions, or expectations, and what was the logical and evidential basis of my ideas?

◆ If there was more than one hypothesis, how are the hypotheses interrelated so that they don't seem fragmented and unconnected?

◆ When I turn to the method section afterward, will it be clear from my introduction that the empirical procedures I used were a natural consequence of the questions I wanted to answer?

4.5 The Method Section

The next step is to think about how you will detail the method (the procedures, the characteristics of the research participants, the research design, the materials that you used, and so on). It is customary to subdivide the method section, possibly in the same way that Jane subdivided her section into "Participants," "Materials," and "Design and Procedure." However, no ironclad rule states that you must use these particular subdivisions if instead you think there is a clearer, more logical, and more fluid way of describing what you did. The APA Manual suggests several options for subsections of the method section, including the three used by Jane and possibly another subsection on "Sampling Procedures," another on "Sample Size, Power, and Precision," another on "Measures" (that is, the measures used and, if relevant, the training and reliability of those who collected the results), and so on.

The first subsection of Jane's report (in appendix A) tells us about the people who participated in her research: the diners and the server. She uses the symbol n to indicate the number of dining parties ($n = 20$) in each of the 4 conditions, ranging in size from 2 to 12, with 3–4 people (on average) in each dining party. Given the nature of the experiment, the level of detail is quite adequate. In other kinds of research situations, more details that describe the characteristics of the research participants may be required to give a sense of the population to which the results are presumed generalizable. For example, if your research had to specifically sample a particular age group, ethnic group, or racial group, it would be important to describe the sample in more detail. In many studies, it might also be appropriate to provide information about the average age of those in each group, the number of males and females, and any other demographic details that could conceivably be picked up again when you are discussing the generalizability of the results in the discussion section of the report.

Most experimenters recruit what have been described as "opportunity samples"—that is, the first individuals (usually the first students) who are available—rather than use special sampling procedures such as those used in polling studies. That is, researchers frequently proceed on the assumption that people are people, and the objective is to draw universal generalizations. Back in the 1940s, however, a prominent psychologist (Quinn McNemar) stressed that the science of human behavior had become largely the science of the behavior of college sophomores, because students in psychology got more than their fair share of opportunities to play the role of research subject. Concerns about the use of students as the model of "persons in general" have been based not only on the obvious differences between college students and more representative persons in age, intelligence, and social class, but also on the suspicion that college students may be more sensitive and responsive to inadvertent task-orienting cues (called the *demand characteristics*, a term that was coined by Martin T. Orne some years ago). More recently, methodologists have also become interested in characteristics associated with the volunteer status of research participants, on the suspicion that volunteers may often be different from nonvolunteers in ways that are related to particular outcomes. (This idea is discussed by John Smith in the section of his review paper in appendix B that is labeled "Two Issues in Intelligence Assessment.") The point is that it is important to think about whether the generalizability of your results might be limited to a specific population (rather than persons in general) and, therefore, to be sure to describe characteristics of the sample that you might want to revisit in the discussion section of your report.

The next subdivision of Jane Doe's report describes the materials that she used in her research (the chocolates) and also tells us how she used a randomizing method to assign each specific condition to the dining parties. If you are using tests or standardized measures of some kind, this is the place to provide information about the validity and reliability of the instruments and how you used them. Even if you used well-known, standardized tests, it is still a good idea to describe them in a few sentences. Including such a description tells the instructor that you understand the nature and purpose of your measuring instruments. Suppose you used Mark Snyder's Self-Monitoring Scale, described in an article he wrote in the *Journal of Personality and Social Psychology* in 1974. Suppose you know from your literature search that research by Briggs, Cheek, and Buss (published in the same journal in 1980) found that Snyder's Self-Monitoring Scale consisted of three dimensions. In the materials subdivision of your method section, your statement could be as follows:

> The study participants were administered Snyder's 25-item Self-Monitoring Scale (1974). The original purpose of this instrument was to measure self-control and self-observation, but Briggs, Cheek, and Buss (1980) found that the scale measures

three distinct factors, described by them as extraversion, other-directedness, and acting. *Extraversion* refers to the tendency to be the center of attention in groups; *other-directedness* refers to a person's willingness to change his or her behavior to suit others; and *acting* refers to liking and being good at speaking and entertaining.

Suppose you needed to report only the nature of a particular measure and not any follow-up inferences by other researchers. Say you used John T. Cacioppo and Richard E. Petty's scale for measuring the need for cognition, which they discussed in an article in the *Journal of Personality and Social Psychology* in 1982. You can succinctly describe this measure in a single clause, if it seems appropriate to do so:

> The participants were administered Cacioppo and Petty's (1982) Need for Cognition Scale, which is an 18-item measure of the tendency to engage in and enjoy thinking.

If you can report information about the reliability and validity of the instrument, mention this information as well (along with an appropriate citation), but be specific. It is vague to say only that "the reliability was $r = .50$" without also indicating whether the measure was the *test-retest reliability* (the stability of the instrument from one measurement session to another), the *alternate-form reliability* (the degree of equivalence of different versions of the instrument), or the *internal-consistency reliability* (the degree of relatedness of items or individual components of the instrument when those items or components are used to give a single score). The same rule applies to the reporting of validity findings; tell which type of validity you mean of those described in Exhibit 13.

EXHIBIT 13 Uses of the term *validity* in research and assessment

construct validity: the degree to which the conceptual variable (or construct) that is presumably measured or studied is what is claimed.

content validity: the adequate sampling of the relevant material or content that a test purports to measure.

criterion validity: the degree to which a measuring instrument is correlated with outcome criteria in the present (its concurrent validity) or the future (its predictive validity).

external validity: the generalizability of an inferred causal relationship over different people, settings, manipulations, and research outcomes.

face validity: the degree to which a measuring instrument "looks as if" it is measuring something relevant.

internal validity: the soundness of statements about whether one variable is responsible for a particular outcome.

statistical-conclusion validity: the accuracy of the statistical conclusions drawn.

The final subdivision of Jane's method section is where she describes in detail the design of her research and her procedure for implementing it. In planning this section in your report, you will describe all the important aspects of the design and implementation of your study. Did you perform a randomized experiment, and if so, what was the nature of the experimental design (for example, a between-subjects or a within-subjects design, a one-dimensional or a factorial design), and how was the random assignment done? If you used another design, what kind was it? If you used a quasi-experimental design, did you anticipate the problem of "nonequivalent groups" and include measures collected at both the beginning and end of the research? If you used a correlational design, what will you say (in the discussion section) about the third-variable problem—the possibility that a "third variable" that is correlated with your two main variables was the reason they were correlated? It is important not to omit details about the design and procedure when omission may mislead the reader.

4.6   The Results Section

In the next major section, the results section, you will describe your findings. Jane begins by telling how she scored the data and defined the dependent variable. She then goes into specific details, beginning with the overall results in each condition. She provides a table of basic summary data, so that an inquisitive reader can recalculate the results. Jane explains why she performed a statistical test that did not address her specific predictions; she did so to check her other calculations, and to demonstrate that she understands certain aspects of other data analyses she reports. Jane's other data analyses are reported next, and in each case, she explains how her hypotheses naturally led her to choose the statistical procedures she used. Jane's discussion of her results—from the most general to the most specific—is, like any good argument, thorough and logically compelling. In chapter 6, we describe four criteria for reporting statistical information; Jane's results section is an exemplar of all four: (a) clarity, (b) accuracy, (c) precision, and (d) enough detail to allow readers to reach their own conclusions.

We will have more to say about the use of tables and figures in chapters 6 and 8. However, to anticipate a little, the APA Manual's distinction between tables and figures is that "tables are almost always characterized by a row-column structure" where "any type of illustration other than a table is referred to as a *figure*" (p. 125). If you plan to include a table or a figure, a fundamental rule is not to make the reader guess what you are trying to communicate. Label the table or figure fully. Don't repeat every single result from the table or figure in your narrative; just tell what the displayed results represent. Ask yourself the following questions as you plan your results section:

- What did I find?
- How can I report the findings in a careful, detailed way?

◆ Is what I am planning to say precise and to the point?
◆ Will what I have said be clear to the reader?
◆ Have I left out anything of importance?

A question that students often ask is how precise they should be in reporting statistical tests (such as the t test, the F test, and chi-square), effect sizes, measures of central tendency (such as means and medians), and measures of variability (standard deviations and variances). A rule of thumb is to round statistical values to two decimal places, as shown in the results section of Jane's report. In her appendix, however, Jane shows the intermediate calculations that she did on a hand-held calculator to more than two decimal places. Precision and accuracy are the reasons that Jane would give for not rounding the intermediate calculations. By analogy, suppose you were an engineer for the National Aeronautics and Space Administration and were trying to figure out how much fuel would be needed to complete a manned mission to Mars. Rounding your intermediate calculations too much could produce results that would send the astronauts on an impossible mission.

Another convention that many students find confusing is how p values are to be presented, as reporting that a result was "statistically significant" or "not statistically significant" is not very informative. For t, F, and chi-square (χ^2) tests, many instructors require their students to report the actual descriptive level of statistical significance. Assuming your instructor does not frown on p values reported to more than two or three decimal places, there are several options. One option is to list a string of zeros, such as "$p = .00000025$." Another option (the one that Jane chose) is to use scientific notation as a more compact way to show a very small p value. Instead of reporting $p = .00000025$, you would report 2.5^{-7}, where the "-7" tells the reader to count 7 places to the left of the decimal in 2.5 and make that the decimal place. In asterisked notes to tables or figures, the convention is to indicate the level of significance reached by a test value as great or greater than the exact p value. So if you indicated by an asterisk that p was less than .001, the asterisk would include *all* p values that are smaller than .001. Notice in Jane's Table 2 that she uses an asterisk to indicate that two of her F tests were statistically significant at p less than .0001.

We will have more to say about how to report statistical results in chapter 6, but we do not want to leave you with the impression that the value of the statistical test and the p value are all that needs to be reported. As the APA Manual cautions, these are only starting points. Providing additional information is imperative, such as effect sizes and, when possible, confidence intervals. Enough information should be reported so that an interested reader can independently draw his or her own conclusions. There are also traps to be avoided, such as concluding that a p value that is not "statistically significant" is synonymous with "zero effect." These are fundamental concerns that we discuss in more detail in chapter 6.

4.7 The Discussion Section

Once you have a critical mass of data, the purpose of the discussion section is to explain what your results told you and how they relate to the hypotheses or questions that you formulated in the introduction. If you had a sudden insight or an unexpected idea, the discussion section is also the place where you will write about it. When discussing any of your sudden insights or unexpected ideas, it is important to emphasize that they were not *working hypotheses* formulated before you collected the data, but are *ad hoc hypotheses* stimulated by insights after you inspected the data. There is an old Bohemian legend about a fabled archer who was offered an empire if he could teach the king how to become a great marksman. The king came upon the archer standing next to a grove of trees. Each tree had a chalked circle and an arrow in the exact center of the circle. One arrow quivered in its circle even as the king approached. "Keep your empire," the archer told the king, "for the secret of my skill is that I shoot first and draw the circle afterward." It also requires little skill to pretend that ad hoc hypotheses were your working hypotheses, but it would be misleading and unethical to do so.

This is not to discredit ad hoc insights or accidental discoveries, as they can be of enormous value. They are traditionally described as *serendipitous,* if they are truly made by accident. Serendipity is actually quite common in science. A famous case involved the discovery of pulsars (pulsating radio sources) in 1967. In England, a research student at Cambridge University was analyzing charts of extraterrestrial noises when she noticed a "bit of scruff" in the sky. At first, she thought it was an accidental glitch or irregularity, but then she noticed a pattern. What she had discovered by luck turned out to be remnants of rapidly spinning neutron stars that had resulted from the collapse of stars in supernova explosions. Of course, serendipity is not limited to scientific discoveries. Another famous example is an accidental discovery made by George deMestral after he was out for a stroll in the Swiss countryside. While picking cockleburs from his jacket, he happened to notice that they were covered with tiny hooks that had become embedded in the loops of the fabric. Suddenly he perceived a way to create something useful out of a nuisance, the Velcro fastener. The lesson is to keep your eyes and mind open to unanticipated findings and novel ways of thinking about them.

Previously, we mentioned using an evidence-based argument when pulling studies together in your introduction. In the discussion section of your report, you will be making another evidence-based argument that has sometimes been described as *defensive* in that researchers have got into the habit of playing their own devil's advocate in presenting their findings. They ask themselves what a skeptical reader might perceive as the other side of the argument or conclusion, and they temper their discussions or they try to blunt the imaginary skeptical reader's counterargument. This is a challenging exercise, because it requires that the researcher detach himself or herself from the research and then, from the point of view of an unconvinced observer, critically think about shortcomings and inconsistencies in the research. All research findings are limited in some ways, and it is better to anticipate specific limitations in your discussion than to naively exaggerate the research implications. You might ask a clever friend to help you by responding critically to what you want to argue or conclude in your discussion. Impress on the friend that you are trying to find any holes in your argument or conclusions.

Here are some questions to consider as you begin to plan what you will be writing in this section:

- What was the purpose of my study?
- How do my results relate to that purpose?
- Were there any serendipitous findings of interest?
- How valid and generalizable are my findings?
- Are there larger implications in these findings?
- Is there an alternative way to interpret my results?
- Do my results raise new questions?

If you think that there are practical or larger implications in your findings, this is the section of your report in which to spell them out. Are there implications for further research? Another option is to follow the discussion section with another section called "Conclusions," or you can divide the discussion section into subsections and end with a subdivision called "Conclusions." In either case, your conclusions should be stated clearly, accurately, and as precisely as required.

4.8 The References Section

Once you have made plans for writing the body of the report, you need to rethink what you want to cite and reference. It is important to cite and reference everything that is essential to your report, but it is also important not to cite and reference materials that are unneeded. Presumably, you have kept a running list of the material that you thought you might want to include as you progressed through the preparation of the proposal and the implementation of the research. Remember that every article, chapter, and book that you cite must be listed in the references section, and that every reference must be cited in the body of your manuscript. If at the last minute you need to recheck the author, title, or publisher of a particular book, remember that you can go to the Library of Congress Web site (http://catalog.loc.gov). If you need to check the volume number or pages of a journal article, you can again use PsycINFO to find this information.

4.9   The End Material

The end material, as the name implies, refers to everything after the references. In Jane's report, the end material includes an appendix, a footnotes page, and two tables. If you were including one or more figures, they would follow the tables in the end material. Because you are submitting a final manuscript rather than a copy manuscript, the instructor might permit you to incorporate the figures within the narrative text. Footnotes are used only if they are absolutely needed and the information cannot be integrated into the body of the narrative. In Jane's report the footnote information could actually be incorporated in the narrative, though the way it is shown in Jane's report will give you an idea of how to handle footnotes in APA style. Unless your instructor has other requirements, you can use Jane's report as a model for your final manuscript.

The purpose of the appendix in Jane's report is to provide information that does not fit into her results section but elaborates on the results. Theses and dissertations also frequently have an appendix for the raw data and research materials, so the information is available to others in the future (e.g., for use in meta-analyses). Some instructors may prefer, however, that appendix-type information in student reports for class assignments be submitted in an electronic file. Had Jane used a questionnaire or a test that she could not adequately describe in the limited space of the method section, the appendix would be where she would include a copy. If you used a standard program to analyze the data in your research, your instructor may ask you to include a printout, or to pare it down to essentials and include the pared-down results in an appendix section in your final paper. But whether or not your instructor requires an appendix, it is important that you save all your background notes and raw data until the instructor has returned your graded report and you have officially received a grade in the course—just in case the instructor might have questions about your work. Nowadays it is convenient to save the raw data and the manuscript in an electronic file.

4.10   Organizing Your Thoughts

The formal structure of the research report provides a skeletal outline that waits to be fleshed out. Nevertheless, most researchers find it essential to organize their thoughts about each section before writing the first draft. There are several ways to do this in your research report:

- ◆ You can scribble on a piece of paper the points you want to cover and, after you have thought about them, make them into a broad outline and then a more specific outline. To learn about outlining, read chapter 5. Even though it is recommended for students writing literature reviews, chapter 5 can also be a useful guide as you go about organizing your thoughts for a research report.

- ◆ You can make notes on separate index cards for each major point you want to cover (for example, the rationale of the study, the derivation of each of your hypotheses, and each background study) and then sort and re-sort the cards until you think you have a clear direction for each section of your first draft.
- ◆ You can also create an electronic file of such notes and then cut and paste them back and forth until you think they provide a logical direction for your first draft. However, if there are a lot of these notes, it may be difficult to see the big picture, so you may end up printing the notes on separate pieces of paper and sorting and re-sorting them as you would index cards.

If you are still having a hard time organizing your thoughts, try dictating ideas into a voice recorder. Take the voice recorder for a walk; tell it what you found in your research. Another possibility is to imagine you are sitting across a table from a friend; tell the "friend" what you found. No matter what approach you favor, make sure that your notes and files are accurate and complete. If you are summarizing or paraphrasing something you read, you must provide a complete citation. If you are quoting someone, put the statement in quotation marks in your notes as a reminder that you copied it exactly, and write down the page numbers since they are required for an exact quote.

5

Organizing the Review Paper

When you are ready to begin drafting your review paper, the first step is to create a rough outline. The imposition of form will help you collect and refine your thoughts as you shape the paper, and you can prepare a more detailed outline after you have thought some more. If you don't outline before you begin the first draft, you should at least do so afterward. If a logical, ordered form does not emerge, the weak spots will become apparent and you can fix them.

5.1 Why You Need an Outline

Once you are ready to think about the first draft of your review paper, it is time to begin outlining your thoughts about how to order your source materials and insights in a systematic way that will shepherd a reader from the introduction, through each section of your paper, and finally to your conclusions. Unlike the research report (chapter 4), which usually adheres to a traditional arrangement of sections, the literature review (with the exception of meta-analytic reviews) is more flexible in its overall structure. A 2-page table in the APA Manual (pp. 251–252) tells what to include in a meta-analytic review, but here we are interested in review papers along the lines of John Smith's paper in appendix B. Like his paper, your final manuscript will have a title page, an abstract, then the narrative text, followed by a list of references, possibly some footnotes (John lists three), and end with any tables and/or figures (in this order) that you want to include (John has one table and one figure). Depending on the argument or thesis that you want to develop in your paper, the narrative text will be divided into sections that take the reader from the introduction to the final conclusions.

If you go back to Exhibit 8 in chapter 3 (see section 3.1), you will remember that Maya sketched out several options for her proposal. After submitting the proposal, she made notes about everything she read and thought a lot more about it within the context of the objective of her review. In sketching a tentative plan for her final paper, she might have thought about going from the Pygmalion experiment to a detailed review of the work on moderator variables, with subsections focused on particular moderators, then into a review of relevant controversial issues, and ending with a set of conclusions. An alternative might be to begin with the Pygmalion experiment and then subdivide the paper into sections corresponding to educational applications and ending with her conclusions. A third idea might be to begin with the Pygmalion experiment, and then to focus on research findings on interpersonal expectations, followed by a discussion of implications and conclusions. So there are a number of options for Maya to consider, each depending on the direction she is considering as the basis of a tentative plan. This range of options presents itself for most review papers. Once the writer has settled on a particular option, it becomes the skeletal framework of the paper. Fleshing out this preliminary framework with more and more particulars will produce the rough outline and then a more detailed outline.

Not having at least a rough outline is like trying to drive from point A to point B in an unfamiliar area without a map. You may end up going around in circles, driving yourself to distraction as you dissipate the motivation and energy you need to complete your assignment on schedule. With a coherent, logical, and realistic outline, you know where your ideas and sentences are heading. One instructor wrote to us: "Some of my students' lit reviews read like catalogs of studies with no real organization. There's a paragraph on X's study, one on Y's study, and then another one on the study by Z." A paper like that is a sure sign that the student did not develop an outline before beginning to write.

In sketching a rough outline, you can do as Maya did, beginning with a cluster outline of different options. Another possibility is a preliminary outline of studies you want to review in chronological order, which will show the temporal sequence in which these research ideas evolved. Another alternative might be to group them by results that supported one hypothesis and then the results that supported an alternative hypothesis. It all depends on the argument or thesis that you want to develop in your paper.

5.2   A Strategy That Will Get You Started

So far, we have given you a general idea of what is required to outline the review paper, and now it is time to get started on a particular strategy and stick with it. You can begin to organize ideas and studies into an informal outline as you retrieve and read your reference material. If you choose this strategy, use comparison and contrast as a way of categorizing components into groups and subgroups. Add or remove components as you pull together the facts, arguments, and studies that seem to document and expand on your subtopics. Like an amorphous mass in a science fiction movie that gradually takes shape out of primordial ooze, the structure of even the most preliminary outline will gradually acquire form and shape if you just keep thinking about it patiently. You don't have to do your organizing in one sitting. In fact, it is better to take a break, go for a walk, work on something else, and then come back to the task with a refreshed mind. Keep in mind that your objective is to produce a logical progression of ideas and a balanced hierarchy of organization that you will expand on and then polish as needed.

If this seems confusing, or you find it difficult to get started, here are three tricks you can try:

- ◆ Think of the outline as a very detailed table of contents based on the headings and subheadings you might want to use in a particular section.
- ◆ Shop around for an interesting quote that encourages fresh thinking (see John's opening quote on page 3 of his paper) or, as Jane Doe did in her research report in appendix B, a pithy fact ("More than two million people in the United States work as waiters and waitresses who serve in restaurants."). Assuming it still is relevant later on, you can use the quote or pithy fact (as John and Jane did) to launch your introduction as well as capture and focus the reader's interest.
- ◆ Another trick is to come up with an image or metaphor or analogy, which you can use as a launching point for other associations (and also possibly use again in your paper). John Smith used the image of a movie theater in which different films are playing to describe the multiplex orientation that he discussed in his review paper in appendix B. However, as Maya's instructor cautioned, "Stay focused." At this point in your writing, you want to kick-start your outline. Later on, the image or metaphor or analogy that helped you do that might also be used to set the tone of the final manuscript.

Before attempting the first draft of your paper (discussed in chapter 7), it is a good idea to revise and polish the rough outline so it reflects the organizational structure of your paper as precisely as possible. The structure can be redrafted or modified as your ideas evolve, so don't be shy about consulting the instructor if your thinking changes and you want to modify the structure of your review. But do consult your instructor about major changes; do not simply show up at the end of the semester with a paper that is unrecognizable from the proposal that the instructor approved.

5.3   The Rough Outline

Your first outline can be simply a numbered list of items you want to cover in the paper. You can then think about the list, put it aside for a day or so, and then think about it some more. Asking yourself the following questions should help you get going:

- How do I want to begin?
- What conclusions do I want to draw?
- What sections do I need between these two points?
- In each section, what do I want to emphasize?
- What illustrations, examples, or quotations can I use?
- What details do I use? In what order?

Turning again to John's paper in appendix B, you can see that all these questions are addressed. If we could go back a couple of steps and ask how John began structuring his paper, we would find that he might have sketched something like the following:

1. Point out that the concept of intelligence is controversial, that the term is used in more than one way, and that certain assumptions can be explained in other ways.
2. Present the issue that assessing intelligence is not without potential problems.
3. Review the history of the traditional (g-centered) theoretical orientation and what I call the multiplex orientation.
4. Explain Gardner's theory of multiple intelligences.
5. Review point-counterpoint criticisms and rejoinders.
6. Sum up the main ideas and say something about future directions or further research.

There is enough here to let John think about the details of each section in order to frame a more meticulous outline. In getting down to specifics, he needs to keep all of his ideas parallel to ensure logical consistency in his arguments. Just as the rough outline can take different forms, the detailed outline that John next constructs can be set down in topics, sentences, or paragraphs—whichever seem to make the most sense as his ideas begin to flow.

5.4   Making Ideas Parallel

For the more detailed outline, whether you decide to work with topics, sentences, or paragraphs, the form you choose should be the only one that you use. In other words, you need to make the ideas parallel. In the following outline fragment, the ideas are not parallel:

I. What is intelligence? What does g-centric mean? What will follow?
II. Two views
   A. Traditional—the general overriding factor of intelligence is measured by every task on an intelligence test

    B. Spearman's psychometric contribution
    C. Developmental psychologists, following Piaget, argue for general mental structures
    D. *The Bell Curve*

The problem with the outline above is that it is a hodgepodge of questions, topics, idea fragments, and a book title. Such an outline will sabotage efforts to put thoughts and notes into a logical sequence. Contrast that incoherent structure with the parallel structure of the following outline:

    I. Two views of intelligence
      A. The traditional approach
        1. General overriding trait (Spearman)
          a. The *g*-centric assumption
          b. The question of heritability
        2. General structures of the mind (Piaget)
          a. Universal developmental sequence
          b. Biological correlates
        3. Societal implications (Herrnstein & Murray)
          a. Assertions
          b. Controversial assumptions

What makes the second outline an improvement over the first is not only that the same form is used throughout but that the ideas are also logically ordered. The second outline looks more polished and inviting and will certainly be easier to use as a writing plan.

5.5   *Putting Ideas in Order*

To create this polished look, whether you use topics, sentences, or paragraphs for your detailed outline, the trick is to try to group your information in descending order, from the most general facts or ideas to the most specific details and examples. You can see this approach clearly in the parallel format of the second outline shown above. The first-level (I) heading ("Two views of intelligence") is the most general. The second-level (A) heading ("The traditional approach") is somewhat more specific. The third-level (1) heading ("General overriding trait") is more explicit, and the fourth-level (a) heading ("The *g*-centric assumption") is the most exact.

    The rule of orderly precision applies whether you are outlining definitions, the assumptions and assertions of a particular theory, evaluation criteria, or arguments and counterarguments. You can see the order and precision in the following outline segment as it proceeds from the general to the most specific:

    II. Gardner's theory of "intelligences"
      A. Definition of intelligence
        1. Problem solving and creative abilities

      2. Evaluation criteria
        a. Isolation if brain-damaged
        b. Existence of exceptional populations
        c. Unique core operations
        d. Distinctive developmental history
        e. Existence of primitive antecedents
        f. Openness to experimentation
        g. Prediction of performance on tests
        h. Accessibility of information content
  B. Kinds of intelligence
      1. Logical-mathematical
      2. Linguistic
      3. Spatial
      4. Bodily-kinesthetic
      5. Musical
      6. Personal
        a. Intrapersonal
        b. Interpersonal

Another convention in making a detailed outline, as illustrated in Exhibit 14, is that if there is a subtopic division, there should be at least two subtopics, never only one. Facts, ideas, and concepts are classified by the use of Roman numerals (I, II, III); capitals (A, B, C); Arabic numerals (1, 2, 3); lowercase letters (a, b, c); and finally, numbers and letters in parentheses. Thus, if you list I, you should list II (and perhaps III and IV and so on); if A, then B; if 1, then 2. The Roman numerals indicate the outline's main ideas. Indented capital letters provide main divisions within each main idea. The letters and numbers that follow list the supporting details and examples. Note the indentation of each subtopic. Any category can be expanded to

EXHIBIT 14   Subdivision of the outline

I.
   A.
   B.
      1.
      2.
        a.
        b.
          (1)
          (2)
            (a)
            (b)
II.

---

fit the number of supporting details or examples that you wish to cover in the paper. Any lapses in logic are bound to surface if you use this system of organization, so you can catch and correct them before proceeding.

For example, look at the following abbreviated outline; item B is clearly a conspicuous lapse in logic:

II. Gardner's theory of "intelligences"
    A. His definition of intelligence
    B. How did the concept of *g* originate?
    C. Seven kinds of intelligence

Item B should be moved from this section of the outline to the one pertaining to the *g*-centric view of intelligence. Some items may require a return to PsycINFO or the library to clarify a point or to supplement parts of the outline with additional reference material.

5.6 Detailed Outline for Writing and Note Taking

The outline is a way not only to organize your thoughts but also to make it easier to start writing. We can see this effect clearly in the following outline fragment:

II. Gardner's theory of "intelligences"
    A. Definition of intelligence
        1. ". . . the ability to solve problems, or to create products that are valued within one or more cultural settings" (Gardner, 1983, p. x)
        2. Intellectual talent must satisfy eight criteria (Gardner, 1983)
            a. Possible identification of intelligences by damage to particular areas of the brain
            b. Existence of exceptional populations (savants), implying the distinctive existence of a special entity

Had our hypothetical outline used complete sentences, the paper would practically write itself:

II. Gardner's theory of "intelligences"
    A. Definition of intelligence
        1. Gardner (1983) conceived of intelligence as "the ability to solve problems, or to create products that are valued within one or more cultural settings" (p. x).
        2. Gardner (1983) argued that a talent must fit eight criteria to be considered "intelligence."
            a. There is potential to isolate the intelligence by brain damage.
            b. Exceptional populations (e.g., savants) provide evidence of distinct entities.

The outline's coding system makes it convenient to go back and code your notes. If your notes refer to section "II.B.1" of your outline, then you will record this code on the card, photocopy, or computer printout. In this way, you bring order to your notes. If you are using cards, for example, you can spread them on a large table and sort through them, sorting them to match the sections in your outline. Keep in mind, however, that the outline is only a guide. Its specific structure may change as you integrate your notes.

5.7   Techniques to Focus Your Thinking

Some students find it difficult to get started drafting an outline because their ideas are not yet really organized in their thinking. Here are a couple of tricks that may help to focus your thinking:

- One technique is to start with a cluster outline. Just as Maya did, you simply write down the core question or theme of your paper and draw a circle (or oval) around it, and then you attach circled ideas to the core question or theme until it all makes sense to you. This procedure is illustrated in Exhibit 15 for John Smith's writing assignment. He began with the central theme ("intelligence") and then added other circled items. The next step is to develop a logical progression of these ideas. The logical progression will become the preliminary outline that is the foundation of a more detailed outline.
- Another technique is to write the tentative section headings on index cards, which you move back and forth until you think they

EXHIBIT 15   Cluster outline for John Smith's project

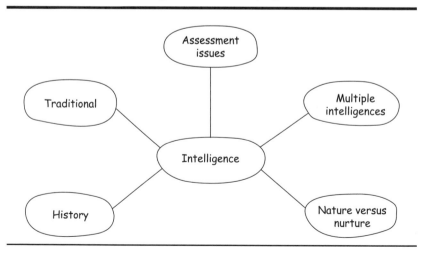

are in the right logical order. Then write each study or idea on a separate index card, and sort these cards to fit under the appropriate section headings. You can color-code the cards to represent possible headings, subheadings, and so forth. The advantage of this technique is that it is also visual, and you can easily rearrange the cards after you have taken a break and can look at the arrangement again from a fresh perspective.

5.8 Outlining After the Fact

Some students write their papers over more than one semester (a senior thesis, for example) and may feel they cannot outline from the outset because they do not know where the final paper will go. When they do sit down to write, they tend to incorporate material from their earlier drafts, but they do not make an outline first. Still other students find the process of making an outline too exacting, preferring to sit at the computer and let the stream of ideas flow spontaneously.

If either case describes you, then try outlining after the fact. To assure yourself that your work has what psychologists call a *good gestalt* (a coherent, psychologically appealing form), make a "mini-table-of-contents" of your final draft, and then do a more detailed outline within the headings and subheadings. Ask yourself:

- ◆ Is my discussion focused, and do the ideas flow from or build on one another?
- ◆ Have I amply developed each idea?
- ◆ Have I provided supporting details for each main idea discussed?
- ◆ Are the ideas balanced?
- ◆ Is my writing to the point?

If you can answer yes to each of these five questions, you have an effective outline and your writing should not go off on a tangent.

6

Communicating Statistical Information

Whether you are summarizing the results of your own data analysis in a research report or commenting on someone else's statistical information in your review paper, it is vital to have a sense of how and what to communicate. This chapter addresses these questions from the perspective of four general guidelines and the ethical implications of adhering to these guidelines. If you are not presenting any statistical information, you may want to skip this chapter and go on to chapter 7. On the other hand, all of us are consumers in a technological culture infused with numbers and statistics, and the topics covered in this chapter may be of general interest to you.

6.1   Knowing "How" and "What" to Communicate

This chapter is for students who have taken an introductory course in statistics or are currently taking one, and who need to report statistical results in a literature review or a research report. For example, in his review paper (appendix B), John Smith quotes the statement that "approximately three fourths of the variance in real-world performance is not accounted for by intelligence test performance." In his footnote 2, John comments that a predictor variable that accounts for approximately 25% of the variance implies an effect size correlation of around .5, which is not unimpressive in psychology. John also cites a supporting reference, which (as he mentions in the author note on the cover page of his paper) was recommended by his instructor. Meta-analytic review papers, on the other hand, consist primarily of the use of statistical and graphical methods to sum up a set of studies (such as Raudenbush's meta-analytic review in chapter 2, Exhibit 6). If you are preparing to write up your research report, you know that detailed statistical analyses are an integral part of the results section, as Jane Doe's report illustrates (appendix A).

Although the statistical information presented by Jane is the kind that is supposed to be routinely reported in journal articles, not every non-APA journal insists on all those details. For example, the APA Manual notes that "researchers in psychology have relied heavily on null hypothesis significance testing (NHST) as a starting point for many (but not all) of its analytic approaches" (p. 33). The APA Manual adds that "APA stresses that NHST is but a starting point and that additional reporting elements such as effect sizes, confidence intervals, and extensive description are needed to convey the most complete meaning of the results" (p. 33). Not all editors or researchers consider NHST a starting point, but most would no doubt agree with the rest of the statement in the APA Manual, that is, the importance of "reporting elements such as effect sizes, confidence intervals, and extensive description." We will have more to say about the distinction between the probability value (the p value) and the effect size later in this chapter. (To help jog your memory of these and other common statistical concepts and symbols, see Exhibit 16.)

Not mentioned in the APA Manual are a number of other useful statistics, such as Rosenthal and Rubin's *counternull value* of the observed effect size (ES). The interval between the null value of the ES and the counternull value of the ES is called the *null-counternull interval*. It is a kind of confidence interval except that the lower limit is zero (the null hypothesis), and unlike confidence intervals (which are based on prespecified levels such as 95% CI or 99% CI), the null-counternull interval is based on the obtained p value. The reason for using the counternull ES is that it is insurance against prematurely believing the null hypothesis of zero to be true when the p value exceeds .05. Rosenthal and Rubin also developed another useful procedure for estimating an effect size when all that is known is the total sample size (N) and the accurate p value, but nothing else. The estimated ES, called $r_{equivalent}$, is similar to a sample point-biserial correlation between the independent variable indicator in a two-group experiment (e.g., treatment vs. control) and an exactly normally distributed outcome on the dependent variable. There are effect sizes for use in designs with more than two groups or conditions and precise predictions (as in Jane Doe's research report), and there are formulas for computing d and g (both defined in Exhibit 16) when the sample sizes are unequal. There are also formulas for estimating the loss of statistical power in designs with unequal sample sizes relative to designs with equal-sized samples.

In the end, of course, reporting significance tests and associated p values alone is not nearly as informative as reporting effect sizes and corresponding interval estimates. Suggested readings are listed at the end of this chapter. To provide a context for thinking about *how* and *what* to report, we turn next to four general guidelines, designated by the acronym CAPE. It stands for *c*larity, *a*ccuracy, *p*recision, and providing *e*nough detail to

EXHIBIT 16   *Common statistical abbreviations and symbols*

Symbol/ abbreviation	Definition
English symbols/abbreviations	
ANOVA	Acronym for *analysis of variance*, a statistical procedure in which the total variance of a set of scores is partitioned into components and *F* tests are used to statistically evaluate differences between variances.
CI	Confidence interval, that is, the lower limit (LL) and upper limit (UL) between which a population parameter is likely to be found, indicated, for example, as 95% CI [LL, UL] or 99% CI [LL, UL].
d	Cohen's effect size index for the difference between two means, a descriptive (as opposed to an inferential) value that is calibrated in standard score (*z*-score) units ranging from zero to positive or negative infinity. When computing Cohen's *d*, the difference between means is divided by the pooled population standard deviation (σ_{pooled}).
df	Degrees of freedom, the number of observations minus the number of restrictions limiting the observations' freedom to vary.
F	Fisher's *F* ratio for his test of significance to evaluate the tenability of the null hypothesis (H_0) of no difference between two or more means or variances.
g	Also known as Hedges's *g* (and Cohen's d_s, which antedated *g*), this is an inferential (as opposed to a descriptive) effect size index for the difference between two means; the effect size is calibrated in standard score (*z*-score) units that can range from zero to positive or negative infinity. When computing Hedges's *g*, divide the difference between means by *S* (the square root of the unbiased estimator of the population value of σ^2).
M	Simple arithmetic average of a set of scores (called the *arithmetic mean*). An older way of symbolizing the arithmetic mean was $\overline{X}$ (still sometimes seen, but not in APA-style journals).
Mdn	Median, the midmost score of a distribution.
MS	The unbiased estimate of the population variance, also symbolized as S^2.
n	The number of scores or observations in one condition or subgroup of a study.
N	The total number of scores or observations in a study.
p level	The probability of rejecting the null hypothesis when it is true (the probability of a Type I error).

EXHIBIT 16 Continued

p_{rep}	Statistic proposed by Peter Killeen, which indicates the probability of replicating a directional effect. Closely tied to the p value, the p_{rep} probability increases as the p value gets smaller and smaller, thus giving us a sense of the robustness of individual studies.
r	Pearson product-moment correlation, an index of the linear relation between a pair of variables.
SD	Standard deviation (σ), an index of the variability of a set of data around the mean value.
SS	The sum of the squared deviations from the mean in a set of scores.
t	An inferential test of significance that is used to judge the tenability of the null hypothesis of no relation between two variables. Also known as Student's t because William Sealy Gosset, who was the originator of this procedure, used the pseudonym Student.
Z score	Score converted to a standard deviation unit, also frequently indicated as z-score.

Greek symbols/abbreviations

α	Alpha, the probability of a Type I error (the error of rejecting the null hypothesis when it is true), where $1-\alpha$ is the confidence level. (The term alpha is also used to designate a measure of internal consistency reliability, known as *Cronbach's alpha*.)
β	Beta, the probability of a Type II error (the error of failing to reject the null hypothesis when it is false), where $1-\beta$ refers to the power of a statistical test (the probability of not making a Type II error).
λ	Lambda, a value in a set of coefficients (weights) that sum to zero and are used to state a prediction (as illustrated in Jane Doe's research report in appendix A).
σ	The standard deviation of a population of scores, also frequently indicated as SD.
σ^2	The variance of a population of scores.
Σ	Instruction telling us to sum (add) a set of scores.
Φ	Phi coefficient, the correlation statistic between two variables, each of which is dichotomous (e.g., treatment vs. control; yes vs. no responses; illness present vs. illness absent). It is also frequently indicated as ϕ.
χ^2	Chi-square, a statistic used to test the degree of agreement between the frequency data obtained and the frequency data expected under a particular hypothesis (e.g., the null hypothesis).

enable readers to reach their own conclusions. Afterward, we turn to the ethical implications of adhering to these general guidelines.

6.2 *Communicating Clearly*

Clarity of reporting statistical information basically means not obfuscating details in obscure or murky visual displays, or using technical terms inappropriately because you do not fully understand them, or talking about one thing when you really mean something else (such as reporting a diffuse data analysis although you hypothesized a specific result, a problem that we return to in the next section). It is vitally important that the structure of your paper enable the reader to easily follow the logic of your reasoning. Submitting the proposal (chapter 3) was your initial attempt to develop a coherent structure. If you are writing a research report, the traditional structure described in chapter 4 was designed to impose coherence on the presentation. If your assignment is to write a review paper, the guidelines in chapter 5 should help you develop a good outline before you begin writing the first draft. Thus, when information is communicated clearly, it is an indication to the instructor that the student has made a concerted effort to organize and plan the report or review paper and, in the specific case of reporting statistical information, that the student has a good understanding of the technical terms and expository language used.

Clear writing usually also means putting your thoughts down on paper concisely or, as the APA Manual reminds us, "less is more" (p. 61). This dictum is also true to an extent in reporting statistical information. However, it is important not to leave out critical details. Properly reporting the summary results of data analyses entails transparency, candidness, and openness, so that no one is misled by partially reported results or, in the worst case scenario, by fabricated results. Later in this chapter, and again in the next a chapter, we will have more to say about the ethics of writing and reporting. A primary responsibility is honesty in all aspects of your work. Fabricating the data or falsifying statistical results is a critical violation of this ethical imperative, and when discovered it is dealt with harshly.

The clear communication of statistical information is also a prime consideration when you are using graphical displays in reports and papers. With the availability of computer graphics, which can transform tabular data into charts and other visual displays quickly, it is easy to be lulled into a false sense of security about the interpretability of your graphical displays. When they are designed properly, bar charts (histograms) and line graphs (frequency polygons) can reveal a pattern of results at a glance. However, as noted above, graphics programs can be mind-numbingly deceptive, and using graphic displays because they are pretty or easy to create is no guarantee they are useful or interpretable. In *Elements of Graph Design* (published by W. H. Freeman in 1994), psychologist Stephen M. Kosslyn wrote on how the brain perceives and processes visual information and the implications for visual displays. Kosslyn mentioned that people are rarely aware of complex spatial relations between parts of a display because of the way in which the human brain has developed. A good reason for reporting information in tables is that exact values can be provided; when the data are summarized in histograms and frequency polygons, we can make only an educated guess about the exact values.

In chapter 9 (section 9.4), when we discuss the use of color in posters in visual displays, we will have more to say about Kosslyn's work on the cognitive processing of visual information. Visual displays that are cognitively impenetrable are simply a waste of the reader's time. Displays that are clear will communicate essential facts directly, simply, logically, and intelligibly. Kosslyn suggested three principles that summed up the psychological basis of graph design:

1. *The mind is not a camera.* That is to say, we do not see things only as they are, because experiential factors and expectancies also come into play. You remember the old proverb that "seeing is believing." Well, it is also true that "believing is seeing," in that people tend to perceive in ways that fit into their expectations.
2. *The mind judges a book by its cover.* That is, people take appearance as a clue to reality. As an extreme example, imagine a bar chart that reports the results of two teams, called the Blue Team and the Red Team. However, the artist uses blue ink to represent the Red Team and red ink to represent the Blue Team. As a result, the bar chart will inevitably create confusion, because the mind will give more weight to physical appearance and, in this case, is very likely to construe the chart inaccurately.
3. *The spirit is willing, but the mind is weak.* By analogy, just as we can bend our arms forward at the elbow but not backward, there are natural limitations on our visual and memory systems, which also must be recognized if visual displays are to be created in forms that can be interpreted correctly.

If you plan to use graphics in your report or paper, use them to enhance what you say in the narrative text. But no matter whether you are planning to use a figure (as John used in his review paper) or tables (as Jane used in her research report), mention that the figure and tables are in the manuscript and be sure to interpret them. Here are four simple guidelines (condensed from the APA Manual) if you are planning to include a bar chart or a line graph in your manuscript:

- ◆ Use a font, lines, labels, and symbols that are large enough, and easy enough to see, so the figure can be read easily, and make sure the lines are smooth and sharp.
- ◆ Use the same sans serif (no squiggles or loops) lettering in all figures, because it is easier to read this "monotonic" style of typeface.

- If you are displaying the relationship between an independent variable and a dependent variable (or between a predictor variable and a criterion or outcome variable), it is customary to put the independent (or predictor) variable on the horizontal axis (the x-axis, called the *abscissa*) and to put the dependent (or criterion) variable on the vertical axis (the y-axis, called the *ordinate*).
- The metric units or values should progress from small to large on each axis.

6.3 Communicating Accurately

In 2009, the National Academy of Sciences published the third edition of its guide to responsible conduct in research ("On Being a Scientist"). Among the responsibilities discussed was that "researchers have an obligation to the public, to their profession, and to themselves to be as accurate and as careful as possible" (p. 12). As stated in the guide: "The best methods will count for little if data are recorded incorrectly or haphazardly" (p. 9). On the other hand, to err is human. Therefore, all we can reasonably ask of students is that a conscientious effort be made to identify and correct any mistakes in measurements, calculations, and the reporting of numbers. Checking the raw data or raw scores is a way to spot *outliers,* the name for scores that lie far outside the normal range. Should you spot any, make sure they are not recording mistakes. Once you know that the scores have been recorded accurately, you may decide to report not only the means, but also the ranges and medians so that readers will not be misled into thinking that the scores were all clustered together. Incidentally, outliers that are not merely recording errors can sometimes provide clues to plausible moderator variables in relational and experimental research. Therefore, it is important not to simply dismiss outliers without examining them more closely, as it is always possible to "explain away" exceptions that may be telling us something of potential theoretical or practical significance.

Accuracy also means choosing the right statistical tools and using them correctly. Suppose you hypothesize a particular pattern of three or more group means, in the way that Jane did in her research in appendix A. If you assess your experimental hypothesis (your *working hypothesis*) by choosing an omnibus statistical test (i.e., a diffuse statistical test) that is not naturally sensitive to patterns in three or more means, your conclusions will be inaccurate because they are based on a data analyses that is not specifically focused on your explicit prediction. You may end up rejecting your working hypothesis prematurely, having not even addressed it statistically. If you're a movie buff and know the old Tarzan movies, where Tarzan swings from tree to tree, you may know that Johnny Weissmuller was the actor who originally played Tarzan. Asked about his philosophy of life, Weissmuller's answer was that "the main thing is not to let go of the vine." This is also good advice for student researchers: Know what you predicted, and hang on to your working hypothesis long enough to accurately evaluate it. (In the suggested readings at the end of this chapter, we list some "how to" articles on the focused testing of specific predictions.)

Accuracy and clarity are sometimes hard to separate, because the accurate reporting of information means describing your study in a way that is transparent rather than vague, including its design, conduct, analysis, and interpretation. As a case in point, randomized clinical trials in medical research have been criticized as being vague in the reporting of vital details about how the subjects or patients were allocated to the groups or conditions. Recommendations for improving the quality of reports of randomized clinical trials have been described in a position paper called "The CONSORT Statement" (available online at http://www.consort-statement.org), which the APA Manual drew upon in formulating reporting standards for journal articles. This medical example is also a reminder that inaccuracy is wasteful of resources, and it can be demoralizing as well, because biased conclusions and misleading recommendations can lead to false hopes. You may be wondering, however, what this discussion has to do with your research study, because you are not conducting a randomized clinical trial. The answer is that, whatever the nature of your study, the grade that you receive on your research report will depend to a significant degree on how accurately and clearly you describe the design, implementation, data analysis, and interpretation of the results.

Another problem to be avoided might be described as "missing the forest for the p," because it concerns how p values can cloud students' perceptions. We will have more to say about p values later in this chapter, but the point is not to act as if there were some special place in the instructor's heart for students with reported p values less than .05, or to think that a nonsignificant p is evidence in itself that the effect size is zero. Your instructor will admire a "statistically nonsignificant" result as much as a "statistically significant" result, as long as the statistical results are reported accurately and honestly, and appropriate implications are drawn. In addition, as we said before, remember that significance tests and their associated p values alone are not nearly as informative as estimates of the effect sizes with their corresponding interval estimates.

6.4 Communicating with Appropriate Precision

Reporting statistical information in appropriately precise detail requires striking a balance between being discursive and being falsely or needlessly precise. *False precision* implies that something that is inherently vague is reported in overly exact terms. Suppose that a standard attitude questionnaire was used in a study and the research participants were asked to respond to pro-and-con statements on a 5-point scale from "strongly agree" to "strongly disagree." Reporting the mean results to a high number of decimal places would be *false precision,* because the questionnaire is not that sensitive to slight variations in attitudes. *Needless precision* implies reporting results more exactly than the specific circumstances require. For example, reporting the weight of mouse subjects to six decimal places is needless precision. Your measuring instrument may be capable of this degree of precision, but the situation does not call for this degree of exactitude. When in doubt, ask the instructor for guidance.

Finally, if you are still wrestling with whether to use a table or a figure (such as a bar chart) in your research report, we mentioned previously that it is frequently better to report complex data in a table in a research report. On the other hand, if you are preparing a poster presentation, it may be better to use a figure in the display. Exhibit 17 shows a bar chart based on the means and confidence interval results in Jane Doe's Table 1 (appendix A). The bar chart shown is intended to draw people's eyes to the poster. Once Jane's poster has attracted a viewer's attention, Jane can speak with the person and give out a copy of her report with a table that provides more exact results (discussed in chapter 9).

EXHIBIT 17   **Bar chart based on Jane Doe's Table 1 (in appendix A)**

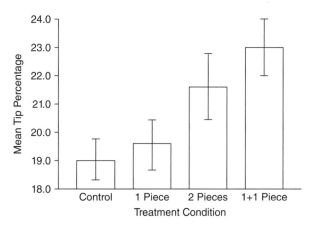

Note. The highest level of the enclosed bar indicates the mean tip percentage (estimated from the ordinate), and the capped vertical line within and above each bar indicates the 95% confidence interval of the mean tip percentage. This bar chart is based on the results in Table 1 of Jane Doe's final report in appendix A. Comparing those precisely reported results in Jane's Table 1 with this bar chart illustrates that exact values can be provided in tables, but readers can make only a rough estimate of the exact values when data are reported in bar charts.

6.5   *Communicating Enough Information*

Earlier in this chapter, we mentioned that the statistical information presented by Jane is the kind that is supposed to be routinely reported in journal articles. It is typical of what the APA Manual considers a "sufficient set of statistics." The APA Manual requires reporting "at least" (a) the number of units, or subjects, in the samples and subsamples; (b) the sample and subsample means or, in chi-square designs, frequencies; and (c) the standard deviations or pooled within-cell variances. For statistical tests such as t, F, and chi-square (χ^2), the APA Manual calls for the reporting of (d) the exact value of the test statistic; (e) the degrees of freedom (df); (f) the statistical probability (p level); and (g) the effect size indices associated with "single degree-of-freedom statistical tests" (by which they mean any t test, F tests with numerator $df = 1$, and 1-df χ^2 tests, or what Jane referred to as *focused statistical tests* in appendix A). The APA Manual also recommends that the researcher use (h) confidence intervals for estimates of population means and effect sizes and that (i) these confidence intervals be based on a prespecified level (such as 95% CI or 99% CI), which is then consistently used in the report. A good way to make sure that you have not left out anything important is to make a checklist. Carefully go through the list in the way that a pilot goes through a detailed checklist before taking off.

We have emphasized the reporting of effect sizes and their corresponding interval estimates. The term *effect size* is used in two ways. It is used to refer to specific measures of the magnitude of effect but is also used as a general term, so it can be confusing unless we know which effect size index is reported. For example, reporting that the effect size value was .5 means something different depending on whether it was r (.5 is often described as a "large" effect size r) or Cohen's d (.5 is often described as a d of "medium" size). Better still, don't use these descriptors at all; instead specify the ES index, report the precise value, and interpret it in the context of the interval estimate. As you probably know, the Pearson product-moment correlation (r) indicates the strength of association between two variables, such as a predictor (or independent) variable and a dependent variable, where $r_{\text{effect size}} = 1$ indicates a perfect linear relationship and $r_{\text{effect size}} = 0$ indicates that neither variable is predictable from the other by use of a linear equation. Cohen's d, on the other hand, indicates the standardized difference between two group means (i.e., resembling a z score), with the values ranging from zero to positive or negative infinity. We assume your statistics text or research methods text contains more information about effect sizes and how they are computed and interpreted, but if not, you will find suggested readings later in this chapter.

Before Jacob Cohen introduced the concept of the effect size in the 1960s, most research reports emphasized only the significance levels (p values) of statistical tests. The problem is that the same magnitude of effect can be statistically significant *or* statistically nonsignificant depending on the number of participants in a study. In other words, it is important to separate these two concepts (the significance level and the effect size) in your mind and in your report. This separation is explained in the accompanying table, which lists correlations (think of each r as an effect size correlation) significant at $p = .05$ (two-tailed), given the particular $N - 2$ values (the degrees of freedom):

$N - 2$	r	$N - 2$	r
1	.997	40	.304
2	.950	50	.273
3	.878	100	.195
4	.811	200	.138
5	.754	300	.113
10	.576	500	.088
20	.423	1,000	.062
30	.349	2,000	.044

In other words, all the r values in the table, whether they are as small as .044 or as large as .997, are significant at $p = .05$ (two-tailed). Notice that what counts most for each of these r values achieving significance at $p = .05$ is the $N - 2$ values. We see that a correlation as small as $r = .044$ is significant at $p = .05$ with a total N of 2,002. By comparison, the table suggests that, with a total N of 12, an r 13 times larger than .044 ($r = .044 \times 13 = .572$) would not be exactly statistically significant at the same p level. The reason is that .572 is smaller than the critical level of .576 for $N - 2 = 10$. Reporting that "the observed effect was statistically significant" would not give us a clue to the size of the effect. Statements like "significant difference" and "nonsignificant difference" can be misleading when we are interested in the size of the effect.

Another useful way of thinking about effect sizes and p values is represented by the following conceptual equation:

$$\text{Significance test} = \text{Effect size} \times \text{Study size.}$$

This equation explains that any significance test (e.g., t, F, or χ^2) can be parsed into two components, the product of which is the calculated value of the significance test. One of the components will be a reflection of the size of the effect, and the other, the size of the study (e.g., the number of sampling units). From your statistics course, you know that the larger the value of the significance test (that is, the bigger the calculated value of the t, F, or χ^2), the smaller (and usually more coveted) will be the p value. As the equation tells us, increasing the effect size and/or the study size will produce a larger calculated value of t, F, or χ^2 and usually, therefore, a more coveted p value.

For example, when the sizes of two independent groups that are being compared by a t test are equal ($n_1 = n_2$), one way to describe an independent-sample t test in terms of the conceptual equation above is

$$t = d \times \frac{\sqrt{df}}{2},$$

where df in this case is usually the total sample size minus 2. The effect size indicator in this example is Cohen's d, defined as

$$d = \frac{M_1 - M_2}{\sigma_{pooled}},$$

where the difference between the two group means (M_1 and M_2) is divided by the pooled population standard deviation.

The statistical example above teaches that the numerical value of t will increase as the difference between means M_1 and M_2 increases, as the variability within groups (i.e., the σ_{pooled}) decreases, and as the total sample size increases. Suppose you are designing a two-group experiment and you want to maximize the statistical power of your t test. One way would be to select the strongest manipulation ethically and practically feasible, on the assumption it will be more likely to drive the means (the numerator of d) further apart and thereby produce a larger numerator value. A second way would be to work with a homogeneous sample of subjects and a standardized procedure, on the assumption that this approach will minimize the variability within groups (the denominator of d) and thereby give a smaller denominator value. Dividing a smaller denominator into a larger numerator will increase the estimate of the effect size. A third way would be to recruit as many participants as you can afford, or as are practical to run, because you will thereby increase the study size. Multiplying the increased effect size by the increased study size will maximize the value of t and, in turn, yield a smaller (and usually more coveted) p value.

Before we leave this discussion of how much information is enough, we need to say something more about the use of confidence intervals for population estimates (such as means, proportions, and effect sizes). As noted in Exhibit 16, the confidence interval tells us the lower and upper estimated limits (or boundaries) of the population value. The confidence level (defined as 1 − alpha) indicates how "approximate" that estimation was. If you increase the level of confidence (say, from a 95% CI to a 99% CI), you widen the confidence interval. Similarly, reducing the level of confidence from a 95% CI to a 90% CI will shrink the confidence interval. To understand why, think of how wide an interval you would need to be 100% sure about some risky event.

6.6 Ethics and Principled Reporting Practices

At the beginning of this chapter we drew a distinction between *what* information is reported and *how* it is reported. However, you can see now that the what and the how are intertwined in that the success of one depends on the success of the other. One way to think about this issue is in terms of ethics. The term *ethics,* derived from a Greek word (*ethos*) meaning "character" or "disposition," refers to the dos and don'ts by which "right" and "wrong" conduct are defined on moral grounds. For example, the golden rule states, "Do unto others as you would have them do unto you." Another golden rule in statistics might be expressed as "Do not lie with numbers." This admonition is encompassed in a general ethical principle that has been described as *integrity*. It implies adherence to the moral principle of honesty and soundness. In science, for example, the advance of knowledge depends on the trust that scientists have in the honesty and soundness of one another's work. Thus, the advance of science is predicated on the assumption that all numbers and statistics have been reported faithfully and truthfully.

In the same way that the principle of integrity is woven into the fabric of a great many professional codes and ethical guidelines, four additional broad principles are also part of many codes and guidelines. Two principles (which reach back to the Hippocratic Oath in medicine) have been described as *nonmaleficence*, or the admonition not to harm anyone, and *beneficence*, the concomitant ideal of maximizing possible benefits to others to the extent possible. For example, the American Statistical Association's code of ethics warns about the dangers to the public that can result from false or misleading statistics. A fourth principle, referred to as *justice,* means being fair and even-handed. In the 2002 APA code of ethics, justice is also equated with ensuring that the biases and the limits of one's expertise "do not lead to or condone unjust practices." And finally, a fifth principle is *respect* for others. In the 2002 APA code, respect for others is equated with guarantees of "privacy, confidentiality, and self-determination."

There are also other professional ethics in addition to these five—including those defining the relationships between teachers and students—but we focus here on integrity, nonmaleficence, beneficence, justice, and respect for others because they are hallmarks of the principled reporting of statistical results. Reporting those results clearly, accurately, with appropriate precision, and in sufficient detail will give readers more opportunity to understand the results with interpretive errors minimized. In certain applied areas (such as randomized clinical trials of medical interventions), studies that meet these standards to a high degree may also have a better chance of doing more good (beneficence) while also minimizing the possibility of harm (nonmaleficence), for example, by identifying sets of individuals who are more likely to be helped or harmed by a given intervention. There are also experimental designs that make an effort to treat the participants in an even-handed way (justice), for example, by assigning them at random to treatment and *wait-list control groups* (i.e., the participants wait to receive the treatment until after it has been given to the treatment group and found to be effective). Principled statistical practices treat the participants with respect by not wasting their valued assistance with inferior data analyses and reporting.

6.7 Suggested Readings

For more about the statistical concepts mentioned in this chapter, the most readily accessible source is your statistics or research methods text. There are also many helpful Web sites, and you will find a list (with links) at http://statpages.org. Another good portal on the Web is Clay Helberg's http://claviusweb.net/statistics.shtml. If you are looking for statistical distribution tables that give exact values for statistical tests, a useful Web site is http://www.statsoft/textbook/distribution-tables.

The readings suggested here were selected on the basis of their accessibility to advanced students. Articles with "how to" instructions or examples are denoted by an asterisk (*). The numbered readings indicate a suggested sequence in which they should be read.

6.7.1 Null Hypothesis Significance Testing
We mentioned that there is disagreement about the proper role of null hypothesis significance testing (NHST). In fact, there has been a spirited debate in which some have even suggested that NHST be banned. In psychology, the debate over NHST began with an article by William Rozeboom in 1960.

1. Rozeboom, W. W. (1960). The fallacy of the null-hypothesis significance test. *Psychological Bulletin, 57,* 416–418. *Rozeboom calls into question the prevalent use of NHST. (Available at PsycARTICLES)*
2. Cohen, J. (1994). The earth is round ($p < .05$). *American Psychologist, 49,* 997–1003. *Jacob Cohen describes NHST as a "mishmash" that "does not tell us what we want to know, and we so much want to know what we want to know that, out of desperation, we nevertheless believe that it does!" (Available at PsycARTICLES)*
3. Wainer, H. (1999). One cheer for null hypothesis significance testing. *Psychological Methods, 4,* 212–213. *Statistician Howard Wainer's insightful proposal for a useful, but diminished, role for NHST (called NHT in the article). (Available at PsycARTICLES)*

6.7.2 Focused Statistical Tests and Effect Size Indicators

The contrasts Jane Doe used (in appendix A) are statistical procedures for asking focused questions of data. Compared to diffuse or omnibus questions, focused questions are characterized by greater conceptual clarity and greater statistical power when used to examine those focused questions. If an effect exists, we are more likely to discover it and to believe it to be real when asking focused rather than omnibus questions.

*1. Rosnow, R. L., & Rosenthal, R. (1988). Focused tests of significance and effect size estimation in counseling psychology. *Journal of Counseling Psychology, 44,* 1276–1284. *Early article on the distinction between focused and omnibus statistical tests (a distinction proposed by the authors in their graduate text four years earlier) and the seminal importance of Jacob Cohen's concept of effect size, which he proposed in the 1960s. (Available at PsycARTICLES)*

*2. Rosnow, R. L., & Rosenthal, R. (2009). Effect sizes: Why, when, and how to use them. *Zeitschrift für Psychologie/Journal of Psychology, 217,* 6-14. *Tutorial on difference-type and correlation-type effect size indicators, confidence intervals, null-counternull intervals, and a systematic approach to comparing and (when there is a theoretical justification for doing so) combining competing predictions expressed in the form of lambda values and effect sizes. (Available at PsycARTICLES)*

6.7.3 Confidence and Null-Counternull Intervals

Confidence intervals generally use fixed intervals such as 95% CI or 99% CI, whereas the null-counternull interval is a kind of "confidence interval," except that it involves the null hypothesis and the obtained p value.

*1. Masson, E. J., & Loftus, G. R. (2003). Using confidence intervals for graphically based data interpretations. *Canadian Journal of Experimental Psychology, 57,* 203–220. *Instructions on, and illustrations of, the use of confidence intervals in figures and graphs. (Available at PsycARTICLES)*

*2. Cumming, G., & Fidler, F. (2009). Confidence intervals: Better answers to better questions. *Zeitschrift für Psychologie/Journal of Psychology, 217,* 15–26. *(Available at PsycARTICLES) For more information and exploratory software for confidence intervals, visit Professor Geoff Cumming's Web site (http://latrobe.edu.au/psy/esci) at La Trobe University in Melbourne, Australia.*

*3. Rosenthal, R., & Rubin, D. B. (1994). The counternull value of an effect size: A new statistic. *Psychological Science, 5,* 329–334. *The counternull statistic, conceptually related to confidence intervals, involves the obtained effect size and null hypothesis* *and is insurance against prematurely believing the null hypothesis of zero to be true when the p value exceeds .05. (Available at www.jstor.org/pss/40063131)*

6.7.4 Ethics and Quantitative Methods
In the next chapter, we return to the subject of the ethical responsibilities of students writing research reports and review papers. The work cited below is specifically focused on ethics and quantitative methods, where we define quantitative methods in the broadest sense to include statistical procedures and also research that employs the quantification of the observations made (quantitative research, as was defined in section 4.1).

1. Rosenthal, R. (1994). Science and ethics in conducting, analyzing, and reporting psychological research. *Psychological Science, 5,* 127–134. *Rosenthal's "waste not, want not" philosophy of research ethics when one is considering a design, analyzing the data, and reporting the results. (Available at www.jstor.org/pss/40063082)*
2. Committee on Science, Engineering, and Public Policy. (2009). *On being a scientist: A guide to responsible conduct in research* (3rd ed.). Washington, DC: National Academies Press. *National Academy of Sciences guide mentioned in section 6.3. (Video and pdf available at http://nap.edu/catalog.php?record_id=12192)*
3. Panter, A., & Sterba, S. (Eds.). (2011). *Handbook of ethics in quantitative methods.* London, England: Routledge Academic. *More technical discussions of the human cost of quantitative decision making from design and data collection, the data analysis, to the reporting of findings. (Web site at http://www.routledge.com/books/details/9781848728554)*

6.7.5 Statistical Illiteracy and Its Consequences
Having all the statistical information in the world would be of no avail if people did not understand the meaning of the numbers and statistics. The readings below focus on the perils of statistical illiteracy or innumeracy in a world in which we are showered with numbers and statistics.

1. Gigerenzer, G., Gaissmaier, W., Kurz-Milcke, E., Schwartz, L. M., & Woloshin, S. (2008). Helping doctors and patients make sense of health statistics. *Psychological Science in the Public Interest, 8,* 53–96. *Describes how most people misperceive and misconstrue the meaning and implications of risk statistics. (Google the exact title for online links.)*
2. Paulos, J. (1988). *Innumeracy: Mathematical illiteracy and its consequences.* New York, NY: Hill & Wang. (Paperback edition published by Vintage Books.) *Fascinating examples of the perils of innumeracy.*

7

Writing the First Draft

Writing a first draft is a little like taking the first dip in chilly ocean waters on a hot day. It may be uncomfortable at the outset but feels better once you get used to it. This chapter provides pointers and examples of basic elements of writing style to buoy you up as you begin writing. We also revisit the issue of ethical standards, which was raised in chapter 6 in the context of the principled reporting of statistical information.

7.1 Sorting Through Your Material

Back in 1947, there was a fascinating story in newspapers and magazines about two brothers, the Collyers, who were found dead in a rubbish-filled mansion at Fifth Avenue and 128th Street in New York City. On receiving a tip that one brother, Homer Collyer, had died, the police forced their way into the mansion with crowbars and axes. They found all of the entrances to the house blocked by wrapped packages of newspapers, hundreds of cartons, and all kinds of junk (14 grand pianos, most of a Model T Ford, the top of a horse-drawn carriage, a tree limb 7 feet long and 20 inches in diameter, an organ, a trombone, a cornet, three bugles, five violins, three World War I bayonets, and 10 clocks, including one 9 feet high and weighing 210 pounds). The rooms and hallways were honeycombed with tunnels through all this debris and booby-trapped so that anything disturbed would come crashing down on an intruder. The police began searching for the other brother, Langley, who had been caring for Homer, as it was thought that he might have phoned in the tip. After 8 weeks of burrowing through the incredible mess, they finally found the body of Langley Collyer wedged between a chest of drawers and a bedspring; he had been killed by one of his own booby traps.

For students writing reviews and research reports, the lesson of the Collyer brothers is that it is not always easy to discard things that you have made an effort to save, including notes, studies, and quotes that you have taken trouble to track down. However, conciseness is one of the keys to clear writing, and quantity cannot replace quality and relevance in the material that you save and use in your final manuscript. Instructors are more impressed by tightly reasoned papers than by those that overflow with superfluous material. It is best to approach the first draft with an open but focused mind, keeping your end goal in view while simultaneously disposing of redundant or irrelevant material (not discarding your raw data or calculations, however).

7.2   Creating a Self-Motivator Statement

Even before you draft the first sentence of your opening paragraph, you will find it useful to write down somewhere for yourself the overall purpose of your paper. In a short paragraph, remind yourself what the paper will be about. We call this the "self-motivator statement" because it is a good way to get you going, keep you clearheaded, and help you to filter out superfluous material. You may also find it helpful when you write the abstract after you have written the rest of your paper. At that point, your self-motivator statement might provide a coherent basis upon which to develop a longer one-paragraph summary following the guidelines in this book.

For example, we can imagine the following self-motivator statement that Jane Doe might have written as she began the first draft of her research report:

> I'm going to describe how I found that tipping increased when diners in a restaurant were given a small gift, and how my manipulation of a reciprocity effect increased the tipping percentage still further. I will open my report with a background review leading into my hypotheses and predictions. In the final discussion, after summing up my findings, I will try to pose ideas for further research.

For John Smith, as he began the first draft of his review paper, we can imagine the following self-motivator statement:

> A theme running throughout my paper will be the elusive nature of the concept of intelligence. I'm going to compare the traditional g-centered view of intelligence with what I am calling the multiplex view. I will mention the foundational work for both views, but I'm going to focus primarily on Gardner's work, criticisms of the multiplex approach, and counterarguments. At the end of the paper, I will try to speculate about future directions.

As you can see from these examples, the trick in writing a self-motivator statement is to keep it relatively brief and to the point. You will be less apt to go off on a tangent if every once in a while you glance at your self-motivator statement to remind yourself of your plan for your paper's direction.

7.3 Writing the Opening Paragraph of Your Introduction

The next step is to write an inviting opening paragraph. You can get some ideas by looking at the opening paragraphs in the sample papers in appendix A and appendix B, and you can also get ideas by glancing at the opening paragraphs in research journals or review journals. For example, the journal *Psychological Science,* published by the Association for Psychological Science (APS), is a good model if you are writing a research report because the journal is read by psychologists and others who work in a wide variety of fields, and the research articles cover a wide range of topics. This journal is also strict about word limits, so the authors of these research articles are aware of the importance of using "economical prose." As you will see, some of the authors seem to be masters at creating good openings that grip our attention and make us want to learn more about their work.

The trick in this case is not to start out ponderously, and there are many ways of creating an inviting opening paragraph. You can start by describing the phenomenon of interest to you in a way that strikes a note of familiarity in the reader. Or you might start with an anecdote, like the one about the strange case of the Collyer brothers and how it is a metaphor for "pack rats." Some writers use a thought-provoking quotation, called an *epigraph,* to set the stage for what follows. Some writers start with a question that begs for an answer. If it is a good question and we think about it, even for a moment, we may find ourselves trying to answer it in our own minds and then wanting to read about what the writer proposes. A good opening not only leads readers into the work but, at its best, should provide momentum for the writer as the words begin to flow.

Paying attention to writing styles, not only in journals, but also in books and other contexts, will teach you how skilled writers express ideas in effective ways. For example, psychologist Sissela Bok wrote a popular book about the ethics of lying (*Lying: Moral Choice in Public and Private Life,* Pantheon, 1978). She opened her book with a set of compelling questions that resonated with immediacy and vibrancy:

> Should physicians lie to dying patients so as to delay the fear and anxiety which the truth might bring them? Should professors exaggerate the excellence of their students on recommendations in order to give them a better chance in a tight job market? Should

parents conceal from children the fact that they were adopted? Should social scientists send investigators masquerading as patients to physicians in order to learn about racial and sexual biases in diagnosis and treatment? Should government lawyers lie to Congressmen who might otherwise oppose a much-needed welfare bill? And should journalists lie to those from whom they seek information in order to expose corruption? (p. xv)

By posing these questions, Bok spoke to readers in the same way that she would if she were opening a dialogue.

Here is another example from the opening paragraph of one of the books cited by John Smith in his review paper (appendix B). The book, written by psychologist Richard E. Nisbett, *Intelligence and How to Get It* (Norton, 2009), takes on the thesis of intelligence as genetically determined and argues instead that intelligence is malleable in ways that can be encouraged. The book begins with a personal reminiscence of Nisbett's:

I began having trouble with arithmetic in the fifth grade, after I missed school for a week just when my class took up fractions. For the rest of elementary school I never quite recovered from that setback. My parents were sympathetic, telling me that people in our family had never been very good at math. They viewed math skills as something that you either had or not, for reasons having most to do with heredity. (p. 1)

You are not writing a book, of course, although maybe in the future you will. But the quoted passages above illustrate the benefit of paying attention to successful writing styles as you develop your own writing skills. Similarly, notice how Jane Doe's report (appendix A) starts with interesting facts, an opening that leads into the persuasive logic of her introduction and, ultimately, to her working hypotheses and specific predictions. John Smith (appendix B) takes another tack, opening his review paper by quoting an old saying and noting its relevance to the theme of his paper. In both student papers, there are smooth transitions from the opening paragraphs into the following sections. We can see how the openings must have provided momentum as the students' words began to flesh out their outlines.

7.4   Settling Down to Write

Should you find yourself still having trouble beginning the introduction, try the trick of not starting with the introductory paragraph. Start writing whatever paragraph or section you feel will be the easiest, and then tackle the rest as your ideas begin to flow. When faced with a blank computer screen and a flashing cursor, some students escape to the blogosphere or to a video game. Recognize these and other counterproductive moves for what they are, because they can drain your writing energy. If you find them irresistible, then use them instead as rewards *after* you have done a good job of writing.

The following are general pointers to ensure that your initial writing will go as smoothly as possible:

- While writing, try to work in a quiet, well-lighted place in 2-hour stretches (dim lighting makes people sleepy). Even if you are under time pressure to finish the paper quickly, it is important to take a break so you can collect your thoughts and make sure you are not writing aimlessly or drifting off in a wrong direction.

- When you take a break, go for a stroll, preferably outside, because the fresh air will be invigorating, and the change of environment will help you think about what you have already written and what you want to say next.

- If you are unexpectedly called away while you are in the middle of an idea, jot down a phrase or a few words that will get you back on track once you return to your writing. (Be sure to save your work before you leave.)

- When you stop for the day, try to stop at a point that is midway through a thought that you are finding difficult to express or complete. When you wake up the next day, your mind will be fresh with new ideas, and your writing will not have to start cold.

- Try to pace your work with time to spare so that you can complete the first draft and let it rest for a day. When you return to the completed first draft after a night's sleep, your critical powers will be enhanced, and you will have a fresh approach to shaping the final draft.

7.5   *Ethical Considerations Revisited*

If you have not read chapter 6, we recommend you read section 6.6 on ethics and principled reporting practices in the communication of statistical information. Whether or not you are reporting numbers and statistics, the most fundamental ethical principle in all scholarly writing is honesty in all facets of the work. As discussed in the earlier chapter, two examples of deliberate dishonesty are the falsification of data and the fabrication of results, both of which constitute fraud. Just as when the professional career of a scientist who falsifies data or fabricates results is compromised, the consequences will be harsh for the student writing a research report in which the data or results are fabricated. Falsely claiming someone else's work as your work is another form of fabrication that will not be tolerated.

In the following section we focus on that issue, but first we want to mention three other issues that have ethical implications. One has to do with the rhetoric of causality in reporting research studies. In chapter 4 (section 4.1), we mentioned that it was important not to make exaggerated claims by implying in relational research that "X is responsible for Y" when all that can be confidently stated is that "X is related to Y." Exaggerating the implications of a study has been described as "hyperclaiming," and the hyperclaiming of a causal relationship when none actually exists has been described as "causism"—terms coined by Robert Rosenthal in his suggested article in section 6.7.4. For example, stating "the effect of," "the impact of," "the consequence of," or "as a result of" implies there is a causal relationship. If the research design and results did not justify a causal inference, the writer who used those expressions would be guilty of hyperclaiming. To avoid this problem, the writer could simply use the appropriate language, expressions like "was related to," "was predictable from," or "could be inferred from." Rosenthal's position was that knowingly implying a causal relationship when none exists constitutes blatant unethical misrepresentation and deception. When a writer hyperclaims a causal relation but is "unaware" of having done so, this (Rosenthal argued) reflects either ignorance or lazy writing.

Another ethical standard in science concerns the sharing of data with those who want to verify published claims by reanalyzing results. Provided the confidentiality of the research participants is protected, and unless legal rights preclude the release of the data, psychologists are encouraged to make their data open to qualified investigators. Any personally identifiable information is expected to be deleted or coded so that the privacy and confidentiality of the research participants is protected. In some cases, there may be proprietary concerns of the investigator or the sponsor of the research, which may also have to be addressed. Although your paper is not a publication, the instructor has the option to ask you to provide the original data on which the work is based. Providing the original data in this case would be in addition to listing the raw scores in the appendix of the research report.

Before we turn to what many instructors consider the most significant concern in student papers—the avoidance of plagiarism—we will mention one further standard with implications for students. It is unethical to misrepresent as fresh data any research results that have already been published or reported. In the case of students who are writing papers for course requirements, it would also be a problem if the same work submitted for credit in one course were then submitted for additional credit in another course. However, suppose a student who had conducted a pilot study in one course and then conducted a follow-up study in a second course was interested in meta-analyzing the two sets of results in the research report for the second course. Or suppose a student who wrote a detailed literature review in one course was then interested in drawing on part of that paper for a research proposal in another course. To avoid a later problem, both students would be advised to discuss their plans with their instructors in advance. With the approval of their instructors, the students could proceed as they had proposed and then acknowledge in the author note (on the cover page of the final paper) the nature of the recycled material and the fact that it was included with the prior consent of the instructor.

7.6   Steering Clear of Plagiarism

The nagging concerns of most instructors who teach writing-intensive courses are conveying the importance of originality and the meaning and consequences of plagiarism. The term *plagiarism,* which comes from a Latin word meaning "kidnapper," refers to the theft of another person's ideas or work. It is crucial that you understand what constitutes plagiarism. Claiming not to know that you committed plagiarism is not an acceptable defense. Simply stated, taking the work of someone else and passing it off as your own is plagiarism. It is wrong to do so, both ethically and legally, and the ensuing penalty in a class assignment or a thesis will be severe.

In fact, it is quite easy to avoid committing plagiarism, even accidentally. All you must be is attentive and willing to make the effort to paraphrase the material in question (and to cite the source exactly), or else to quote the material word for word and then put quotation marks around it (and, of course, cite the source and page number). If a passage you want to use is 40 or more words (illustrated by the passages that we quoted earlier from Bok's and Nisbett's books), then quotation marks are not used. Instead the passage is set off as a *block quotation*—indented about a half inch from the left margin, with the page number indicated in parentheses after the final period.

To illustrate plagiarism and how easily it can be avoided, assume that a student writing an essay came across Bok's book and copied down the following passage for future reference:

> Deceit and violence—these are two forms of deliberate assault on human beings. Both can coerce people into acting against their will. Most harm that can befall victims through violence can come to them also through deceit. But deceit controls more subtly, for it works on belief as well as action. Even Othello, whom few would have dared to try to subdue by force, could be brought to destroy himself and Desdemona through falsehood. (Bok, 1978, p. 18)

There would be no problem if the student reproduced the passage as it appears above, because the student has copied the passage accurately, has clearly indicated that it is quoted from Bok's work (by indenting the entire passage), and has properly noted the page on which it appeared. The plagiarism problem would arise if the student decided to change a word or two to make the passage sound a little different and then passed it off as an original thought: No need to mention Bok's book, the student thinks, because it's not a recent book that the instructor is likely to be familiar with. No one will bother to check, but even if the instructor should happen to recognize this passage, why, the student can plead "forgetting" to give Bok full credit—or so the student thinks.

Suppose the student submits a paper with the following passage incorporated into the narrative text (that is, it is not indicated as a quote with a few words changed):

> Deceit and violence are two forms of deliberate assault on human beings. Both can coerce people into acting against their will. Most harm that can happen to people through violence can also happen to them through deceit. However, deceit controls more subtly, because it works on belief as well as action. Even Othello, whom few would have dared to try to subdue by force, could be brought to destroy himself and Desdemona through falsehood.

Although it might seem like an A paper to the student, the incorporated passage, when read in the context of the rest of the paper, will stick out like a sore thumb, and instructors are sensitive to blatant inconsistencies like these.

Another word of caution: One instructor mentioned to us that, "although changing a word or two of an author's writing, failing to cite the source, and just passing it off as one's own work is certainly egregious, it is not the problem that many instructors run into more frequently." A more frequent problem, this instructor told us, is that students start off with something like "According to Bok (1978)," then change some words, and repeat a passage without indicating that it is *almost* a word-for-word quote. Changing a word or two in each sentence is not legal paraphrasing; it's plagiarism. The student needs to put the author's ideas into his or her own words and his or her own sentence structure.

Of course, if you believe that someone else has said something much better than you can ever hope to say it, quote (and cite) or paraphrase (and cite) the other source. For example, here is how the student might have incorporated Bok's ideas without falling into plagiarism:

> Bok (1978) made the case that deceit and violence "can coerce people into acting against their will" (p. 18). Deceit, she argued, controls more subtly because it affects belief. Using a literary analogy, Bok observed, "Even Othello, whom few would have dared to try to subdue by force, could be brought to destroy himself and Desdemona through falsehood" (p. 18).

Electronic plagiarizing is no more acceptable than plagiarizing from printed matter. It is also easier to catch. Remember that if you find something on the Internet that you want to include in your work, the same considerations of honesty apply. There is a specialized search engine using algorithms that are constantly updated, which an instructor can use to look for plagiarism. Because it is now used by thousands of high schools and colleges, the likelihood of not getting caught plagiarizing written assignments is diminishing rapidly. As noted before, it is a good idea to keep your notes, outlines, and rough drafts, because instructors ask students for such material if a question arises about the originality of their work.

7.7 Not Falling Into Lazy Writing

On hearing that quotations and citations are not construed by definition as plagiarism, some lazy students submit papers peppered with quoted material. Unless you feel it is absolutely essential, avoid quoting lengthy passages throughout a paper. What, then, would be appropriate occasions for quoting someone? If you are describing two competing views, for example, and want to be sure to represent both positions fairly, you may want to use direct quotations. Or someone's language may be so expressive and convincing that you believe quoting a portion of it will improve your presentation.

Thus, on some occasions, it may be advisable to quote someone (with a citation, of course). However, quoting a statement that is not particularly momentous or poignant signals lazy writing. Your instructor expects your paper to reflect *your* thoughts after you have examined and synthesized material from sources you found pertinent. Lazy writing does not carry as severe a penalty as plagiarism, but it will usually mean a reduced grade in writing-intensive courses. The reason for a lowered grade is that lazy writing conveys the impression that the student has not put much effort into the assignment. Furthermore, if you really cannot say something in your own words, the instructor will conclude that you do not understand it well enough to write about it.

7.8 Creating the Right Tone

As you write, keep in mind certain basic style points. The *tone* of your paper is the manner and attitude reflected in the way you express your ideas. The writing should not sound affected, self-important, or flowery, and it also should not be monotonous or mind-numbingly tedious to read. How can you create an appropriate tone in a scholarly essay or research report in psychology? It takes patience, practice, and a desire to learn from others. You can learn by paying attention to how researchers and other academic scholars who communicate clearly and effectively express their ideas in an appropriate tone.

Here are some tips on how to create the right tone:

◆ Strive for an explicit, straightforward, interesting, but not emotional way of expressing your thoughts, findings, and conclusions (as illustrated in the sample papers).

- Try not to sound stilted or uncomfortably formal (instead of saying, "In the opinion of this writer," just state your opinion—period).
- Don't write in a nonchalant or slapdash way ("Here's what Jones and Smith say" or "So I told the research participants"), and try not to sound like the glib reports on TV or the slick writing in tabloids and advertisements.
- Strive for an objective, direct tone that keeps your reader subordinate to the material you are presenting. Instead of saying, "The reader will note that the results were . . . ," say, "The results were . . ."
- If your instructor finds it acceptable, don't be afraid to use the first person (but don't use it routinely throughout your paper), and don't refer to yourself as *we* unless you are clearly referring to a collaborative effort with someone else.
- Avoid wordiness. In a famous writing manual, William Strunk Jr. and E. B. White's *The Elements of Style,* a highly quoted admonition is "Omit needless words. Omit needless words. Omit needless words."

7.9 The Problem of Sexist Language

The problem of *sexist language* and its negative consequences has been a matter of some sensitivity among writers for a number of years. A reason to be concerned about sexist language is that words can frequently influence people's thoughts and deeds, on both a conscious and an unconscious level, and we do not want to reinforce stereotypes and prejudiced behavior. One way to avoid this problem is to encourage gender-free language when it is appropriate. Sometimes, of course, there are good reasons not to use gender-free nouns and pronouns. Suppose a new drug has been tested only on male patients. If the researcher used only gender-free pronouns when referring to the patients, the readers might mistakenly infer that the results applied equally to men and women. The lesson, of course, is to choose your words carefully.

When the issue of sexist language first gained prominence, writers used contrived words such as *s/he* and *he/she* to avoid the word bias problem. Not only are those forms awkward, but if the actors in question were of one sex, the use of *s/he* and *he/she* would mislead the readers into thinking that the actors included both sexes. Another contrived practice, which is still popular, is to mistakenly use the plural pronoun *they* as a singular pronoun. For example, it would be grammatically incorrect to write:

> When a *person* [singular] takes an idea from a published source, *they* [plural pronoun, used instead of using the contrived *he/she* or *s/he*] must cite that source appropriately.

There are grammatically acceptable alternatives, assuming that you want to refer to both sexes. One acceptable (but wordy) alternative is to write *she or he* rather than *they:*

> When a *person* takes an idea from a published source, *she or he* must cite that source appropriately.

A less wordy alternative is to make the entire sentence plural. That is, you would use both plural nouns and plural pronouns:

> When *people* [plural noun] take ideas from published sources, *they* [plural pronoun] must cite those sources appropriately.

7.10   Subjects Versus Participants

Some psychologists have argued that the term *subject* is another example of word bias because, they claim, it demeans those who play a role as research participants in our studies. Interestingly, some early psychologists used the term *reagents* to refer to people who participated in psychological research. The term was borrowed from chemistry, where it refers to a substance that, when carefully mixed with another substance under specified conditions in a clean test tube, produces a predictable reaction. However, the "test tubes" (research settings) and "reagents" (the subjects or participants) in research studies in psychology are not at all like those in chemistry. People are sentient and active beings, and their needs, expectations, anxieties, and other characteristics come into play when they participate in our research settings.

Although the term *subject* long ago replaced the term *reagent*, the APA Manual (going back to the previous edition) has wrestled with whether those who participate in our research might be better described as *participants,* because they are active agents rather than passive reagents. The current edition of the APA Manual gives the following advice: "Write about the people in your study in a way that acknowledges their participation but is also consistent with the traditions of the field in which you are working" (p. 73). What is essential, we would only add, is that you describe the research participants or subjects (we use both terms in this book) clearly, accurately, with appropriate precision, and in enough detail. If your instructor has a strong preference, let that be your guide when you refer to the participants or subjects in a research investigation. (Jane Doe uses the term *participants*, but she specifically describes them also as *dining parties*.)

7.11   Achieving the Right Voice

The verb forms you use in your writing can speak with one of two voices: active or passive. You write in the *active voice* when you represent the subject of your sentence as performing the action expressed by your verb

("The children who participated in the study responded by . . ."). You write in the *passive voice* when the subject of your sentence undergoes the action expressed by your verb ("The response was made by the children who participated in the study . . .").

Active Voice (Good)

If you rely mainly on the active voice, your writing will have a more vital, compelling style:

> Eleanor Gibson (1988), a pioneer in perception studies, argued that perceptual development in humans is "an ever-spiraling path of discovery" (p. 37).

Passive Voice (Not as Good)

If you rely mainly on the passive voice, your writing will not be as compelling as when you write in the active voice:

> It was argued by Eleanor Gibson (1988), a pioneer in perception studies, that perceptual development in humans is "an ever-spiraling path of discovery" (p. 37).

This quoted passage also illustrates when it is advisable to quote. The reason the student chose to quote "an ever-spiraling path of discovery" was that it seemed eloquent and the student felt incapable of paraphrasing the quoted passage with the same flair and expressiveness. Another reason for quoting the passage was that Eleanor Gibson was an eminent authority whose words gave weight to the student's development of a particular argument.

7.12 Choosing an Appropriate Verb Tense

The verb tenses you use in your paper can get into a tangle unless you observe the following two basic rules: First, use the *past tense* to report studies that were done in the past ("Jones and Smith found . . ."). If you are writing a research report, both the method and the results sections can usually be written in the past tense because your research has been completed ("In this study, data *were* collected . . ." and "In these questionnaires, there *were* . . ."). Second, use the *present tense* to define terms ("Multiplex, as I propose to use this term, *means* . . ." and "A stereotype *is* defined as . . ."). The present tense is frequently used to make a general claim ("Winter days *are* shorter than summer days").

Some researchers save the *future tense* for the section of their research reports in which they discuss implications for further investigation ("Future research *will be* necessary . . ."). However, it is not essential to use the future tense. Instead, you can use the present tense in this case to say, "Further investigation *is* warranted. . . ."

Notice that three spaced periods appear at the end of some of the examples above. These periods are called *ellipses* or *ellipsis points*, and they are used in these examples to indicate that the sentences continue. Though as a general rule ellipsis points are not used at the end of a quotation, we used them here to introduce you to this punctuation mark. Typically, ellipsis points are used somewhere in the middle of a lengthy quoted passage to indicate that selected words have been omitted. For example, the following is partially quoted from the longer quote taken from Sissela Bok's book in section 7.3; the ellipsis points indicate that words have been omitted:

> Should professors exaggerate the excellence of their students . . . in order to give them a better chance in a tight job market? . . . And should journalists lie to those from whom they seek information in order to expose corruption? (p. xv)

7.13   *Making Sure That Subject and Verb Agree*

Each sentence in your paper must express a complete thought and have a *subject* (in general terms, something that performs the action) and a *verb* (an action that is performed or that indicates a state of being).

Verb and Subject Correctly Agree

In the following example, the subject is plural (*study participants*) and, therefore, the verb form used (*were*) is also plural. Thus, the verb and subject agree, a basic rule of grammar:

> The study participants [the subject is plural] were [the verb is plural] introductory psychology students who were fulfilling a course requirement.

Plural and Singular Verbs with Collective Nouns

In most sentence forms, achieving this agreement is a simple matter, but trouble sometimes arises. For instance, when you use *collective nouns* (those that name a group, for example, *committee, team, faculty*), they can be either singular or plural. When you think of the group as a single unit, use a singular verb ("The union *is* ready to settle"). In the rarer case where you want to show that you are referring to components of a group, use a plural verb ("The faculty *were* divided on the issue").

Patricia T. O'Connell, in the third edition of her popular book, *Woe Is I* (Random House, 2009), offered a helpful tip on how to decide whether to use a singular or a plural verb when the word used for the subject of a sentence can be interpreted as either singular or plural. If the word is preceded by "the" (*the* team, *the* committee, *the* couple), it is a clue that the subject of the sentence should be viewed as singular and a singular verb is needed. If the word is preceded by "a" (*a* team, *a* committee, *a* couple), it is a clue that the subject of the sentence should be viewed as plural and a plural verb is needed. O'Connell reminds us that *all, any,* and *none* can be singular or plural, depending on how you use them. If you use a word to mean "all of it," or "any of it," or "none of it," then a singular verb is needed. If you use a word to mean "all of them," or "any of them," or "none of them," then a plural verb is used (p. 51).

Trouble may also pop up when words come between subject and verb, as in the following grammatically correct example:

Therapy [singular subject], in combination with behavioral organic methods of weight gain, exemplifies [singular verb form] this approach.

The reason the example above is correct is that the subject is singular (*therapy*) and the verb that goes with that noun is also singular (*exemplifies*). It would be grammatically incorrect to write something like the following, in which the subject is singular but the verb form is plural:

Therapy [singular subject], in combination with behavioral organic methods of weight gain, *exemplify* [plural verb form] this approach.

Using the correct verbs with words such as *everyone* and *nobody* can be puzzling as well. The rule of grammar is to use a *singular verb form* when the subject to which the verb refers is signified as "each," "either," "everyone," "someone," "neither," or "nobody." Here is a correct usage:

When everyone *is* (singular verb form) ready, the experiment will begin.

7.14 Other Common Usage Errors

7.14.1 Confusing Homonyms
The inside front cover of this book lists similar sounding words (*homonyms*) that are often confused with one another. Word-processing spelling checkers will not catch these errors, so you have to proofread your manuscript very carefully. One instructor's recommendation was that students proofread their papers *aloud* before submitting them, avoiding the kind of skimming that misses usage errors.

For example, one such pair of homonyms is *affect* and *effect*. Here are several tips to help you sort out these two words:

- ◆ In their most common form, the word *effect* is a noun meaning "outcome" (as in "Aggression is often an *effect* of frustration"), whereas *affect* is a verb meaning "to influence" (as in "The level of frustration *affects* how a person behaves").

♦ However, *effect* can also be used as a verb meaning "to bring about" (as in "The clinical intervention *effected* a measurable improvement").

♦ And *affect* can also be used as a noun meaning "emotion" (as in "Several of the patients participating in this clinical trial exhibited positive *affect*").

7.14.2 Singular and Plural of Familiar Terms

Another potential source of problems is the incorrect use of the singular and plural of some familiar terms. The following list shows the correct singular and plural forms:

Singular	Plural
analysis	analyses
anomaly	anomalies
appendix	appendices or appendixes (both are correct)
criterion	criteria
datum	data
hypothesis	hypotheses
phenomenon	phenomena
stimulus	stimuli

For example, one common usage error in student papers is the confusion of *phenomena* (plural term) with *phenomenon* (singular term). It would be incorrect to write, "This [singular pronoun] phenomena [plural subject] is [singular verb] of interest." The correct form is either "This phenomenon is . . ." (singular subject and singular verb) or "The phenomena are . . ." (plural subject and plural verb).

The word *data* can also be a source of confusion, and most grammarians feel that they have lost this battle. In *The New York Times* and most other mass media publications, *data* appears as both a singular and a plural noun. Strictly speaking, the word *data* is plural and the word *datum* is singular, but *datum* has almost vanished from popular usage. One way around this problem is to use the term *data set* to refer to the singular and *data sets* to refer to the plural. However, if you prefer to use *data* as a noun (rather than an adjective as noted above), then avoid using a singular verb. That is, don't write: "The data [plural subject] indicates [singular verb] . . ." or "The data shows . . ." Instead write: "The data indicate [plural verb] . . ." or "The data show . . ."

7.14.3 Between and Among

In the past, another common source of confusion was in the use of the words *between* and *among*. We were taught in high school English to use *between* when referring to two items only, and to use *among* when there are more than two items. This distinction seems to be another that has gone out of style, however. For example, *Webster's* (the 10th edition as well as the 11th edition) denies the correctness of the distinction of the words *between* and *among*. When referring to analysis of variance (abbreviated ANOVA), the convention in statistics is to speak of the "between sum of squares" and "between mean square," even if the number of conditions being compared is more than two.

7.14.4 Prefixes

Other common problems concern the use of some *prefixes* in psychological terms:

◆ The prefix *inter-* means "between" (for example, *interpersonal* means "between persons"); the prefix *intra-* means "within" (for example, *intrapersonal* means "within the person").

◆ The prefix *intro-* means "inward" or "within"; the prefix *extra-* means "outside" or "beyond." The psychological term *introvert* thus refers to an "inner-directed personality"; the term *extravert* indicates an "outer-directed personality." (*The New York Times* and other mass media publications spell *extravert* as *extrovert,* which makes no sense.)

◆ The prefix *hyper-* means "too much"; the prefix *hypo-* means "too little." The term *hypothyroidism* refers to a deficiency of thyroid hormone. *Hyperthyroidism* means an excess of the thyroid hormone, and a *hyperactive* child is one who is excessively active.

7.15   Numbers, Numerals, Digits, Figures

We use the terms *figures* and *digits* to refer to the symbols for numerals (1, 10, 100, etc.), and we describe them as "expressed in words" when they are "spelled out" (one, ten, one hundred, etc.). In general, the APA recommends expressing single-digit numbers in words (*one, two, three, four, five, six, seven, eight, nine*) and using figures for numbers with more than one digit (*10, 20, 30, 40*). For example, Jane Doe speaks of "two million people" in the opening sentence of her introduction. Here are seven APA rules to help you decide when to express numbers in words and when to use figures for numbers:

1. Although it is recommended that you not begin a sentence with a number, if you must do so, express it in words ("Twenty-nine students volunteered for this study" or "Fourteen percent of all the participants responded in the affirmative").

2. Numbers expressed as words in phrases and sentences should be spelled out (as in "two-tailed test" or the sentence "Only two of the participants refused to go further in the study").

3. Spell out *zero* and *one* when they are easier to understand than *0* and *1* ("zero-sum game" or "one-word response").

4. When single-digit numbers are part of a group, use figures (for example, "5 of the 25 participants failed to answer this question").

5. Use figures for all numbers—even one-digit numbers—that immediately precede a unit of measurement (for example, 3 cm or 9 mg).

6. Use figures for units of age and time (4-year-old, 3 months, 2 days, 9 minutes), units of measurement (3%), and numbers used in reference lists (pp. 4–6, 2nd ed., Vol. 4).

7. Use whatever is the universally accepted style for well-known expressions (the Ten Commandments).

Three additional APA rules, for reporting singular and plural numbers, long sequences of numbers, and physical measurements, are the following:

8. When reporting the plurals of numbers, add an *s* without an apostrophe. So the plural of *1990* is *1990s*, and the plural of *20* is *20s*.

9. Commas are used between groups of three digits (1,000,000), except for page numbers (page 1225), binary digits (001001), serial numbers (345789), degrees of freedom, and numbers to the right of a decimal point (3.14159).

10. When reporting physical units, use the metric system. Thus, 1 foot is reported as .3048 m (or meter), and 1 inch becomes .0254 m. To avoid confusion, you might put a zero before the decimal (0.3048 m or 0.0254 m).

7.16   More on Punctuation

7.16.1 Periods

Besides the proper use of commas in reporting numbers, there are various other rules for the use of punctuation marks in your writing. Notice above that there was no period after the *m* (no italics) symbol for *meter*, because the APA style is not to use a period after a symbol, except when a symbol is at the end of a declarative sentence (because a period is always used to end a declarative sentence). Periods are also used following an abbreviation other than a physical unit, as in the following common abbreviations of Latin words:

cf.	from *confer* ("compare")
e.g.	from *exempli gratia* ("for example")
et al.	from *et alia* ("and others")
et seq.	from *et sequens* ("and following")

ibid.	from *ibidem* ("in the same place")
i.e.	from *id est* ("that is")
op. cit.	from *opere citato* ("in the work cited")
viz.	from *videlicet* ("namely")

If you continually write "eg" or "et. al," you will be telling the instructor, "I don't know the meaning of these terms!" The reason (as indicated above) is that *e.g.* (with no italics) is the abbreviation of two words, not one. Writing "eg" is an announcement that you believe (mistakenly) it is the abbreviation of one word. Putting a period after "et" is an announcement that you also believe (again, mistakenly) it is an abbreviation, which it is not; it is an entire Latin word.

With the exception of *et al.* (but don't use italics), if you use any of these Latin abbreviations, the APA Manual recommends that you use them in parentheses and/or tabular material, and that you otherwise spell out the abbreviations. Take the expression "for example"; in parentheses you would write it as "e.g." as in the following:

Herrnstein and Murray's (1994) book was widely debated (e.g., Andery & Serio, 1997; Andrews & Nelkin, 1996; Carroll, 1997).

When not in parentheses, spell the phrase out ("for example") rather than abbreviate it as "e.g.":

Herrnstein and Murray's (1994) book was widely debated; see, for example, work by Andery and Serio (1997), Andrews and Nelkin (1996), and Carroll (1997).

Other abbreviations that are followed by a period are the short forms of English words, as illustrated by the following:

anon.	for *anonymous*
ch.	for *chapter* (also Ch.)
diagr.	for *diagram*
ed.	for *editor* (also Ed.) or *edition*
fig.	for *figure*
ms.	for *manuscript*
p.	for *page*
pp.	for *pages*
rev.	for *revised*
v.	for *versus* (in references to and text citations of court cases)
vol.	for *volume* (also Vol.)
vs.	for *versus, against*

7.16.2 Abbreviations Without Periods

Another APA rule is that, except for common abbreviations like those above, most abbreviations for terms are first spelled out for the reader. Many abbreviations of technical terms are not followed by a period, however. Suppose you frequently refer to reaction time or to an instrument called the Humboldt Upside-Down Test. You would write "reaction time (RT)" or "Humboldt Upside-Down Test (HUDT)" at the first mention and use the abbreviation RT or HUDT in the rest of your paper.

The APA Manual's exception to spelling out abbreviations is that those listed as word entries in *Merriam-Webster's Collegiate Dictionary* do not need to be defined first. For example, IQ, REM, AIDS, HIV, and ESP do not need to be either spelled out or set off in parentheses the first time they are used in a psychology paper.

7.16.3 Commas and Semicolons

We have already covered the use of commas in numbers. Some other uses of the *comma* are the following:

1. Use commas to separate each of three or more items in a series ("Smith, Jones, or Brown"; "high, medium, and low scorers").
2. Use commas to set off introductory phrases in a sentence ("In another experiment performed 10 years later, the same researchers found . . .").
3. Use commas to set off thoughts or phrases that are incidental to, or that qualify, the basic idea of the sentence ("This variable, though not part of the researchers' main hypothesis, was also examined").
4. Put a comma before coordinating conjunctions (*and, but, or, nor, yet*) when they join independent clauses ("The subject lost weight, but he was still able to . . .").

A common error in student papers is to insert a comma before a transitional expression such as *however, moreover,* or *therefore* when it is used to connect two complete clauses in a compound sentence. For example, writing the following would be grammatically incorrect:

The participants voiced no concerns, however, it was quite obvious that they were uncomfortable.

To avoid making that grammatical mistake, you have several choices. One option is to use a *semicolon* (;) before *however,* instead of a comma:

The participants voiced no concerns; however, it was quite obvious that they were uncomfortable.

A second option for avoiding the misuse of the comma would be to divide the compound sentence into two sentences:

The participants voiced no concerns. However, it was quite obvious that they were uncomfortable.

A third option is to replace the transitional expression *however* with the conjunction *but,* preceded by a comma:

> The participants voiced no concerns, but it was quite obvious that they were uncomfortable.

As a general rule, a semicolon is called for when the thoughts in the two independent clauses are close, and the writer wishes to emphasize this closeness or to contrast the two thoughts. The following sentence is an example of the grammatically correct use of the semicolon to connect thoughts:

> Anorexia nervosa is a disorder whose victims literally starve themselves; despite their emaciated appearance, they consider themselves overweight.

In most instances, however, these longer sentences can be divided into shorter ones and made clearer:

> Anorexia nervosa is a disorder whose victims literally starve themselves. Despite their emaciated appearance, they consider themselves overweight.

7.16.4 *The Colon*

Generally, the *colon* (:) is used to indicate that a list will follow, or to introduce an amplification. The colon tells the reader, "Note what follows." Here is an example in which we see a colon used to indicate that a list follows:

> Subjects were given the following items: (a) four calling birds, (b) three French hens, (c) two turtle doves, . . .

An example of the amplification use of a colon is the title of John Smith's review paper in appendix B ("The Elusive Concept of Intelligence: Two Diverse Orientations"). Here is another example of amplification:

> Gardner (1983) postulated two forms of the personal intelligences: interpersonal and intrapersonal intelligence.

For another use of the colon, notice in the reference lists of the two sample papers that a colon is inserted between the place of publication of a book and the name of the publisher, for example, "Englewood Cliffs, NJ: Prentice Hall" and "Cambridge, MA: Harvard University Press."

7.17   Uses of Punctuation in Quoted Passages

We mentioned ellipses (. . .) used in quoted passages to indicate that selected words have been intentionally omitted. You will sometimes also see in quoted passages the use of brackets ([ ]) with words inside. The brackets tell us that the words are not part of the original quotation but were inserted by the writer using the quoted material. A potential problem is that omitting some words may make a quoted passage grammatically incorrect or may make the quoted passage unclear, but either of these problems can be easily fixed by the insertion of a few connecting words in brackets.

Earlier, we also mentioned the importance of putting quotation marks around words that are quoted. An exception is a quotation of 40 or more words, in which case the quotation is set off from the body of the text by means of indented margins, and quotation marks are omitted. If there is an internal quotation within the set-off quotation, then *double quotation marks* ("...") are inserted around the quote within the longer quote, as in the following example:

> What practical implications did Rosenthal and Jacobson (1968) draw from their research findings? They wrote:
>
> > As teacher-training institutions begin to teach the possibility that teachers' expectations of their pupils' performance may serve as self-fulfilling prophecies, there may be a new expectancy created. The new expectancy may be that children can learn more than had been believed possible, an expectation held by many educational theorists, though for quite different reasons. . . . The new expectancy, at the very least, will make it more difficult when they encounter the educationally disadvantaged for teachers to think, "Well, after all, what can you expect?" The man [*sic*] on the street may be permitted his opinions and prophecies of the unkempt children loitering in a dreary schoolyard. The teacher in the schoolroom may need to learn that those same prophecies within her [*sic*] may be fulfilled; she is no casual passer-by. Perhaps Pygmalion in the classroom is more her role. (pp. 181–182)

When a quoted passage is fewer than 40 words, double quotation marks are used, and the passage is simply inserted in the text as part of the narrative. If a smaller quote appears within the quoted passage, then *single quotation marks* ('...') are used to set off the quote within a quote, as in the following sentence:

> Participant B responded, "My feeling about this difficult situation was summed up in a nutshell by Jim when he said, 'It's a tough job, but somebody has to do it.'"

As this example also illustrates, if the appropriate punctuation is a period (as shown at the end of the sentence), the period falls *within* the quotation marks. The same rule applies to a comma; it is inserted within the quotation marks. But if the appropriate punctuation is a colon or a semicolon, it is inserted *after* the closing quotation marks.

In the lengthy quote above, which begins, "As teacher-training institutions . . ." and ends ". . . in the classroom is more her role," notice that the numbers of the pages on which the passage appears in Rosenthal and Jacobson's book are shown in parentheses at the end. Notice also that the word *sic* (Latin, meaning "thus") is inserted in brackets in two places; it indicates that a word or phrase that appears strange or incorrect is quoted verbatim. If you wanted to make the point that a quoted passage ignores gender, you would insert in brackets the word *sic* as shown. But observe that we did not insert *sic* after every gender term. In the fourth sentence of the quotation, the masculine pronoun *his* was not set off by *sic* because the reference is "man on the street." In the fifth sentence, the feminine pronoun *she* is also not set off, because the referent is "within her."

7.18 *Safeguarding the Draft Manuscript*

In the next chapter we consider the details of producing a final manuscript, whereas in this chapter we focused on the draft manuscript. If you have ever lost a computer file, you are not alone. This time you are working under a strict deadline, and losing your work will be a scary setback. You never know when the power will suddenly go out or someone will playfully or accidentally hit a wrong key, or you might be distracted and hit a wrong key and send your latest work into oblivion. So remember to safeguard your work against possible losses.

One way to do this is to have your word-processing program do it automatically on the hard drive and/or on a backup drive. Another way is to do it yourself whenever you are ready to call it quits for the day, or whenever you decide to take a break. We do both, backing up our work on a flash memory and, when it is time to stop for the day, on a backup drive. If you work on a desktop computer, think about investing in a backup battery that will warn you (by beeping) when there is a sudden power outage and will give you ample time to save your work and shut down the computer.

8

Producing the Final Manuscript

This chapter provides you with guidelines and tips for polishing the draft manuscript and producing a final version. The layout and production of the final manuscript are like the icing on a cake. If the underlying structure is sound, the result will be smooth and predictable in accord with the standards described in this book.

8.1   Polishing the Draft Manuscript

The purpose of the preceding chapter was to guide you through the first draft of your research report or review paper, and the next step is to polish that first draft. Polishing is best done after you have been able to leave the draft manuscript entirely. When you approach your writing after taking such a break (ideally, 24 hours or more), your critical powers will be sharper. You will see clearly any syntax errors, lapses in logic, and other problems, so that polishing your writing will be straightforward and simple.

As you reread, consider the following suggestions:

- Make sure your writing gets right to the point of what you want to say.
- Break up long paragraphs containing a lot of disparate ideas into smaller, more coherent paragraphs.
- Be specific and appropriately precise.
- Choose words for what they mean, not just for how they sound.
- Don't use a long word when a short word will do.
- Don't let spelling, grammatical, or punctuation errors mar your writing.

The spelling checkers and grammar checkers that are built into word-processing systems are designed to flag mistakes, suggest alternatives, and let you choose whether to make a change or to ignore the recommendations. These checkers are not infallible, so do not let them lull you into a false sense of security, thinking they are a substitute for careful proofreading. Your spelling checker is based on a word inventory in the word-processing system, and not all technical terms that psychologists and other professionals use are part of every word-processing inventory. Spelling checkers frequently suggest word changes that mix up tenses and singulars and plurals, so take every suggested spelling change with a grain of salt. Have a good dictionary nearby to refer to when you are in doubt about the suggested word change. Commonly misspelled words are also listed on the inside front and back covers of this book. If you peruse those lists, some of the words may catch your eye as possible mistakes in your paper that you and the spelling checker missed.

Grammar checkers are designed to flag a sentence, phrase, or clause that violates a particular grammar or style rule. When the grammar checker encounters what it has been programmed to define as a problem, it suggests one or two alternatives, and you are asked whether you want to accept one of the suggestions or ignore them all. Sometimes it turns out that grammar checkers respond to typos that they interpret as grammatical mistakes, but at least they have alerted you to a typo that needs correcting. Grammar checkers can be maddening, however, because they frequently "catch" acceptable stylistic variations and fail to recognize actual stylistic errors. Many experienced writers turn off the grammar checker. You can, if you wish, use the grammar checker only when you want it, or you can set it to automatically flag "violations" as they are encountered. It is also useful to have one or two good grammar books handy, such as the latest editions of Strunk and White's *The Elements of Style* and O'Connell's *Woe Is I*.

8.2   *Formatting and Organizing Your Final Manuscript*

We now turn to the formatting of your final manuscript. The following are some general pointers based on the specifications in the APA Manual:

- If you have read chapter 6, you may remember that the APA style is to use sans serif lettering (no squiggles or loops) in all graphics or figures. For the rest of the manuscript, the APA Manual recommends using a serif font, such as Times New Roman, with 12-point font size.
- Use double-spacing between all text lines, and double-space every line in the title, headings, footnotes, quotations, references, and figure captions. The exceptions to this APA rule are that triple- and quadruple-spacing are acceptable in "special circumstances" (such as the title page or before and after a displayed equation).

- Leave margins of at least 1 inch at the top, bottom, and both sides of every page.
- Use a maximum line length of 6 ½ inches.
- Leave the right margin uneven (called a *ragged* margin), and don't divide words or use hyphenations to break a word at the end of the line.
- The APA Manual suggests setting the tab key at ½ inch or five to seven spaces to indent the first line of every paragraph, though the default setting in most word-processing programs is also acceptable.

Jane Doe's research report (appendix A) illustrates the following arrangement of the pages of the final manuscript of a research report, with the exception of figures (Jane has two tables but no figures):

Title page (numbered page 1)
Abstract (numbered page 2)
Narrative text begins (start on page 3)
Method (no page break)
Results (no page break)
Discussion (no page break)
References (start on a separate page)
Footnotes (start on a separate page)
Tables (start each on a separate page)
Figures (start each on a separate page, and show the caption on the same page as the figure)
Appendix (start on a separate page)

John Smith's review paper (appendix B) illustrates the following arrangement of the pages of a literature review:

Title page (numbered page 1)
Abstract (numbered page 2)
Narrative text begins (start on page 3)
References (start on a separate page)
Footnotes (start on a separate page)
Tables (start each on a separate page)
Figures (start each on a separate page, and show the caption on the same page as the figure)

Once the pages are in their proper order, they should be numbered consecutively in the upper right corner, beginning with the title page. This should be done by using the word processor's automatic function for inserting a header with a page number. Notice in Jane's and John's manuscripts that the header (called a *page header*) is a few words taken from the full title and is flush left in capital letters on the same line as the page number on the right. The page header will make it easier to identify each manuscript page if some hard copy pages become separated from the rest.

As you make these changes in your manuscript, save and back up your work. Our habit is to make a printout periodically. Even if you are submitting your final manuscript as an e-mail attachment, having a printed copy will make it easier for you to inspect and modify the layout to make sure it all looks the way you want it to. If you are submitting a printed copy, the printout will allow you to polish your writing in the same format that you will be submitting to your instructor. Sometimes the computer screen makes spelling errors less apparent, as well as passages that might be unclear, inaccurate, imprecise, or lacking some needed detail. These problems are more likely to jump out as your eye traverses a printed page.

8.3   Formatting the Title Page

Glance again at the title pages of Jane's report in appendix A and John's review paper in appendix B. The title summarizes the main idea of the project and is centered near the top of the page. (Notice that the title appears again on page 3 of each sample paper.) A good title is succinct and yet adequately describes to the reader the gist of the work. If you arrived at a working title at an earlier stage, that title can now be modified and made more specific if you think it is no longer accurate or completely descriptive of the finished paper. The APA Manual style is to capitalize prepositions of four or more letters in titles and headings, so you would capitalize the word *With* or *From* if it is used in the title of your paper. Notice that the words *of* and *on* are not capitalized in the titles of Jane's or John's papers.

The student's name (called the *byline*) appears below the title. Below the byline is the name of the academic institution.

In the Author Note, the student takes responsibility for the originality of the work and indicates the name of the instructor and the name of the course. This note gives you an opportunity to acknowledge the assistance provided by others as well. The note concludes by providing contact information, such as your e-mail or mailing address.

The date that the paper was submitted to the instructor is typed at the bottom of the title page.

8.4   Formatting the Abstract

You write the abstract, which appears on a separate page (page 2), after you finish the report or review paper. It summarizes the manuscript in a single paragraph. In chapter 4 (section 4.3), you will find specifics for a research report's abstract. Notice in Jane's and John's final manuscripts that the word *Abstract* is centered, in boldface, and is not italicized.

8.5 Formatting the Headings

It is customary to break up the text of a lengthy paper into sections and to provide a brief but informative heading for each section. One purpose of these headings is to provide a sort of conceptual map that will enable readers to understand exactly where they are as they proceed through a sequence of topics or issues in the paper. Another purpose is to organize the writer's thinking, so that topics that belong in one section do not accidentally stray into another section where they do not belong. A third purpose is to guide the readers through the logical flow of the paper, from the most important to the least important (but still relevant) topics, issues, or other information.

If you are writing a review paper, thesis, or some other kind of term paper, you should be able to derive these headings from the outline of your paper or thesis. Observe, for example, how John Smith's headings and subheadings lend symmetry to his review paper, showing its progressive development in concise phrases. John's paper uses two formatting arrangements of headings: center and flush left. These are also described as *levels of headings*. In the APA style, *center headings* are first-level headings, which are used to separate the paper into major sections. As illustrated by Jane's and John's final manuscripts, these first-level headings are centered and in bold uppercase and lowercase letters.

The next level of headings (the second level) is flush left and in bold uppercase and lowercase letters. The third level of headings is indented and in boldface; only the first letter is in uppercase, and the heading ends with a period. John used only first- and second-level headings in his review paper. Jane, on the other hand, used all three levels of headings in her research report, as illustrated below:

Results

Scoring and Calculations
Overall Findings
    Basic data.
    Omnibus F test.
Focused Statistical Tests
    Hypothesis 1.
    Hypothesis 2.
    Hypothesis 3.
    Contrast F test.

The symbol F was capitalized and italicized in two of Jane's third-level headings (above) because it is the proper name of the statistical test discussed in that subsection. If you need to use more than three levels of headings, the APA style for a fourth-level heading is that it is similar to a third-level heading except that it is italicized. A fifth-level heading is similar to a fourth-level heading except that it is not in boldface.

8.6   Other Uses of Italics

◆ Besides the use of italics in some headings and in your reference list (chapter 3), here are further guidelines to help you decide when to use italics:Conventional usage calls for italicizing the titles of books and periodicals in the narrative text. For example, here is a quote from John Smith's paper: "In the 1990s, a controversial reanalysis of IQ data by Herrnstein and Murray (1994), in a book entitled *The Bell Curve,* ignited a spirited debate about . . ."

◆ Letters in English used as statistical symbols are italicized: *F, N, n, P, p, t, z,* and so forth. Note that some symbols are in lowercase and others in uppercase. This distinction can be very important. For example, an uppercase N indicates the total number of sampling units, whereas a lowercase n indicates the number of units in a subsample of N.

◆ Words that you want to emphasize are italicized ("Effective teaching, the authors asserted, will come from the teachers' firm belief that their pupils *can* perform"), but use this device sparingly.

◆ Words used to illustrate are italicized ("the term *knowing* . . ." or ". . . is called *knowing*").

Incidentally, notice in the opening sentence of John's introduction that foreign phrases (John quotes an old French saying) are not italicized. Nor are nonstatistical subscripts italicized even though the statistical symbol is italicized. For example, Jane (in her research report) repeatedly uses the symbol $r_{\text{effect size}}$. The r is italicized because it is the statistical symbol, but the subscript "effect size" is not italicized.

8.7   Citations and References Revisited

In chapter 3 we provided examples of the conventions for citing (section 3.3) and referencing (section 3.4) material in the APA style. Remember that Exhibit 9 is a summary list of citations illustrated in section 3.3, and Exhibit 10 is a summary list of references illustrated in section 3.4. When you are creating your reference list, we suggest you refer to those two exhibits and the discussions and examples in chapter 3. You will find some similar items in Jane's reference list (appendix A) and John's reference list (appendix B) keyed to the corresponding examples in chapter 3. Notice again that the reference section begins on a new page and the word *References* is centered and in bold (but not in italics). The references are all double-spaced, and all but the first line of each reference is indented (called a *hanging indent*). Remember that the APA rule is not to list any publications in your list of references that you did not cite in your paper (whether it was in the narrative text, in a footnote in the text, in a note in a table or a figure, or in an appendix).

EXHIBIT 18 Postal abbreviations for states and territories

Location	Abbreviation	Location	Abbreviation
Alabama	AL	Montana	MT
Alaska	AK	Nebraska	NE
Arizona	AZ	Nevada	NV
Arkansas	AR	New Hampshire	NH
California	CA	New Jersey	NJ
Colorado	CO	New Mexico	NM
Connecticut	CT	New York	NY
Delaware	DE	North Carolina	NC
District of Columbia	DC	North Dakota	ND
Florida	FL	Ohio	OH
Georgia	GA	Oklahoma	OK
Guam	GU	Oregon	OR
Hawaii	HI	Pennsylvania	PA
Idaho	ID	Puerto Rico	PR
Illinois	IL	Rhode Island	RI
Indiana	IN	South Carolina	SC
Iowa	IA	South Dakota	SD
Kansas	KS	Tennessee	TN
Kentucky	KY	Texas	TX
Louisiana	LA	Utah	UT
Maine	ME	Vermont	VT
Maryland	MD	Virginia	VA
Massachusetts	MA	Virgin Islands	VI
Michigan	MI	Washington	WA
Minnesota	MN	West Virginia	WV
Mississippi	MS	Wisconsin	WI
Missouri	MO	Wyoming	WY

Also, as we mentioned in chapter 3, the names of U.S. states and territories should be abbreviated in the reference list (or anywhere else in your manuscript where you refer to the location of a U.S. publisher). The abbreviations should be those used by the U.S. Postal Service, which, for your convenience, are listed in Exhibit 18.

8.8 Footnotes

Jane's and John's final manuscripts also illustrate the placement and formatting of footnotes. If you feel the need to have footnotes, they begin on a separate page following the list of references. The word *Footnotes* is capped and centered (not in italics or bold), and each footnote is numbered as shown in the sample reports. As the APA style for manuscripts is to tuck the footnotes away after the references, they can be a nuisance if the reader has to jump back and forth from the text to footnotes. Therefore, use footnotes sparingly, if at all, and think of the sample manuscripts as illustrating the formatting style and not as recommending the use of footnotes. When students approach their draft manuscripts after having taken a break, they often find that the information in a footnote can be condensed and integrated into the text if it is vital information, or they find that it was superfluous information to begin with and is expendable.

8.9 Formatting Tables and Figures

As discussed earlier in this book, tables and figures can be used to augment the presentation of the results. Often, however, when students include tables in their research reports, they are merely presenting their raw data in a neat format. If you are writing such a report, save your raw data for the appendix of your report (as illustrated in Jane's final manuscript). Keep in mind that statistical tables in results sections of research reports are intended to *summarize* the data and the statistical results. As we noted earlier, each table starts on a separate page after the footnotes section or, if you have no footnotes, after the references. If you include one or more figures (there are none in Jane's research report, but there is one in John's review paper in appendix B), each belongs on a separate page immediately following any tables.

Jane used two tables to summarize some of her statistical results, and John used a single table to define Howard Gardner's original seven types of intelligence. Notice that the tables are numbered, and below the number appears the title of the table, in italics. The title is in upper- and lowercase, and both the table number and the title are flush left. If you want to include a note explaining something, the word *Note* (italicized and followed by a period) precedes what you want to say, and the entire note is flush left without a paragraph indentation. Jane's Table 2 also has an asterisked footnote indicating that two of the F values in the table were statistically significant at $p < .0001$. (Using an asterisked footnote in this way was discussed in the next to last paragraph in section 4.6 in chapter 4.)

The APA style is to use superscript asterisks (* ** ***) or superscript lowercase letters ([a] [b] [c]) to add specific annotations to a table. Suppose you wanted to indicate more than one significance level using an asterisk notation:

$$*p < .05 \qquad **p < .01 \qquad ***p < .0005$$

Or suppose you want to use superscript lowercase footnotes to indicate sample sizes that varied:

$$^a n = 50 \qquad ^b n = 62$$

If you are using tables, notice also in the sample manuscripts that each column in a table has a heading that defines the items in that column. The important thing is to keep your table headings clear, concise, and informative, so that a reader can understand what is in the table. If you are using a figure, notice in John Smith's review paper that the term *Figure 1* is italicized and followed by a period, and the title of the figure (called the *caption*) is not italicized; it reads like a phrase and ends with a period.

8.10 Appendix in Student Papers

The final section in Jane Doe's research report, the appendix, also starts on a new page. It is possible (although unusual) to include an appendix in a review paper. Because the material included in an appendix can vary greatly from one research report to another, the formatting style of the appendix should be determined by the material to be included. The only rule is that there should be a separate appendix for each general type of information or material. As there is only one appendix in Jane's report, there is no need to label it as anything more than "Appendix," centered and in boldface (without the quotation marks). But suppose you have used a questionnaire in your research and the instructor requires that a copy be included in your final report. You can label one "Appendix A" and title it "Raw Scores and Statistical Calculations," and you can label the second "Appendix B" and title it "Questionnaire Used in the Research."

8.11 Proofing and Correcting

We now come to the final steps before you submit your manuscript: proofing and correcting. Read your finished paper more than once, preferably aloud (so you can catch errors like *too* for *to*—which bypass spelling checkers and some grammar checkers). Ask yourself the following questions:

- ◆ Are there omissions?
- ◆ Are there misspellings?
- ◆ Are the numbers correct?
- ◆ Are the hyphenations correct?
- ◆ Do all the references cited in the paper (including those in footnotes, tables, figures, and an appendix) also appear in the references section?

The first time you read your final draft, the appeal of the neat, clean copy may lead you to overlook errors. Put the paper aside for 24 hours, and then read it carefully again. After you have corrected any errors, give the paper a final look, checking to be sure all the pages are there and in order. If you adhered to the guidelines in this manual, you should feel confident that the paper will receive the serious attention that a clear, consistent, and attractive manuscript deserves.

9

Preparing Posters and Concise Reports

The poster is a visual display used to convey the nature and major findings of your research in the setting of a public forum. It is customary for poster presenters also to provide interested visitors with a brief report of the research. The exercise of boiling down your research to its most pertinent components, without sacrificing vital details, will teach you the art of selecting critical information.

9.1 Posters and Handout Reports

It is becoming increasingly common for students doing empirical research not only to prepare a detailed written report of their findings, but also to present their results in poster form. Some posters may even be presented at conferences. This format has its own set of conventions and requirements, although they are not uniform; they depend on the parameters set forth by the organizer of each specific conference.

If you have an opportunity to attend a poster session, you can assess the visual impact of the presentations. Which posters draw your eye? What is it about some posters that makes them more visually accessible than others? Poster presenters planning to do further research, or planning to write up their results for submission to a journal, find the feedback they obtain invaluable. If people are not drawn to the poster, however, there is no opportunity for feedback or discussion. Therefore, it is important to construct a poster that is visually inviting, and in this chapter we provide guidelines to help you.

To supplement the information that is presented visually in the poster, a concise handout is usually prepared. The report you prepared for class would be inappropriate as a handout. It is too costly to reproduce a lot of copies of a lengthy paper. Moreover, it contains more information than anyone but your instructor will want. Therefore, we will also illustrate how to condense Jane Doe's detailed research report in appendix A into a concise (but informative) report for distribution.

9.2 Guidelines for the Poster

The way a poster session usually works is that you are asked to show up with your material in a large room or auditorium full of rows of display boards. For example, if you were presenting a poster at an APA convention, you would find poster boards mounted on stands; the poster presenter's place among the poster boards would be indicated by an alphanumeric code next to the paper in the convention program. (If you are presenting a poster at a meeting and have not been assigned a particular board, it will be first come, first served, so arriving early is definitely to your advantage.) Pushpins and Velcro hooks are usually available for attaching the pages to the display board. In advance of the meeting, some presenters, having arranged and pasted their pages on a cardboard poster, simply attach the whole poster to the display board. You are not allowed to write, paint, or use paste on the display board, and you must have your display set up in the time allotted (generally around 10 minutes). Your display must be removed after the poster session, and the display board left neat and presentable for the next set of presenters.

Exhibit 19 illustrates how the guidelines for poster presentations differ from one organization to another. The exhibit provides a comparison of poster elements suggested by the American Psychological Association (APA), the Association for Psychological Science (APS), and the American Association for the Advancement of Science (AAAS). For example, the APS's and AAAS's poster board surfaces are two feet wider than the APA's; the larger the surface, the more the information that can be displayed. Notice that the APA and APS guidelines call for an abstract of the research to appear in the upper-left corner of the poster.

It is impossible in this chapter to anticipate every special requirement that you may encounter. This information is generally available on the Web site of the organization that is sponsoring the meeting, and you can ensure that your proposal will be suitable by finding out the special requirements before you begin to design your poster. Within these requirements, there is usually some flexibility of poster arrangements. For example, Exhibit 20 shows three sample arrangements provided on the APA Web site for presenters at its annual convention. Of course, not every poster presenter will plan to have two tables and one figure. You might also ask yourself which of the sample arrangements you would find most inviting if you were a viewer, or how you might want to modify the arrangements when presenting your own research.

EXHIBIT 19   APA, APS, and AAAS poster design standards

Poster element	APA	APS	AAAS
Poster board	4' high, 6' wide	4' high, 8' wide	4' high, 8' wide
Legibility	At a 3' distance or more	At a 3' distance	At about a 5' distance
Sequence	Abstract (300 words or less) in upper-left corner, followed by ordered material	Abstract (300 words or less) in upper-left corner, followed by ordered material	Conclusions, then supporting text, ending with brief summary
Title and author(s)	1" high, at least	At least 30-point font	2–3" high
Lettering of text	3/8" high, preferably boldface font, or hand-lettered with regular felt-tipped pen	20-point font or larger	24-point font, but color as well as different sizes and proportions can be used
Section headings	Clearly labeled	At least 30-point font	½–1" high subheadings
Tables and figures	Simple, clear, and easily visible	Clearly readable	Graphics preferred to tables
Handouts	50 copies of concise report	50 copies or more of concise report	Abstract (number unspecified)

9.3   Sample Content and Arrangement

The example in Exhibit 21 arranges the information and the poster panels in a way that seems less cluttered and easier for the eye to follow. The abstract still appears in the upper-left corner, as required by both the APA and the APS, but the other panels are relabeled and also numbered. If you choose this approach, we would suggest that the abstract not be simply a reiteration of what would typically appear in a research report (as described in section 4.3 in chapter 4) but be written more concisely, in a way that draws people to the poster. Once a person's attention is drawn to the poster by the title and the abstract, the numbered panels in Exhibit 21 are designed to walk the person through the study with more technically detailed information.

Exhibit 22 fills in the content panels of Exhibit 21 with the information from Jane Doe's research. All that is missing from Exhibit 22 is the title of Jane's poster, her name, and her e-mail address, all of which would be in boldface. In Exhibit 22, you can see that Jane's poster captures the highlights of her research study. She will also have 50 or more paper copies of a handout (described later in this chapter) that she will offer to interested viewers. Once you have created your poster, stand back a few feet and see

EXHIBIT 20   APA sample poster arrangements

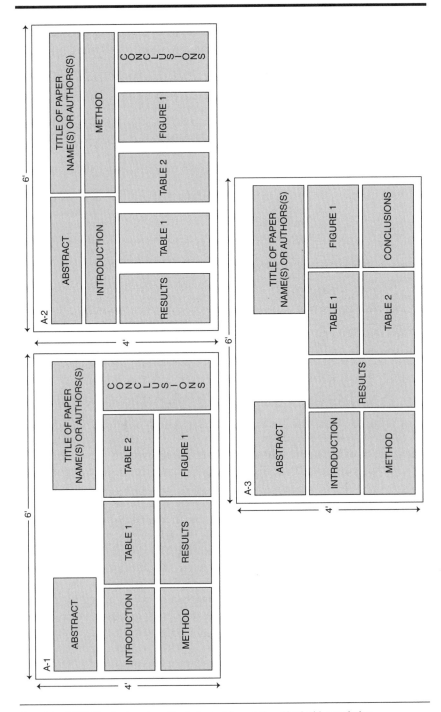

EXHIBIT 21   Modified poster arrangement

Abstract	TITLE OF PAPER AUTHOR(S) e-mail address

1. The Problem	2. Hypotheses	3. Research Procedure

4. Summary of Results	5. (Labeled Figure or Table)	6. Conclusions

EXHIBIT 22   Sample content for modified poster

Abstract

Are dining parties in restaurants likely to reward servers with bigger tips when diners are presented with a chocolate candy with the check? When presented with two chocolate candies, will the tips be bigger still? Suppose the offer of a second chocolate candy is a generous afterthought on the part of the server. Will it be reciprocated by an even more generous tip? The results of the randomized experiment described in this poster suggested the answer to each of these questions is yes.

1. The Problem

Over 2 million people in the U.S. work as waiters and waitresses who serve in restaurants. Their major source of income is usually the tips they receive from customers. Research on tipping behavior has found that the following techniques used by servers can increase tipping:

- Touching the recipient of the check on the palm of the hand for a fraction of a second.
- Giving diners who are sitting alone a large, open-mouth smile.
- Squatting to the eye level of the dining party.
- Telling the diners one's first name during the initial visit to the table.
- Drawing a happy face or writing "thank you" on the check.

All these techniques seem to have in common that the servers are also doing something that may increase customers' impressions of friendliness. In this study, another such technique was experimentally manipulated— offering the customers an after-meal miniature chocolate candy.

EXHIBIT 22 Continued

---

2. Hypotheses

There were three experimental hypotheses:

1. On the assumption that the offer of a miniature chocolate candy would be perceived by diners as a gesture of friendliness, it was hypothesized that the candy offer would encourage tipping behavior, in comparison with a no-candy control condition.

2. On the further assumption that this effect is cumulative (up to a point), it was hypothesized that offering each diner two chocolate candies would encourage tipping even more.

3. Research on reciprocity has found that individuals often feel obliged to return a favor to the person perceived as responsible for the favor. Thus, it was hypothesized that diners' perceptions that the offer of a second candy reflected the server's spontaneous generosity would encourage tipping still further.

---

3. Research Procedure

A waitress in an upscale restaurant in central New Jersey was provided with a small basket filled with wrapped miniature chocolates. She was given a stack of 80 index cards, each of which indicated one of the following four conditions (in a random sequence):

Control condition: The server brought the check (not the basket of candies) at the end of the meal, thanked the dining party, and left the table.

1-piece condition: The server brought the basket of candies when presenting the check, invited each person to select one candy, then thanked the dining party and left the table.

2-piece condition: The server brought the basket of candies when presenting the check, invited each person to select two candies, then thanked the dining party and left the table.

1+1 condition: The server brought the basket of candies when presenting the check, invited each person to select one candy, said, "Oh, have another piece"—as if this were a generous afterthought—and then thanked the dining party and left the table.

EXHIBIT 22   *Continued*

4. Summary of Results

The dependent measure was the tip percentage, which was obtained for each dining party by division of the amount of the tip by the amount of the check before taxes, and then multiplication by 100. The height of the bars in Figure 1 indicates the mean tip percentage in each condition, and the thin error bars denote the 95% confidence intervals around those mean tip percentages.

As the bar graph shows, the mean tip percentage increased from the control to the 1-piece to the 2-piece to the 1+1 condition. Consistent with this observed trend, a linear contrast was highly significant ($p < .0001$), and the 95% confidence interval for the effect size ranged from $r = .45$ to .73.

Independent-sample t tests of simple effects were also highly significant ($p < .0001$ one-tailed) for the comparison between (a) the control group and the 2-piece condition and (b) the control group and the 1+1 condition (both effect size $rs > .5$). However, the t test comparing the control group and the 1-piece condition was not statistically significant ($p = .17$ one-tailed, effect size $r = .15$), but power was less than .5.

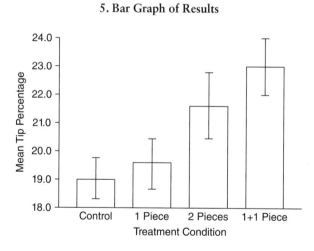

5. Bar Graph of Results

Figure 1. Mean tip percentages and their 95% confidence intervals (based on 20 dining parties in each condition).

EXHIBIT 22   Continued

---

6. Conclusions

Offering diners an after-meal chocolate candy increased the tip percentages, and offering two candies increased tips more than offering one. This finding is consistent with the idea that a token gift conveys friendliness, and that, in return, people give larger tips as a sign of their appreciation,

Results in the 1+1 condition were consistent with reciprocity theory, in that people gave the largest tip percentages after being led to believe they had benefited from the server's generous impulse.

Further research is needed to explore the generalizability of these results, as well as research to confirm the mediational roles of friendliness and generosity that were presumed to be operating in this study.

if you can read it easily. You can also show it to your instructor, and to any others willing to give candid opinions about its readability and design.

9.4   Further Guidelines for the Poster

In whatever arrangement you choose, remember that you are trying to draw attention to your study. You also want to chat with people who are interested in learning more about it, as well as to ferret out issues and ideas that can help you anticipate problems if you expect to submit the research to a journal or to continue doing research on this topic. One instructor told us that he cautioned students to be prepared for a cramped area with relatively poor lighting, a lot of distracting noise, and other sensory intrusions. He also gave his students the following tips:

◆ Choose a font size that is big enough for tired, middle-aged viewers with failing eyesight to see from a distance.
◆ Keep the tables and figures simple, because people don't usually want to stand around and study them.
◆ Keeping it simple also means being selective in what you report, but it doesn't mean being evasive or misleading, only straightforward and concise.

Besides reviewing the specifics provided by the organizer of your poster session, consider these further tips on how to format the poster:

◆ Use a typeface that is easy to read, such as Arial or Times New Roman, not a fancy one that has squiggles or loops.

- Make sure that you use a font size that is visible at a distance, such as 24 points (one-quarter inch high; as recommended by the AAAS) or even 32 points.
- Don't overcomplicate tables or figures, and don't use jargon or exotic terms that are likely to be unfamiliar to your viewers.
- Make your figures and illustrations bold and self-explanatory, and be sure the details are easy to see.
- Organize and label the sequence of information in a way that leads the viewer through the poster, and leave some space to separate the parts of the poster.

You may remember that in chapter 6 (section 6.2) we referred to the work of Stephen M. Kosslyn on how the brain perceives and processes visual information and the implications when you are preparing graphical displays. If you are planning to use color in your poster, it is best to use it sparingly and also to keep in mind the following tips from Kosslyn's book, *Elements of Graph Design* (W. H. Freeman, 1994):

- Choose colors that are well separated in the spectrum, because those close together are harder to discriminate. The colors perceived as being most separated are reddish purple, blue, yellowish gray, yellowish green, red, and bluish gray.
- Colors that, according to popular wisdom, are never confused (unless the person is color-blind) are white, gray, black, red, green, yellow, blue, pink, brown, orange, and purple.
- Use only a few of these colors, however, because using a lot of colors in the same visual display can be distracting and confusing.
- Avoid juxtaposing red (which has a relatively long wavelength) and blue (which has a relatively short wavelength), as they may be perceived as shimmering.
- Avoid cobalt blue, which is actually a mixture of blue and red and is hard to keep in focus. As an example, you may recall seeing a halo around blue streetlights at night, and you may have thought it was due to fog; it was a visual phenomenon caused by your eyes' inability to focus the image properly.

9.5   Guidelines for the Concise Report

Even the most interested viewers are unlikely to want to take extensive notes. Therefore, it is necessary to have a printed report they can take with them. The most economical approach is to try to confine the vital information to two pages, so that you can make copies of a one-page handout with information on both sides of the paper. Exhibit 23 illustrates such a handout based on Jane's research. A comparison with her full report in appendix A will reveal Jane's inclusion of the most essential information. Notice the space provided for Jane's e-mail address and institutional mailing address, should anyone wish to communicate with her about this

EXHIBIT 23 *Concise report for distribution*

Effects of Offering After-Meal Candy on Restaurant Tipping

Jane Doe*
(Institutional affiliation and contact information)

*This report is based on a poster of the same title, which I presented at
(the name of the meeting, location of meeting, and date of presentation).*

Background and Hypotheses

More than two million people in the U.S. work as waiters and waitresses in restaurants (Bureau of Labor Statistics, 2010–2011). As tips are important to the livelihood of most servers, knowledge about the conditions that can affect tipping practices is valuable. Empirical research has demonstrated that a variety of techniques used by servers can increase tipping, such as (a) briefly touching a diner twice on the palm of the hand (Hornik, 1992); (b) giving a diner who is sitting alone a large, open-mouth smile (Tidd & Lockard, 1978); (c) squatting to the eye level of diners (Lynn & Mynier, 1993); (d) introducing oneself by one's first name at the initial visit to the table (Garrity & Degelman, 1990); and (e) writing "thank you" or drawing a happy face on the check (Rind & Bordia, 1995, 1996).

These techniques seem to have in common that the servers are doing something that may increase customers' impressions of friendliness. This study examined another such technique in a randomized experiment, guided by the following three hypotheses:

1. Proceeding on the assumption that presenting customers with a chocolate candy with the check would be viewed as a gesture of friendliness, this *1-piece condition* was hypothesized to increase tipping, in comparison with a no-candy *control condition*.

2. Assuming this effect is cumulative, it was hypothesized that presenting two pieces of chocolate candy with the check (called the *2-piece condition*) would further increase tipping.

3. As people often feel obligated to reciprocate when they have received a favor (Regan, 1971), it was hypothesized that creating the impression that the favor of a second candy was a generous impulse on the part of the server would increase tipping even more (the *1+1 condition*).

Method

A waitress in an upscale restaurant in central New Jersey was provided with a basket of wrapped miniature chocolates, which (in all but the control condition) she brought to the table when presenting the check. She was also given a shuffled stack of 80 index cards, each indicating the particular condition, and the waitress then drew a card blindly from her apron pocket when it was time to present the check. In the *control condition,* she presented the check, thanked the dining party, and left the table. In the *1-piece condition,* she offered each person 1 chocolate candy of his or her choice, then thanked everyone and left. In the *2-piece condition,* she offered each person 2 candies, then thanked everyone and left. In the *1+1 condition,* she offered each person 1 candy and said, "Oh, have another piece" (thus making it appear that the favor was a generous afterthought); she then thanked everyone and left. Once the dining party had left the restaurant, the waitress recorded (on the card used to determine the treatment condition) the amount of the tip, the amount of the bill before taxes, and the party size.

Results

The dependent variable was the tip percentage (i.e., the amount of the tip divided by the amount of the check before taxes, and then multiplied by 100). The table below summarizes the results in each condition; it shows the mean (M) tip percentage, the 95% confidence interval around M, the standard deviation (SD), and the number (n) of dining parties in each condition:

EXHIBIT 23   *Continued*

Results	Treatment conditions			
	Control	1-piece condition	2-piece condition	1+1 condition
Mean (M)	18.95	19.59	21.62	22.99
95% CI	$M \pm 0.70$	$M \pm 0.82$	$M \pm 1.17$	$M \pm 1.02$
SD	1.46	1.71	2.45	2.43
Sample size (n)	20	20	20	20

Tip percentages in the experimental and control conditions were compared by means of t tests and the pooled error term of $S^2 = 4.45$ ($df = 76$). These t tests were statistically significant for the comparison of (a) the 2-piece condition and the control and (b) the 1+1 piece condition and the control (p values $< .0001$, effect size rs of $.54$ and $.70$, respectively), but not for (c) the 1-piece condition and the control ($p = .17$ one-tailed, effect size $r = .15$). A more powerful test was also possible because it was predicted that the tip percentage would increase from the control to the 1-piece to the 2-piece to the 1+1 condition. Addressing this prediction by a linear contrast (lambda weights of $-3, -1, +1, +3$ for those 4 conditions, respectively) resulted in $F(1,76) = 44.97$, $p = 3.1^{-9}$, and the effect size $r = .61$ (the 95% CI ranged from $r = .45$ to $.73$).

Conclusions

The observed pattern of tip percentages (and the linear contrast) was consistent with the prediction that the offer of a token gift of miniature chocolate candy would increase tipping, that offering two candies would increase it further, and that a "generous impulse" offer of a second candy would increase tipping the most. Nonetheless, further research is needed to explore the generalizability of these results, and additional study is also needed to confirm the presumed roles of friendliness and generosity.

References

Bureau of Labor Statistics. (2010–2011). *Occupational outlook handbook.* Information retrieved from http://www.bls.gov/oco/ocos162.htm

Garrity, K., & Degelman, D. (1990). Effect of server introduction on restaurant tipping. *Journal of Applied Social Psychology, 20,* 168–172. doi:10.1111/j.1559-1816.1990.tb00405x

Hornik, J. (1992). Tactile stimulation and consumer response. *Journal of Consumer Research, 19,* 449–458. Retrieved from http://www.jstor.org/stable/2489401

Lynn, M., & Mynier, K. (1993). Effect of server posture on restaurant tipping. *Journal of Applied Social Psychology, 23,* 678–685. doi:10.111/j.1559-1816.1993.tb01109.x

Regan, D. T. (1971). Effects of a favor and liking on compliance. *Journal of Experimental Social Psychology, 7,* 627–639. doi:10.1016/0022-1031(71)90025-4

Rind, B., & Bordia, P. (1995). Effect of server's "thank you" and personalization on restaurant tipping. *Journal of Applied Social Psychology, 25,* 745–751. doi:10.1111/j.1559-1816.1995.tb01772.x

Rind, B., & Bordia, P. (1996). Effect on restaurant tipping of male and female servers drawing a happy, smiling face on the backs of customers' checks. *Journal of Applied Social Psychology, 26,* 218–225. doi:10.1111/j.1559-1816.1916.tb01847.x

Tidd, K., & Lockard, J. (1978). Monetary significance of the affiliative smile: A case for reciprocal altruism. *Bulletin of the Psychometric Society, 11,* 344–346.

[*]This research was performed to satisfy a course requirement in Dr. Bruce Rind's research methods class at (name of college or university). I would like to thank Dr. Rind for his guidance throughout this project, and I thank the owner of the restaurant and the server (both of whom requested anonymity) for making it possible to conduct this study.

research. Although her poster in Exhibits 21 and 22 did not contain a list of references, the handout in Exhibit 23 does.

Jane did not use a ragged right margin or double spacing; instead she designed her brief report to resemble a published paper. Experimenting with the final format used in the sample paper in Exhibit 23, Jane was interested in conserving space so the report would fit neatly on both sides of a single piece of paper. Of course, Jane's primary objective was to give people a clear, accurate, precise understanding of how her research was done, what she found, and what she concluded. She also needed to provide sufficient information to let readers reach their own conclusions and, if they wished, to analyze the results based on the detailed information that she provided.

Finally, take with you a manila envelope, labeled "HANDOUTS." Slip 50 or more copies of your concise report inside, and attach it to the poster board, making your research readily available to visitors who would like a copy.

A

Jane Doe's Research Report

RESTAURANT TIPPING

Pages are numbered consecutively, beginning with the title page, and contain a short heading (called the page header) of two or three words from the title.

1

Effects of Offering After-Meal Candy on Restaurant Tipping

Jane Doe

(Name of College or University)

The title, student's name and college are centered between the left and right margins (8.3).

Use a serif font, such as Times New Roman, with 12-point font size.

Author Note

I have written this report of my original research to satisfy the requirements in Dr. Bruce Rind's

Research Methods course (Psych 333). I would like to acknowledge the generous assistance of

the owner of the restaurant where this research was conducted and the server who helped me by

putting the treatment conditions into practice. Both requested anonymity but asked that I share

my findings with them.

The student take responsibility for the originality of the paper and also acknowledges assistance.

Contact information.

If there are any questions about this study or this research report, I can be reached at (provide an

e-mail address or other contact information, and alternative contact information if you anticipate a

change of address in the near future).

Leave margins of at least one inch at the top, bottom, and both sides.

(Indicate the date you submitted this report to the instructor.)

Date the paper is submitted to the instructor.

The abstract is not indented.

The abstract begins on a new page.

Abstract

Previous research findings were consistent with the idea that restaurant servers can increase their tips by simple techniques that create an impression of the server's friendliness. The experiment reported here was inspired by this idea. The general procedure consisted of having a server offer the diners an after-meal candy (i.e., a miniature chocolate) when presenting the check to them. In the *1-piece condition,* the server offered each member of the dining party one chocolate candy of his or her choice, and my prediction was that the tip percentage would be greater in this condition than in the control condition. In the *2-piece condition,* the server offered each diner two candies, and the prediction was a further increase in the tip percentage. In the *1 + 1 condition,* the server offered each diner one candy and then said, "Oh, have another piece"; this condition was intended to emphasize the server's generosity and friendliness and was predicted to result in the largest tip percentage. In the *control condition,* the server presented the check but brought no candies to the table. Though tip percentages in the control group differed significantly only from the 2-piece and 1 + 1 conditions, there was, as hypothesized, an increase in tipping percentages from the control to the 1-piece to the 2-piece to the 1 + 1 condition. The linear trend was significant at $p < .0001$, the effect size was $r = .61$, and the 95% confidence interval ranged from $r_{\text{effect size}} = .45$ to .73. The limitations to the study and suggestions for further research are discussed.

The abstract, which is written after the rest of the paper has been written, is a concise summary of the paper (8.4).

In research reports, the abstract tells why the research was done, what was hypothesized, the findings, and what else appears in the discussion.

The text begins on a new page and opens with a repetition of the title.

3

Effects of Offering After-Meal Candy on Restaurant Tipping

More than two million people in the United States work as waiters and waitresses who serve in restaurants (Bureau of Labor Statistics, 2010–2011). Although they are generally paid for their service by their employers, their major source of income is usually the tips they receive from the dining parties (Lynn & Mynier, 1993). Because tips are important to the livelihood of most servers (i.e., waiters and waitresses), knowledge about conditions that affect customers' tipping practices is valuable. Several studies have examined the conditions hypothesized to affect tipping behavior. Such studies have shown that servers can increase their tipping percentages by simple techniques (Lynn, 1996).

Some of these techniques involve interpersonal action on the part of the server, such as smiling at or touching the diner. Hornik (1992) had three waitresses at two restaurants not touch the diners, touch them for half a second on the shoulder, or touch them twice on the palm of the hand for half a second each time. The monetary values of the tips ranged from 12% to 14% to 17% in those three conditions, respectively. Tidd and Lockard (1978) had a waitress present a large, open-mouthed smile or a small closed-mouthed smile to diners sitting alone. In the first condition, diners tipped on average more than twice as much as in the second condition. Lynn and Mynier (1993) had servers bend to the eye level of their customers or stand erect during the initial visit to the table; bending down resulted in increased tips. Garrity and Degelman (1990) reported that a server earned higher tips when introducing herself by her first name during her initial visit to the table (23% average tip) than when she did not introduce herself (15% average tip).

Other techniques reported as effective used an indirect stimulus. Rind and Bordia (1996) had two servers either draw or not draw a happy face on the backs of customers' checks before presenting them. The happy face resulted in increased tips for the female server but not for the male server, for whom the customers may have stereotypically dismissed this practice as gender-inappropriate. Rind and Bordia (1995) also found that writing "thank you" on the backs of checks resulted in an increase in tips from 16% to 18%. McCall and Belmont (1995) had servers present

---

Institutional author (3.3.1).

Indent the first line of every paragraph (8.2).

Double-space every line.

Writing the opening paragraph (7.3).

Leave the right margin ragged (8.2).

The student uses the past tense to report studies that were done in the past (7.12).

Semi-colon (7.16.3).

Coauthors of cited work (3.3.5).

Double quotation marks are because "thank you" is the verbatim expression used.

RESTAURANT TIPPING   4

checks either on a tray with credit card emblems on it or on a tray with no emblems; the tipping
percentages were higher in the first condition.

These techniques, except for the last one, would seem to have in common that the servers
behaved in ways that seemed friendly. The experiment described here explored another technique
to create the impression of server friendliness. When presenting the check to the dining party, the
server sometimes offered a treat of assorted miniature chocolates. Three hypotheses were tested.
First, on the assumption that the treat would be perceived by diners as a gesture of friendliness, it
was predicted that the presentation of the treat would elicit higher tipping than in the no-candy
control condition. Second, on the further assumption that this effect is cumulative (up to a point),
it was predicted that offering more than one candy would stimulate tipping even more. Third, it
was predicted that creating the impression that a candy treat was a special favor reflecting the
server's impulsive generosity and friendliness would increase the tipping still further. This third
prediction was based on Regan's (1971) conclusion that individuals feel especially obligated to
return a favor to the person perceived to be responsible for the favor.

Introduction concludes with the student's hypotheses (4.4).

Method

All major sections of the text follow without a break.

Participants

How to format headings (8.5).

The participants consisted of 80 evening dining parties at an upscale restaurant in central
New Jersey, with $n = 20$ dining parties in each treatment condition. The total number of diners
was 293, with a mean of 3.67 per dining party ($SD = 1.97$); the size of the dining parties ranged
from 2 to 12. The server, a waitress, implemented the four experimental conditions described
below.

Materials

The server was provided with a small wicker basket that was filled with assorted wrapped
miniature chocolates. The chocolates were of four types: (a) dark chocolate, (b) milk chocolate,
(c) rice-and-chocolate, and (d) peanut butter-and-chocolate. A stack of index cards, thoroughly

Writing the method section (4.5).

shuffled beforehand, was placed in the server's apron pocket. Each card described one of the four

conditions of the experiment.

Design and Procedure

When it was time for her to present the check, the server reached into her apron pocket

and blindly selected an index card. In the control condition, the card instructed the server simply

to present the check, not to bring the basket of candy, and to thank the dining party and leave the

table immediately to avoid any nonessential interaction. In the three other conditions, the server

was to take along the basket of candy when presenting the check. In the 1-piece condition, the

server was to offer each person in the dining party one miniature chocolate of his or her choice,

then to thank the diners after their selection of candies and to leave the table. In the 2-piece

condition, the server was to offer each person in the dining party two miniature chocolates, then

to thank the diners after their selection and to leave the table. In the 1+ 1 condition, the server was

to offer one chocolate and say, "Oh, have another piece," implying that the favor of a second

piece reflected the server's generous afterthought; the server then thanked the diners and left the

table. After each dining party left the restaurant, the server recorded (on the card used to

determine the treatment condition) the amount of the tip, the amount of the check before taxes,

and the party size.

Writing the results section (4.6).

Results

Scoring and Calculations

Once all this information had been collected, I calculated the tip percentages by dividing

the amount of the tip by the amount of the check before taxes; I then multiplied the result by 100

to yield a percentage. The raw data and a description of the analyses can be found in the appendix

at the end of this report. I used a computer program to perform the overall calculations, and I used

a scientific calculator for some analyses. The reason that I chose to do some analyses by hand on

a calculator was that the procedures were unavailable on the computer program.

Overall Findings

RESTAURANT TIPPING   6

Basic data. Table 1 shows the average tip percentages in the four conditions, indicated by the means (*M*) of the columns of values shown in the appendix. As was predicted, the mean tip percentage increased from the control group (the no-candy condition) to the 1-piece condition, to the 2-piece condition, and to the 1 + 1 condition. Also shown in this table are a set of values that, added to and subtracted from the means, indicate the upper and lower limits, respectively, of the 95% confidence intervals. Below that row of values are the standard deviation (*SD*) and then the number of dining parties (*n*) in each condition. For example, for the control group, there is a 95% probability that the estimated population mean falls between 18.95 - 0.70 = 18.25 (lower limit of the estimated population mean) and 18.95 + 0.70 = 19.65 (upper limit of the estimated population mean).

Omnibus *F* test. Although an overall analysis of variance (ANOVA) did not address my previously stated predictions, I performed such an analysis for two reasons. One was that it was another way to obtain the mean square error (*MSE*) and thereby served as a check on my other calculations (in the appendix of this report). The other reason was that, given the overall ANOVA used to compute the omnibus *F*, I could create a summary table showing how the sum of squares (*SS*) of the contrast *F* test can be carved out of the overall between-groups *SS* (shown in Table 2). The omnibus *F* (numerator *df* = 3, denominator *df* = 76) was 15.51, $p = 5.8^{-8}$, the same result that I would have obtained had the four groups been in any other order.

Focused Statistical Tests

I tested the predictions associated with the three hypotheses in this study by three focused statistical tests[1], with the following results:

Hypothesis 1. The first prediction was that the tipping behavior would be greater in the 1-piece than in the control condition. Table 1 shows the direction of the means to be consistent with this prediction. However, an independent-sample *t* test comparing the two groups was not statistically significant even with a one-tailed *p*, where *t*(76) = .95 and one-tailed *p* = .17. The

What does the APA Manual consider a "sufficient set of statistics" (6.5)?

Use of footnotes (8.8).

justification for a one-tailed p was that I predicted the direction of the effect to be in one tail of the t distribution. The corresponding effect size r, obtained from the t statistic, was .15, and 95% CI [-.17, .44], which leaves open the possibility of a small effect in the opposite direction from that predicted in the interval containing the population effect size.

Hypothesis 2. On the assumption that the effect of the server's gift giving on subsequent tipping is cumulative, the second prediction was that the tipping would be still greater in the 2-piece than in the control condition. The means in Table 1 are again consistent with the hypothesis. The difference between the control condition and the 2-piece condition was significant with $t(76) = 3.99$, $p = 7.5^{-5}$ one-tailed. The effect size r associated with this result was .54, 95% CI [.28, 73]. There is a 95% probability that the range of values contains the population value of the effect size r reflecting membership in the control group versus the 2-piece group as a predictor of observed tip percentages.

Hypothesis 3. The third prediction, which I derived from reciprocity theory, was that creating the impression that the server was spontaneously generous (the $1 + 1$ condition) would produce the greatest increment in tipping. The t test comparing the $1 + 1$ condition with the control group yielded $t(76) = 6.05$, $p = 2.5^{-8}$ one-tailed, 95% CI [.50, .83].

Contrast F test. To provide a focused evaluation of the increase in tipping from control to 1-piece to 2-piece to the $1 + 1$ condition, I computed a linear contrast. In a contrast analysis, the prediction of interest is represented by fixed coefficients (lambda weights) that must sum to zero. In this case, the coefficients that represent the linear prediction were -3, -1, + 1, + 3 for the increase from the control to the 1-piece to the 2-piece to the $1+ 1$ groups. Results are summarized in Table 2, which shows the linear contrast that was carved out of the overall between-groups SS. As indicated in the table, the linear contrast F, with 1 and 76 degrees of freedom, was 44.97, with $p = 3.1^{-9}$ and $r_{effect size} = .61$, 95% CI [.45, .73].

Discussion

Margin notes:

Third-level heading (8.5).

Statistical test results and effect sizes are rounded to two decimal places in the text.

Thinking about effect sizes and p values (6.5).

Lower and upper limits of confidence interval (see Chapter 6).

Use of scientific notation (4.6).

Common statistical symbols are defined in Exhibit 16 (see section 6.1).

RESTAURANT TIPPING   8

Discussion
begins by
noting the
predictions
and the
results.

It was hypothesized that the server's offering an after-meal candy to restaurant diners at the same time she presented the check would have the effect of encouraging tipping. It was also hypothesized that the more candy offered, the greater the resulting tip. The largest tip percentage was predicted for the condition in which the server was intended to be perceived as spontaneously generous. The four group means (Table 1) were consistent with these hypotheses and predictions. The linear contrast F was consistent with the implied linear increase in tipping. The independent-sample t test comparing the control and 1-piece conditions was not statistically significant. The power of the t test that I used to detect the effect between the control group and 1-piece conditions was much lower than the recommended level of .80.

Writing the
discussion
section (4.7).

There are many ways to improve statistical power, including strengthening the treatments and increasing the sample size. One way to strengthen the treatments would have been to increase the difference between the numbers of candies offered, which would also have allowed a further exploration of the idea of a cumulative effect. Because this study had to be completed well before the end of this semester, there was not time to conduct an exploratory replication. Had there been time to replicate the study, another way to improve statistical power would have been to estimate the overall p value after pooling the results meta-analytically.

Statistical
power is
explained in
Chapter 6
(see section
6.5).

Further research is needed to examine the reliability of the findings and the separate and interacting roles of reciprocity and friendliness. There is also no direct evidence that perceived friendliness was a mediating variable. This lack of direct evidence could be addressed in future research by asking some diners to rate the server's friendliness after the bill has been paid and they are about to leave the restaurant. It is also important in future research to use more than just one server and to use male as well as female servers, other types of restaurants, and other token gifts besides chocolates. There may also be regional differences in tipping.

Concludes
with the
limitations
and the
implications
for future
research.

*The references begin
on a new page.*

RESTAURANT TIPPING   9

References

Bureau of Labor Statistics. (2010–2011). *Occupational outlook handbook.* Retrieved from

http://www.bls.gov/oco/ocos162.htm

Garrity, K., & Degelman, D. (1990). Effect of server introduction on restaurant tipping. *Journal

of Applied Social Psychology, 20,* 168–172. doi:10.1111/j.1559-1816.1990.tb00405.x

Hornik, J. (1992). Tactile stimulation and consumer response. *Journal of Consumer Research, 19,*

449–458. Retrieved from http://www.jstor.org/stable/2489401

Lynn, M. (1996). Seven ways to increase servers' tips. *Cornell Hotel and Restaurant

Administration Quarterly, 37*(3), 24–29. doi:10.1177/001088049603700315

Lynn, M., & Mynier, K. (1993). Effect of server posture on restaurant tipping. *Journal of Applied

Social Psychology, 23,* 678–685. doi:10.111/j.1559-1816.1993.tb01109.x

McCall, M., & Belmont, H. J. (1995). Credit card insignia and tipping: Evidence for an

associative link. *Journal of Applied Psychology, 8,* 609–613. doi:10.1037/0021-9010.81.5.609

Regan, D. T. (1971). Effects of a favor and liking on compliance. *Journal of Experimental Social

Psychology, 7,* 627–639. doi:10.1016/0022-1031(71)90025-4

Rind, B., & Bordia, P. (1995). Effect of server's "thank you" and personalization on restaurant

tipping. *Journal of Applied Social Psychology, 25,* 745–751.

doi:10.1111/j.1559-1816.1995.tb01772.x

Rind, B., & Bordia, P. (1996). Effect on restaurant tipping of male and female servers drawing a

happy, smiling face on the backs of customers' checks. *Journal of Applied Social Psychology,

26,* 218–225. doi:10.1111/j.1559-1816.1916.tb01847.x

Rosnow, R. L., & Rosenthal, R. (2008). *Beginning behavioral research: A conceptual primer* (6th

ed.). Upper Saddle River, NJ: Pearson Prentice Hall.

Tidd, K., & Lockard, J. (1978). Monetary significance of the affiliative smile: A case for

reciprocal altruism. *Bulletin of the Psychometric Society, 11,* 344–346.

*Digital version
of work by
institutional
author (3.4.4).*

*Pagination
by journal
volume
(3.4.16).*

*Pagination
by issue
(3.4.23).*

*Digital Object
Identifier
(2.4).*

*No period
after doi
(3.4).*

*More than
one edition
(3.4.1).*

*Hanging indents
are used for all
references.*

*Every article and book
that was cited in the
report is listed in the
references, and every
reference is cited in the
report.*

The footnotes begin on a new page.

Footnotes

Italics for these defined terms.

[1]The term *focused tests* means that certain statistical tests are precisely oriented to the prediction, that is, as opposed to *omnibus tests*, which are diffuse and unfocused. All F tests with numerator $df = 1$ and all t tests are examples of focused tests, whereas all F tests with numerator $df > 1$ are omnibus tests. When there is a specific prediction regarding the direction of the results and the prediction involves more than two groups or conditions, focused tests are more powerful and more precise than omnibus tests (Rosnow & Rosenthal, 2008).

The student uses the present tense to define terms (7.12).

The footnotes are part of the end material (4.9).

*Each table begins
on a new page.*

Table 1

Mean Tip Percentage (M), 95% Confidence Interval (CI) of Mean, Standard Deviation (SD), and

Number of Sampled Dining Parties (n)

*See Exhibit
16 in section
6.1 for
definitions
of symbols.*

*How to format
tables (8.9).*

Results	Treatment conditions			
	Control	1 piece	2 pieces	1 + 1 piece
M	18.95	19.59	21.62	22.99
95% CI	$M \pm 0.70$	$M \pm 0.82$	$M \pm 1.17$	$M \pm 1.02$
SD	1.46	1.71	2.45	2.43
Sample size (n)	20	20	20	20

Note. The mean (*M*) value in each condition is the average tip percentage in the condition. The

95% CI is the confidence interval around the estimate of the population mean. Tip percentages

were calculated for each dining party by division of the tip amount by the bill amount before

taxes, then multiplication by 100. The standard deviation (*SD*) is the variability of $n = 20$ tip

percentages around the sample mean.

*Statistical tables
in research reports
are intended to
summarize the data
and analyses.*

The APA style is to round values to two decimal places in tables to make the tables easier to read.

Table 2

Analysis of Variance with Linear Contrast

Source	SS	df	MS	F	$r_{\text{effect size}}$
Between groups	207.06	3	69.02	15.51*	–
Linear contrast	200.12	1	200.12	44.97*	.61
Noncontrast	6.94	2	3.47	0.78	–
Within error	338.22	76	(4.45)		

Note. The value in parentheses (under *MS*) is the mean square error (*MSE*). No effect sizes are reported in this table for the two omnibus *F* tests (i.e., numerator *df* > 1) as "the rule of thumb is to report effect sizes for focused statistical procedures and not for omnibus statistical procedures, because effect size indicators are far more interpretable for focused procedures" (Rosnow & Rosenthal, 2008, p. 321).

Asterisks for notes to tables (4.6 and 8.7).

*p < .0001.

168   APPENDIX A

Appendix begins
on a new page.

RESTAURANT TIPPING   13

Appendix

Shown below are the tip percentages for each dining party, obtained by division of the tip

amount by the check amount before taxes, and then multiplication by 100:

	No candy	1 piece	2 pieces	1+1 pieces
	18.92	18.87	22.78	17.38
	18.43	20.49	15.81	23.38
	18.67	17.54	19.16	25.05
	18.27	19.35	19.01	21.83
	18.92	20.65	21.60	24.43
	17.84	19.17	18.45	21.11
	19.57	19.73	23.41	25.09
	19.12	17.88	21.37	24.35
	18.67	21.00	22.01	25.37
	22.94	22.33	20.65	21.87
	19.26	19.75	20.92	23.87
	19.49	20.79	26.17	22.62
	19.12	20.52	23.31	26.73
	15.90	22.66	23.85	21.81
	19.29	18.60	22.30	23.60
	19.12	18.60	21.34	23.06
	21.70	20.07	18.89	24.05
	16.72	14.64	23.47	16.72
	17.75	19.01	25.69	22.43
	19.35	20.08	22.12	25.08
M	18.9525	19.5865	21.6155	22.9915
S	1.4948	1.7525	2.5092	2.4898
σ	1.4570	1.7081	2.4457	2.4268

The purpose of this appendix is to provide the instructor with detailed information that does not belong in the results section but elaborates the results (8.10).

All the formulas and the discussion in this appendix are based on the instructor's lectures

and the course textbook. The 95% confidence intervals (CI) for group means were obtained by

use of the following formula:

RESTAURANT TIPPING   14

$$M \pm \frac{(t_{(.05)})(S)}{\sqrt{n}},$$

and $t_{(.05)} = 2.093$ for $n - 1 = 19$. For example, for the control group, where $S = 1.4948$, the 95% CI

was

$$\pm \frac{(2.093)(1.4948)}{\sqrt{20}} = \pm 0.6996.$$

Subtracting and adding 0.6996 from and to the $M = 18.9525$ indicated a 95% probability that the

estimated population mean fell between LL = 18.2529 and UL = 19.6521.

The pooled error term (*MSE*) is the average of the squared S values, so $S^2_{pooled} = 4.4502$.

The sum of squares between groups ($SS_{between}$) is the total squared weighted deviations (weighted

by sample size, n_k) between the four condition means (M_k) and the grand mean of $M_G = 20.7865$:

$$\begin{aligned} SS_{between} &= \sum [n_k (M_k - M_G)] \\ &= 20(18.9525 - 20.7865)^2 + 20(19.5865 - 20.7865)^2 \\ &\quad + 20(21.6155 + 20.7865)^2 + 20(21.9915 - 20.7865)^2 \\ &= 207.0564. \end{aligned}$$

In the summary ANOVA in Table 2, the omnibus F (numerator $df = 3$ and denominator

$df = 76$) was defined as follows:

$$F = \frac{SS_{between} / (k-1)}{S^2_{pooled}} = \frac{207.0564 / 3}{4.4502} = 15.5091.$$

Independent-sample t tests, using the pooled error above and $df = N - k$ (corresponding to

this mean square error term), compared the 1-piece versus control, the 2-piece versus control, and

the 1 + 1 piece versus control by the following formulas:

$$t = \frac{M_1 - M_2}{\sqrt{\left(\frac{1}{n_1} + \frac{1}{n_2}\right) S^2_{pooled}}} \quad \text{and} \quad r_{effect\,size} = \sqrt{\frac{t^2}{t^2 + df}},$$

where df for the effect size $r = n_1 + n_2 - 2$. When the data for the 1-piece versus control

comparison were substituted in these formulas, the analyses were

The results, although rounded to two decimal places in the text of the report, are reported more precisely in the appendix.

$$t = \frac{19.5865 - 18.9525}{\sqrt{\left(\frac{1}{20} + \frac{1}{20}\right)} 4.4502} = 0.9504 \text{ and } r_{effect\ size} = \sqrt{\frac{(.9504)^2}{(.9504)^2 + 38}} = .1524.$$

Contrast weights for the hypothesized linear increase in tipping from control to 1-piece to 2-piece to 1 + 1 condition were -3, -1, + 1, + 3. Correlating the weights with the four group means yielded $r_{alerting} = .9831$. Squaring this value indicated the proportion of $SS_{between}$ that accounted for the linear contrast. Multiplying the squared alerting r (.9665) by $SS_{between}$ (207.0564) gave the sum of squares for the contrast (Table 2). The effect size r for the contrast was obtained as follows:

$$r_{effect\ size} = \sqrt{\frac{F_{contrast}}{F_{contrast} + F_{contrast}(df_{noncontrast}) + df_{within}}} = \sqrt{\frac{44.9688}{44.9688 + 0.7793(2) + 76}} = .6058.$$

The calculations are reported by the student in a way that walks the reader through the logical sequence, clearly explaining how the summary results in the report were obtained.

B

John Smith's Review Paper

Pages are numbered consecutively, beginning with the title page, and contain a short heading (called the page header) of two or three words from the title.

THE CONCEPT OF INTELLIGENCE   1

Amplification use of a colon in the title (7.16.3).

The Elusive Concept of Intelligence: Two Diverse Orientations

John Smith

(Name of College or University)

The title, student's name, and college are centered between the left and right margins (8.3).

Use a serif font, such as Times New Roman, with 12-point font size.

The student takes responsibility for the originality of the paper and also acknowledges assistance.

Author Note

I have written this review paper to satisfy the requirements in Dr. Anne Skleder's Psychological Testing course (Psych 222). I thank Professor Skleder for explaining the problem with the percentage-of-variance interpretation of effect size and directing me to the statistical reference cited in footnote 2. I thank Prof. Rosenthal at the University of California, Riverside, for permission to reproduce the graphic shown in Figure 1 (R. Rosenthal, personal communication, April 10, 2010).

Contact information.

If there are any questions about this literature review, I can be reached at (provide an e-mail address or other contact information, and alternative contact information if you anticipate a change of address in the near future).

Leave margins of at least one inch at the top, bottom, and both sides.

(Indicate the date you submitted this report to the instructor.)

Date the paper is submitted to the instructor.

THE CONCEPT OF INTELLIGENCE   2

Abstract

Although the study of intelligence has a long history in psychological and educational research, the

concept of intelligence remains one of the most elusive. Going back to the psychometric work of Charles

Spearman, many psychological and educational researchers have regarded intelligence as g-centered,

which means that they assume a general trait (g) lies at the core of every valid measure of intelligence.

More recently, leading researchers, such as Howard Gardner, Robert J. Sternberg, and Stephen J. Ceci,

have theorized the existence of distinct facets of intelligence that are not all g-centered. The purpose of

this review is to examine these two diverse theoretical orientations, with the focus on Gardner's theory of

multiple intelligences as a prominent example of the more recent orientation. I discuss criticisms and

rejoinders with respect to the theoretical notion of multiple intelligences, and the paper concludes with a

brief summation and overview of the principal theme of this review.

The abstract begins on a new page.

The abstract, which is written after the rest of the paper has been written, is a concise summary of the paper (8.4).

The text begins on a new page and opens with a repetition of the title.

THE CONCEPT OF INTELLIGENCE   3

Foreign phrases are not italicized see 8.6 on uses of italics.

The Elusive Concept of Intelligence: Two Diverse Orientations

There is an old French saying that goes: "The more things change, the more they remain the same" (Plus ça change, plus c'est la même chose). The saying seems to apply to the concept of intelligence. By tradition, intelligence is said to include "abstract reasoning, problem-solving ability, and capacity to acquire knowledge," and many experts in the field of intelligence "also believe that memory and mental speed are part of intelligence" (Nisbett, 2009, p. 4). There are, however, experts who argue that IQ tests overlook other "intelligences" (e.g., Gardner, 1983; Sternberg, 1985). In the textbook we use in this course, the authors remark that "of all the major concepts in the field of testing, intelligence is among the most elusive" (Kaplan & Saccuzzo, 2009, p. 230). Much has changed in the way that the experts conceive of intelligence, but what has remained the same is the elusiveness of the concept.

The purpose of this review is to examine two theoretical orientations regarding the nature of intelligence. One orientation, the traditional view, is the idea that a general trait (symbolized as g) defines the core of every valid measure of intelligence. The second orientation, the more recent view, is the idea that there are distinct types of intelligence that are not g-centered. I begin by discussing two issues in intelligence testing. I then turn to the g-centered (or g-centric) view of intelligence and, next, to the more recent orientation, which I describe as "multiplex" (defined later). The focus of my discussion of the multiplex orientation is the work of Howard Gardner as a seminal example. After discussing criticisms of the multiplex orientation, I conclude by noting the trend toward broad, interdisciplinary work on the elusive concept of intelligence.

Each major section in the text follows the previous section without a break.

Two Issues in Intelligence Assessment

Before a specific discussion of the two theoretical orientations that are the focus of this review, it is important to note that the assessment of intelligence is problematic to some degree. A number of years ago, in an encyclopedia article on intelligence testing, Gilbert (1971) stated, "Since human beings are complex, observing or measuring intelligence is no simple matter" (p. 129). Gilbert gave the following case in point:

Writing the opening paragraph (7.3).

Abbreviation for exempli gratia ("for example"). see 7.16.1 for other examples.

Citation of the author's name at beginning of a clause and a sentence (3.3.1).

THE CONCEPT OF INTELLIGENCE   4

Observe star quarterback Joe, for example. It is Friday afternoon, last period, social studies. The

teacher, Mr. Jones, is expounding his pet topic, "The Obsolete Electoral College: Or Is It?," while

For quotations within a block quotation, see 7.17.

Joe's mind is on tomorrow's game. When Mr. Jones asks, "Joe, what do you think?" Joe is about

to say, "Pass to the right end," but he returns to reality and mumbles something about not being

sure of the answer. (p. 129)

As Gilbert (1971) explained, someone who did not know Joe might have quickly concluded from his

mumbled response that he was neither especially bright nor motivated. In fact, Joe was bright *and*

strongly motivated. However, his motivation and intellect were consumed by his anticipation of the next

day's football game and his role as quarterback, not by Mr. Jones's pet topic. Joe was running complex

football plays through his mind. "Pass to the right end" was almost his reply to the teacher's question.

Thus, as Gilbert (1971) stated, "observing or measuring intelligence is no simple matter" (p. 129).

A second basic problem in the assessment of intelligence concerns the generalizability of

population norms in the tables of values that are available for standard tests of intelligence. Such norms

are used to decide where an individual's performance falls relative to the performance of the general

population. Suppose a researcher with a limited budget has developed a set of items for a new test of

Footnote (8.8).

academic IQ.[1] To establish the population norms, the researcher issues a call for volunteers to take the

test. However, it has been found that people who volunteer to participate in research may not be entirely

representative of the general population, and "When there is a significant relationship reported, and very

often there is, it is overwhelmingly likely to show volunteers to be more intelligent" (they score higher)

than the general population (Rosenthal & Rosnow, 2009, p. 727). This idea is illustrated in Figure 1 (at

Mention of figure (8.9).

the end of this paper), which shows, approximately, the positive bias predicted to result from using a

volunteer sample instead of doing random sampling from a national probability data set. The distribution

labeled X represents a theoretical normal distribution of the IQs of volunteers for the researcher's IQ test,

Abbreviation that does not need to be spelled out (7.16.2).

and the distribution labeled Y represents a theoretical distribution of the IQs of people in general. The

difference between the estimated mean of X and the true value mean of Y reflects the amount of bias in

the volunteer sample. It implies that the use of volunteers could lead to underestimates of vital population parameters. In this case, Figure 1 implies that standardizing the new test only on volunteers will probably

result in overestimated population norms.

First-level heading is centered, whereas second-level heading is flush left (8.5).

The Traditional Theoretical Orientation

Early Contributors

I turn now to the traditional theoretical orientation, a view that is sometimes described as *g*-

centered or *g*-centric. The origin of this view goes all the way back to the intelligence-testing movement

and the measures developed by Sir Francis Galton (1822–1911) in England and James Cattell (1860–

1944) in the United States (Gilbert, 1971). The objective was to predict school performance. It was

"theorized that intelligence depended upon sensory input and speed of reaction time; hence sensorimotor

tests should reveal significant differences between individuals in ability to behave intelligently" (Gilbert,

1971, p. 130). Galton came up with the idea of the correlation coefficient, a concept that was then

mathematically refined by the statistician Karl Pearson. One by-product of the development of the

correlation coefficient was that it was shown that the early measures used in the intelligence-testing

movement were not strongly correlated with school performance. Early paper-and-pencil scales were

developed by Alfred Binet and Henri Simon in France "to help diagnose the existence of mental

retardation" (Gilbert, 1971, p. 130). Gilbert (1971) also noted that although "intelligence testing

originated in Europe in at least two separate movements . . . the greatest development of intelligence tests

bears a distinct 'made in U.S.A.'" (p. 130). Henry Goddard first adapted Binet's testing method for the

American Marketplace, but the Stanford-Binet adaptation and its use by Lewis Terman in 1916 (revised in

1937) are far better known. In 1939, David Wechsler, at Bellevue Hospital in New York, developed an

individual intelligence test for adults. This test, called the Wechsler Adult Intelligence Scale, or WAIS,

was revised in 1955 (Kaplan & Saccuzzo, 2009).

Second-level heading (8.5).

The *g*-Centered View

Influenced by the psychometric contributions of Charles Spearman (1927), who viewed

intelligence as a general factor (*g*), psychological and educational researchers in the intelligence test

movement accepted the *g*-centric idea. A number of prominent researchers, such as Arthur Jensen (1969),

No break, because this is another major section of the text.

Quotation within a quotation (7.17).

THE CONCEPT OF INTELLIGENCE

6

argued that individual differences in g were largely attributable to genetic factors as opposed to the role of environmental and/or cultural influences. Child development researchers, inspired by the theoretical and empirical work of Jean Piaget, also argued for the idea of general structures of the mind, structures that developed in a similar way in all children (Siegler & Richards, 1982). In the 1990s, a controversial reanalysis of IQ test data by Herrnstein and Murray (1994), in a book entitled *The Bell Curve*, ignited a spirited debate about the role of g in the lives of individuals and in the larger social order.

Book title in text is italicized (8.6).

SAT is spelled out the first time it is used (7.16.2).

It has been argued that the Scholastic Assessment Test (SAT) is basically a surrogate measure of general intelligence (g) and that it can be used to predict cognitive functioning (Frey & Detterman, 2004). In one study, Frey and Detterman (2004) extracted a measure of g from the Armed Services Vocational Aptitude Battery and found the correlation with SAT scores to be $r = .82$ (.86 corrected for nonlinearity) in a sample of 917 subjects aged 14–21 from a national probability data set. In a second study, Frey and Detterman recruited 104 undergraduate students through the psychology subject pool in order to investigate the relationship between SAT scores and scores on another test, called Raven's Progressive Matrices (a test of reasoning skills), and found $r = .483$ (or .72 corrected for restricted range). Ceci (1996), not a proponent of the traditional orientation, argued that the traditional orientation can be reduced to "five easy facts" (p. 4). First, virtually all people tend to score relatively consistently on different tests of intelligence. Second, when a statistical procedure called factor analysis is used, there emerges a first principal component (g) that reflects the average correlation among the test scores, which is generally around .30. Third, g is considered a proxy for general intelligence. Fourth, there are impressive correlations between g and academic and social accomplishment. Fifth, intelligence is inherited to a considerable degree.

Ordinarily this result would be reported to two decimal places, but John reports .483 to be faithful to how it was reported in cited work.

Ceci (1996) then mounted an attack on the implications of each of the "five easy facts," arguing that a plausible alternative model existed for each fact. "Intelligence is a multifaceted set of abilities," Ceci stated, and any "specific facet might become more or less effective as a result of the physical, social, cultural, and historical contexts in which it has been crystallized and the contexts in which it is subsequently assessed" (p. 8). Recently, Nisbett (2009) argued that traditional g-centered "intelligence is

Quoted passage and page number.

THE CONCEPT OF INTELLIGENCE   7

highly modifiable by the environment" (p. 2). Nisbett added: "And whether a particular person's IQ—and academic achievement and occupational success—is going to be high or low very much depends on environmental factors that have nothing to do with genes" (p. 2). Another side to this argument is not whether *g*-centered intelligence is due to nature or nurture, but whether intelligence is more complex and multifaceted than what is summed up in *g*. Although controversy continues to surround the meaning of intelligence as well as its relationship to real-world skills, experts in psychology apparently agree on a list of "knowns" about intelligence (Neisser et al., 1966), such as Ceci's "five easy facts," although the implications are disputable.

When there are six or more coauthors, the first author's name followed by et al. is used in citation (3.3.7).

The Multiplex Theoretical Orientation

In the 1980s and 1990s, the idea of multiple intellectual aptitudes was taken in an exciting new direction by other prominent psychologists. Robert Sternberg (1990) has argued that the nature of the information processing measured by standard IQ tests is quite different from that involved in certain kinds of complex reasoning in everyday life. A fascinating case in point was Ceci and Liker's (1986) finding that skill in handicapping racehorses cannot be predicted from scores on the WAIS. Sternberg, Wagner, Williams, and Horvath (1995) stated that "even the most charitable estimates of the relation between intelligence test scores and real-world criteria such as job performance indicate that approxomately three-fourths of the variance in real-world performance is not accounted for by intelligence test performance" (p. 912).[2]

Four coauthors, first citation (3.3.6).

Footnote number.

Still, Sternberg et al.'s (1995) point is well taken and certainly supportive of the argument that intelligence consists of "various, relatively independent, abilities" (Gilbert, 1971, p. 129). Sternberg's (1985) "triarchic theory" and Ceci's (1996) "bioecological treatise" are representative of the exciting new direction of work on the elusive concept of intelligence. This theoretical orientation might be described as *multiplex*, inasmuch as it encompasses several distinct types of intelligence.[3] Another prime example of this orientation, the focus of the remainder of this review, is the theory of multiple intelligences proposed by Howard Gardner (1983).

Footnote number.

Gardner's Idea of Multiple Intelligences

Another major section of text, no break.

THE CONCEPT OF INTELLIGENCE   8

Eight Criteria of Intellectual Talents

Gardner (1983) argued against the assumption of a single general characteristic and used the term *intelligences* (plural) to convey the notion of multiple intellectual aptitudes. Gardner's general idea of intelligence was that it encompasses "the ability to solve problems, or to create products that are valued within one or more cultural settings" (p. x). He went on to argue that not every real-life skill should be considered under the label of *intelligence*, though any talent deemed "intellectual" must fit the following eight criteria:

1. The potential must exist to isolate the intelligence by brain damage.

2. Exceptional populations (such as savants) whose members manifest outstanding but uneven abilities should exhibit the distinctive existence of the particular type of intelligence.

3. There must be identifiable core operations, that is, basic information-processing operations that are unique to the particular abilities.

4. There must be a distinctive developmental history, that is, stages through which individuals pass, with individual differences in the ultimate levels of expertise achieved.

5. There should be locatable antecedents (more primitive, less integrated versions) of the intelligence in other species.

6. The intelligence must be open to experimental study, so that predictions of the construct can be subjected to empirical tests.

7. Although no single standardized test can measure the entirety of the abilities that are deemed intellectual, standardized tests should provide clues about the intelligence and should predict the performance of some tasks and not others.

8. It must be possible to capture the information content in the intelligence through a symbol system, for example, language or choreographed movements.

Seven Types of Intelligence

Using as a base the eight criteria listed above, Gardner argued the importance of studying people within the "normal" range of intelligence, and also of studying those who are gifted or expert in various

Page number of quote (3.3.3).

Numbering sets off the items for clarity.

Possessive citation (3.3.1).

THE CONCEPT OF INTELLIGENCE   9

domains valued by different cultures. Drawing on the criteria above and the research results from four

major disciplines (i.e., psychology, sociology, anthropology, and biology), Gardner (1983) initially

proposed the existence of the seven types of intelligence defined in Table 1 (i.e., logical-mathematical,

linguistic, spatial, bodily-kinesthetic, musical, intrapersonal, and interpersonal). Subsequently, he raised

the possibility of additional types of intelligence (Gardner, 1999), but this review focuses on his original

seven types.

    The examples noted in the second column of Table 1 draw partly on Gardner's work and also on

my own intuitive hypotheses. Traditional intelligence, which is language-based and easy to quantify by

conventional measures, encompasses what are described as logical-mathematical and linguistic

intelligence. It would seem these skills are also what Frey and Detterman (2004) extracted from the tests

they correlated with the SAT. As mentioned in the note to Table 1, the final two types of intelligences

(intrapersonal and interpersonal) are what Gardner collectively referred to as the "personal intelligences."

Using Gardner's (1983) idea of a developmental progression in interpersonal intelligence as a launching

point for a set of empirical studies, psychologists implied that the assessment of interpersonal intelligence

may be complicated by intrinsic differences in the cognitive complexity of intention–action combinations

that we experience in our everyday lives (Rosnow, Skleder, Jaeger, & Rind, 1994).

Independence of Abilities

    Crucial to Gardner's formulation is the assumption that the various intellectual "talents" are not

necessarily linked. Someone may perform poorly in one area (e.g., logical-mathematical intelligence) and

yet perform well in others (e.g., spatial intelligence). This discrepancy calls to mind the stereotype of the

brilliant but absent-minded scientist, who cannot find his or her car in the parking lot but can describe in

intricate detail the workings of atoms. Different intelligences can coexist and can also be measured quite

independently of one another, according to Gardner's theory. Because logical-mathematical and linguistic

intelligences are valued so highly in our society, tests designed to measure a variety of intelligences still

rely heavily on these particular skills to the exclusion of other intellectual talents, Gardner (1999) noted.

Abbreviation for id est ("that is"); see 7.16.1.

The student mentions the table note to call attention to it.

Second mention of SAT, which was previously spelled out.

Four coauthors (3.3.6).

See 7.16.1 for other abbreviations.

THE CONCEPT OF INTELLIGENCE   10

In other words, Gardner's argument is that conventional tests of intelligence measure essentially the same intelligences in only slightly different, and perhaps trivial, ways. Therefore, it is hardly surprising that Spearman (1927) found a medium-sized correlation among certain abilities (implying the *g* factor), so that individuals who score higher in verbal intelligence tend to score higher than average in reasoning ability. Knowing someone's linguistic intelligence, however, does not automatically tell us very much about the person's skills with people or music, or about the person's intellectual talents in any other realm, according to this argument.

The independence of abilities is also suggested by the fact that, although intelligence tests can predict school grades reasonably well, the tests are less useful in predicting routine successes outside the school setting. For example, barring low levels of traditional IQ, good managerial skills may be related more to the ability to manage oneself and the task completion of others, or to the ability to interpret the actions and intentions of others, than to the ability to score high on a standard IQ test or some surrogate measure of academic intelligence (Aditya & House, 2002; Sternberg, 1988). Sternberg (1988) referred to these extracurricular skills as "practical intelligence" and distinguished them from academic IQ (p. 211); such practical intelligence seems to depend heavily on what Gardner called the "personal intelligences."

Some Criticisms and Rejoinders

Nontraditional Orientation

Some criticisms of multiplex theories of intelligence appear to rest on the distinction between innate ability and performance skills that have been traditionally characterized as *talent* (Walters & Gardner, 1986). Ericsson and Charness (1994) argued that expert performance does not usually reflect innate abilities and capacities but is mediated predominantly by physiological adaptation and complex skills. Gardner's (1995) response was that the issue is not whether children are born with innate abilities or capacities, but whether a child who has begun to work in a domain finds skill and ease in performance that encourages the child to persevere in the effort. That most people do not usually think of performance skills as "intellectual" is just a red herring in this debate, the reflection of our continued attachment to the

Italics used for emphasis (8.6).

traditional idea of intelligence, Gardner argued. Sternberg (1990) noted that a person who has experienced

an injury that causes a loss of bodily-kinesthetic ability is not viewed as "mentally retarded."

In short, Gardner's argument is that all the forms of intelligence he proposed should be given

equal consideration with the logical-mathematical and linguistic forms so highly valued in Western

cultures (Walters & Gardner, 1986). As he put it, "When one revisits the psychological variable that has

been most intensively studied, that of psychometric intelligence or *g,* one finds little evidence to suggest

that sheer practice, whether deliberate or not, produces large ultimate differences in performance"

(Gardner, 1995, p. 802). Perhaps it is because so many experts have chosen to regard *g* and the "academic

intelligences" as more important than the personal intelligences that terms like *socially retarded* are not

common. Nonetheless, interest in social proclivities appears to be leading to increased attention to the

interplay of the personal intelligences and behavior in different situations, such as predicting achievement

or success in executive roles in organizations (e.g., Aditya & House, 2002).

Structure and Amenability to Operationalization and Assessment

Another criticism of multiplex theories of intelligence is that, given their seemingly amorphous

nature, there would appear to be unlimited possibilities of adding to the number of intelligences. As

noted, Gardner himself raised the possibility of more than seven intelligences and considered the original

seven "working hypotheses" that are fully amenable to revision after further investigation (Walters &

Gardner, 1986). For example, Gardner (1999) alluded to the "naturalist intelligence" of a Charles Darwin

and the "existential intelligence" of a postmodern philosopher. One may wonder whether these additions

might eventually be psychometrically reduced to general types, an idea that may suggest the return to a

(Spearman-like) general factor (as well as specific factors). However, whether this criticism is perceived

as reasonable probably depends on one's willingness to regard the concept of intelligence as even more

inclusive of human talents than it is now.

Also, it has been argued that the standard psychometric approach has the distinct advantage of

being more amenable to testing and measurement than is Gardner's theory of multiple intelligences.

Gardner, on the other hand, contended that his seven intelligences are measurable but that conventional

The student sets off each set of criticisms and rejoinders by a second-level heading within the major section (8.5).

THE CONCEPT OF INTELLIGENCE   12

tests are inadequate for the job. He proposed measurements that are closely linked to what people do in

their daily lives. For example, in applying his theory to education, Gardner (1991) reported assessing

children's intelligences by studying their school compositions, choice of activities in athletic events, and

other aspects of their behavior and cognitive processes. Although this approach is certainly more complex

and time-consuming than the older approach, such measurements are essential from the standpoint of

Gardner's theory.

Conclusions

Words used to illustrate are in italics (8.6).

Another major section of the text.

In everyday parlance, some people are *book smart,* a synonym for the *g*-centered type of

traditional academic intelligence. Some people are called *street smart,* a term implying that they are

intellectually shrewd in the ways of the world, another distinct type of intelligence. In theory, there are

other distinct types as well. For example, some people are said to have a "business savvy" or "political

Colloquial phrases in quotes.

sense" or "the ability to read people like a book," phrases implying intellectual abilities that involve

interpersonal aptitudes not directly assessed by traditional tests of academic IQ. In this review, I focused

on underlying orientations of these notions, with particular emphasis on the traditional *g*-centered view of

intelligence and what I described as a multiplex theoretical orientation (as exemplified by Gardner's

theory of multiple intelligences). Both orientations are associated with a substantial, and still growing,

body of research and speculation, and both have proponents and detractors in the intelligence research

Cited as listed in the references.

community. Indeed, enough has been said and written about the elusive concept of intelligence to fill an

encyclopedia (*Encyclopedia of Human Intelligence,* 1994). Gardner's theory encompasses certain

traditional aspects of the work on intelligence and, at the same time, moves our conceptualization of

intelligence far beyond the classic boundaries. That Gardner's theory is broader than the traditional notion

of intelligence is viewed by some psychologists as problematic, because the broader the theory, the more

difficult it is to disprove. I have a sense that there is a trend toward broad, interdisciplinary formulations

and definitions of intelligence or, in Sternberg's (1997) description, whatever mental abilities are

necessary to enable persons to shape and adapt to their environment.

Within such a broad theoretical orientation, researchers have been exploring ways of assessing and improving performance skills that in the past were ignored or considered far less significant than academic intelligence (e.g., Aditya & House, 2002; Gardner, 1991, 1999; Sternberg, Torff, & Grigorenko, 1998). Another direction of recent work on intelligence was discussed by Anastasi and Urbina (1997), who mentioned that, in the field of developmental psychology, researchers have found "substantial correlations between ratings of infant behavior on personality variables and subsequent cognitive development" and also that "studies of the environmental-mastery motive in infants have revealed some promising relations to subsequent measures of intellectual competence" (p. 302). The challenge remains not only to improve our understanding of the elusive concept of intelligence but, as Wesman (1968) put it, to do "intelligent testing" (p. 267). It is important to develop innovative approaches, no matter how complex and nontraditional, to measure the different facets of intellectual capabilities (Gardner, 1999; Neisser et al., 1996; Sternberg, 1992) and, fundamentally, to recognize that intelligence is "a result of one's total life experience" (Gilbert, 1971, p. 135).

More than one cited work by this author (3.3).

This final major section wraps up the paper, reviewing the objective first and ending with the student's impressions of trends and future directions.

While raising some issues, the final paragraph of the paper clearly ends the discussion.

The references begin on a new page.

THE CONCEPT OF INTELLIGENCE   14

References

Chapter in edited book (3.4.19).

Aditya, R. N., & House, R. J. (2002). Interpersonal acumen and leadership across cultures: Pointers from the GLOBE study. In R. E. Riggio, S. E. Murphy, & F. J. Pirozzolo (Eds.), *Multiple intelligences and leadership* (pp. 215–240). Mahwah, NJ: Erlbaum.

Anastasi, A., & Urbina, S. (1997). *Psychological testing* (7th ed.). Upper Saddle River, NJ: Prentice Hall.

Use of colon in title (7.16.4).

Ceci, S. J. (1996). *On intelligence: A bioecological treatise on intellectual development* (Expanded ed.). Cambridge, MA: Harvard University Press.

Ceci, S. J., & Liker, J. (1986). Academic and nonacademic intelligence: An experimental separation. In R. J. Sternberg & R. Wagner (Eds.), *Practical intelligence: Nature and origins of competence in the everyday world* (pp. 119–142). New York, NY: Cambridge University Press.

No author or editor listed (3.4.31).

Encyclopedia of human intelligence. (1994). New York, NY: Macmillan.

Ericsson, K. A., & Charness, N. (1994). Expert performance: Its structure and acquisition. *American Psychologist, 49,* 725–747. doi:10.1037/0003-066x.49.8.725

Digital Object Identifier (2.4).

Frey, M. C., & Detterman, D. K. (2004). Scholastic assessment or *g*? The relationship between the Scholastic Assessment Test and general cognitive ability. *Psychological Science, 15,* 373–378. doi:10.1111/j.0956-7976.2004.00687.x

Gardner, H. (1983). *Frames of mind: The theory of multiple intelligences.* New York, NY: Basic Books.

Gardner, H. (1991). *The unschooled mind: How children think and how schools should teach.* New York, NY: Basic Books.

Quoted material in title.

Gardner, H. (1995). "Expert performance: Its structure and acquisition": Comment. *American Psychologist, 50,* 802–803. doi:10/1037/0003-066x.50.9.802

Gardner, H. (1999). *Intelligence reframed: Multiple intelligences for the 21st century.* New York, NY: Basic Books.

Encyclopedia with more than one volume (3.4.32).

Gilbert, H. B. (1971). Intelligence tests. In L. C. Deighton (Ed.), *The encyclopedia of education* (Vol. 5, pp.128–135). New York, NY: Macmillan & Free Press.

Hanging indents are used for all references.

Herrnstein, R. J., & Murray, C. (1994). *The bell curve: Intelligence and class structure in American life.*

New York, NY: Free Press.

Jensen, A. R. (1969). How much can we boost IQ and scholastic achievement? *Harvard Educational*

Review, 39, 1–123.

Kaplan, R. M., & Saccuzzo, D. P. (2009). *Psychological testing: Principles, applications, and issues* (7th

ed.). Belmont, CA: Wadsworth/Cengage Learning.

Neisser, U., Boodoo, G., Bouchard, T. J., Jr., Boykin, A. W., Brody, N., Ceci, S. J., . . .Urbina, S. (1996).

Intelligence: Knowns and unknowns. *American Psychologist, 51,* 77–101.

doi:10.1037/0003-066x.51.2.77

Nisbett, R. E. (2009). *Intelligence and how to get it.* New York, NY: W. W. Norton.

Random House dictionary of the English language (Unabridged ed.). (1996). New York, NY: Random

House.

Rosenthal, R. (1990). How are we doing in soft psychology? *American Psychologist, 45,* 775–777.

doi:10.1016/0160-2896(94)90056-6

Rosenthal, R., & Rosnow, R. L. (1975). *The volunteer subject.* New York, NY: Wiley.

Rosenthal, R., & Rosnow, R. L. (2009). *Artifacts in behavioral research.* New York, NY: Oxford

University Press.

Rosnow, R. L., Skleder, A. A., Jaeger, M. E., & Rind, B. (1994). Intelligence and the epistemics of

interpersonal acumen: Testing some implications of Gardner's theory. *Intelligence, 19,* 93–116.

Siegler, R. S., & Richards, D. D. (1982). The development of intelligence. In R. J. Sternberg (Ed.),

Handbook of human intelligence (pp. 897–971). New York, NY: Cambridge University Press.

Spearman, C. (1927). *The abilities of man.* New York, NY: Macmillan.

Sternberg, R. J. (1985). *Beyond IQ: A triarchic theory of human intelligence.* New York, NY: Cambridge

University Press.

Sternberg, R. J. (1988). *The triarchic mind: A new theory of human intelligence.* New York, NY: Viking.

More than six coauthors (3.4.18).

Dictionary, no author or editor indicated (3.4.31).

Four coauthors (3.4.17).

Multiple references by same author are arranged by date; continues on next page.

More than one edition of book (3.4.1).

THE CONCEPT OF INTELLIGENCE   16

Sternberg, R. J. (1990). *Metaphors of mind: A new theory of human intelligence.* New York, NY:

Cambridge University Press.

Sternberg, R. J. (1992). Ability tests, measurements, and markets. *Journal of Educational Psychology, 84,*

134–140. doi:10.1037/0022-0663.84.2.134

Sternberg, R. J. (1997). The concept of intelligence and its role in lifelong learning and success. *American*

Psychologist, 52, 1030–1037. doi:10.1037/0003-066x.52.10.1030

Sternberg, R. J., Torff, B., & Grigorenko, E. L. (1998). Teaching triarchically improves school

achievement. *Journal of Educational Psychology, 90,* 374–384. doi:10.1037/0022-0663.90.3.374

Sternberg, R. J., Wagner, R. K., Williams, W. M., & Horvath, J. A. (1995). Testing common sense.

American Psychologist, 50, 912–927. doi:10.1037/0003-066x.50.11.912

Walters, J. M., & Gardner, H. (1986). The theory of multiple intelligences: Some issues and answers. In

R. J. Sternberg & R. K. Wagner (Eds.), *Practical intelligence: Nature and origins of competence in*

the everyday world (pp. 163–181). New York, NY: Cambridge University Press.

Wesman, A. G. (1968). Intelligent testing. *American Psychologist, 23,* 267–274. doi:10.1037/h0026192

No period after doi (3.4).

Chapter in edited book (3.4.19).

Footnotes begin
on a new page (8.8).

Footnotes

[1] *IQ* stands for "intelligence quotient," which goes back to how intelligence was first defined as the mental age (measured by the IQ test) divided by chronological age, and multiplied by 100. For example, a 10-year-old with a tested mental age of an 11-year-old would have an IQ of (11/10)100 = 110. Nisbett (2009) noted that "modern IQ tests arbitrarily define the mean of the population of a given age as being 100 and force the distribution around that mean to have a particular standard deviation" (p. 5).

[2] It can be noted, though, that finding a predictor variable that accounts for approximately one quarter of the variance (i.e., an effect size correlation of around .5) is not unimpressive in psychological research (Rosenthal, 1990). However, Sternberg et al.'s (1995) point that conceptual and psychometric limits exist in the traditional model of intelligence is well taken and supportive of the argument that intelligence consists of "various, relatively independent, abilities" (Gilbert, 1971, p. 129).

[3] I chose the word *multiplex* because all these theories of multiple intelligences reminded me of a movie theater in which different films are playing to different audiences in auditoriums that are all clearly separated from one another and yet are housed in the same building. The first definition of *multiplex* in the *Random House Dictionary of the English Language* (1966) is "manifold; multiple" (p. 940).

Footnotes
are part
of the end
material
(8.2).

Use footnotes
only sparingly,
if at all (8.8).

Each table begins on a new page (8.9).

THE CONCEPT OF INTELLIGENCE   18

Table 1

Howard Gardner's Original Seven Types of Intelligence

The column headings define what is in this table.

Name	Defining characteristics
Logical-mathematical intelligence	Reasoning and computational skills (e.g., correlated with the SAT)
Linguistic intelligence	Adept with words and language (e.g., multilingual people, writers)
Spatial intelligence	Ability to perceive and steer through the spatial world with ease (e.g., navigators, architects, sculptors)
Bodily-kinesthetic intelligence	Skills carrying and moving one's body (e.g.. dancers, athletes, neurosurgeons)
Musical intelligence	Ability to discern themes in music, sensitive to qualities of melody such as pitch, rhythm, and timbre (e.g., musicians, composers)
Intrapersonal intelligence	Adept at self-understanding (i.e., people who have a sense of their own abilities, aspirations, and limitations)
Interpersonal intelligence	Adept at reading other people's intentions and actions (i.e., "people persons")

The note is flush left, with no paragraph indentation.

Note. Gardner (1983) characterized intrapersonal and interpersonal intelligence as the "personal intelligences," or the talent to detect various shades of meaning in the emotions, intentions, and behavior of oneself (intrapersonal intelligence) and of others (interpersonal intelligence).

The figure and caption, together, are on a new page.

Figure 1. Two curves representing a theoretical normal distribution of IQ scores in the general population (*Y*) and a theoretical normal distribution of IQ scores among volunteer subjects (*X*). From *The Volunteer Subject* (p. 128), by R. Rosenthal and R. L. Rosnow, 1975, New York, NY: Wiley. Copyright © by the authors. Reprinted with permission of R. Rosenthal (personal communication, April 10, 2010).

Formatting figures (8.9).

Figure (or table) reproduced from another source calls for permission from copyright owner.

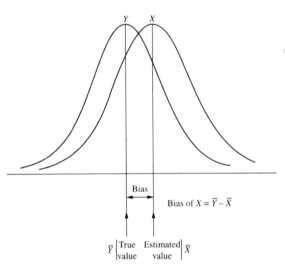

Index